Praise for *FOREGROUND MUSIC: A LIFE IN 15 GIGS*

"Duff captures perfectly that sense of teenage wonder at first being exposed to the spectacle, the power, the joy and the sheer physical noise of those exhilarating live shows that left indelible marks on our adolescent souls."
– Mark Radcliffe

"*Foreground Music* is such a vividly written account of Duff's growing up in public places loudly assaulted by amplified music that any reader is at serious risk of contracting tinnitus." – Chris Bohn, *Wire* magazine

"A very funny and moving music memoir. The Joy Division chapter in particular is gold dust." – Lucy O'Brien, author of *Madonna: Like An Icon*

"Duff's prodigious memory and gift for detail take the reader back to concerts that live again thanks to this book."
– Richard Witts, author of *Nico: Life & Lies of an Icon*

"Academics ponder, but fans want to feel the moment, want to know what it smelt like, how scary it was and what everyone was wearing! Duff captures the time and place, the tension and the joy."
– John Robb, author of *Punk Rock: An Oral History*

"Mixing personal insight with a geek's knowledge of who played what, where and why, the book delivers on numerous levels. Best of all, Duff has the knack of saying the most serious things in a light voice. It's a rare gift."
– Jeff Noon, author of *Vurt*

"A fantastic chronicle of a musical life. It's so warmly and wisely written, I genuinely wanted to have a conversation with it."
– Thomas Patterson, *Shindig* magazine

FOREGROUND MUSIC

A LIFE IN 15 GIGS

GRAHAM DUFF

Foreground Music: A Life in Fifteen Gigs
by Graham Duff

Published by Strange Attractor Press 2019

Text and photographs copyright © Graham Duff 2019

ISBN: 9781907222825

Layout by Rachel Sale

Strange Attractor Press
BM SAP, London, WC1N 3XX, UK
www.strangeattractor.co.uk

Distributed by The MIT Press, Cambridge, Massachusetts.
And London, England.
Printed and bound in Estonia by Tallinna Raamatutrükikoda.

CONTENTS

INTRODUCTION

Mark Gatiss

Music for pleasure.

That was what the red label said in the middle of so many of those glossy black LPs, though, as a kid, I did wonder what else music might be for. Misery? Violence? Pain? As Graham Duff demonstrates in this gloriously entertaining memoir, it can sometimes be all those things…

I'm somewhere in Leeds. About 1984. Definitely a squat. And a basement. Well, when I say basement, I mean a too-low-to-stand-upright, black-mould-creeping-over-the-walls-like-a-goth's-lace-gloves firetrap packed with about a hundred young people. It's the sort of health and safety nightmare now only seen in YouTube videos about the Third World. The ones where people dive into septic tanks in search of missing mobile phones.

Everyone is silhouetted against the bright light of the makeshift stage. If you could see the crowd properly they'd be achingly familiar. Girls with black lipstick, pink tights and DMs. Boys with black lipstick and skinny jeans, swamped in cobwebby mohair jumpers and crimped hair that looks like it's been through a Breville toaster. Everyone clutching cans. Or Thunderbird wine. Or flimsy plastic pint glasses overflowing with piss-weak lager that would take a month to get drunk on.

And then the band come on to whoops and cheers. They're young. Kohl-rimmed eyes. The smooth pink cheeks that bloom for about eighteen months during those golden and never-to-be recaptured teens. There's something in the air. And it's not just damp spores. It's an electricity. A pulse. Music, drenched in expectation, rebellion, the promise of something other. Music for… *pleasure*…

Like Graham Duff, ours was not a very musical household. There was an old dansette with a white rubber turntable on which we'd play ancient copies of 'Living Doll', 'All Kinds of Everything' and Pinky and Perky (slowed down to 78 mph so that they sounded spookily like ordinary people). Then, sandwiched to the side of our optimistically named 'music centre' the soundtrack to *South Pacific* (my Mam's favourite), Shirley Bassey (my Dad's), Neil Sedaka (everyone's) and a handful of Top of the Pops LPs (my sister's) from which I learned and have never quite forgotten the lyrics to 'Wigwam Bam' and 'Knock Three Times'. Perhaps best off all, though, was Geoff Love's *Big War Themes* with its marvellous painted cover featuring Peter O'Toole, Michael Caine and John Wayne engulfed in a fiery holocaust. As Graham demonstrates, this was an eccentric way into music. But it was a way in. A gateway.

It wasn't, however, the live experience.

My Dad worked at a mental hospital and it formed a huge part of our lives. I met Rolf Harris there when I was four – though I couldn't tell if he had an extra leg (or indeed any other, subsequently revealed proclivities). We'd go swimming at the hospital, go to the pictures there and – every summer – to the big summer fete. In my memory it's all a blur of sun-drenched super 8 with a side order of northern gothic. Tombola, hoopla and massive, stained white tents that ponged of grass. But, for some reason though, the hospital authorities would spend a ton of money on booking a big group. Once it was the Glitter Band (Just the band. Not Gary. This is becoming a theme.) and, incredibly one year Slade. ***Slade!!*** I don't remember much about it but this DEFINITELY counts as my first gig.

I think there's a tipping point. A moment. Something that changes inside you and you think – this is mine. This could be for me. It could be a book, a film but I think, most potently it's music. And suddenly, as I turned 13 I started to become aware of music in a different way. Blondie, Tubeway Army. Squeeze. My brother bought '*Germfree Adolescents*' and played it incessantly. Music suddenly seemed exciting – and a little bit forbidden. And then people at school started talking about going to see a band. I bought a massive black overcoat from a jumble sale and grew my fringe so long that it gave me an eye infection. I looked like a thumb in a coat – all cheekbones and eyeliner and electropop sneering. I got into Ultravox (and, retrospectively, Ultravox!), the Teardrop Explodes, the Specials and, my great hero, John Foxx. Everything was suddenly about the *NME*, haunting record shops and queuing in the cold and rain (invariably) for the gig.

What Graham captures so wonderfully in *Foreground Music* is the whole experience. From his first fumblings via a Cliff Richard gospel concert to the glorious epiphany of The Fall, you'll recognise your own musical journey here in loving detail. This isn't, though, simply a book for music geeks. There's a truth and a joy to the writing that speaks to all of us. Of being young, the first flush of adolescent yearning, the desire to escape. Then having 'opinions'. Your favourite band becoming too popular. Then a kind of maturity. An awareness of time passing. Of moments lost. Of eras and movements and stars. I think my favourite part is his account of the David Bowie gig. Knowing that this wasn't vintage Bowie. But knowing, all the same, that it was BOWIE! And now, as the years have rolled inexorably on, of how special it was to have seen him at all.

Foreground Music is an absolute gem. Charming, very funny and often achingly melancholy, Graham's memoir is suffused with a genuine passion for live music and its (occasionally eccentric) power. From the birth of New Wave right up to the present, he falls in love with going to gigs and, along the way, so do we. To anyone raised on battered 7" singles and mix tapes, anyone who's ever stood too close to a speaker or queued in the drizzle as their carefully crimped hair dissolved into cold misery, this book will delight.

Music for… *pleasure.*

London
April 2019

CLIFF RICHARD

KING GEORGE'S HALL, BLACKBURN

FRIDAY 30TH OCTOBER 1974

(AGE 10)

People who like music are stupid. By the age of ten, I've said this so many times, in my mind it's become a fact.

Music isn't a big thing at my parents' house. Never has been. Mum and Dad have maybe 25 LPs: Ray Conniff, Jim Reeves, Mrs. Mills, middle of the road kind of stuff. But the albums never get played anyway. Although the turntable does see some action, when I discover Mum's old comedy LPs: *The Best of Bob Newhart* and best of all, two Tony Hancock albums. I play these to death. Learn them off by heart.

We watch *Top of The Pops* from time to time, but certainly not religiously. Then, on Thursday 6th July 1972, David Bowie appears on the show, performing his new single 'Starman'. He looks alien yet sexy, with his spiked orange hair and bright blue guitar. And, when he sings the line "*I had to phone someone, so I picked on you-oo-oo*", he looks directly into the camera and seems to point right out of the screen. But he isn't pointing at me. Because I'm not there. I'm out riding around on my bike.

I don't have an older brother to teach me about pop and rock. I have three younger sisters: Carolyn, Gillian and Susan. So over the last year, by far the most played album in our house has been *Wombling Songs* by The Wombles.

The only non-Womble pop stars I'm vaguely aware of are David Cassidy, Alvin Stardust and The Osmonds. None of them has captured my imagination. And, as I say, all the kids I know who are really into pop music are stupid. And that's a fact. So I have confidently and arrogantly closed off pop as an avenue of investigation.

But it doesn't matter anyway. Because last year, I discovered something better. Something more powerful. Something more sophisticated. And most importantly of all, something far more adult: James Bond soundtracks.

From a very young age, I'd loved the theme tunes to TV spy and detective shows. *The Saint*, *The Avengers*, and especially the music from the string of fantasy espionage shows made by ITC: *Randall & Hopkirk (Deceased)*, *The Champions* and *Department S*. Best of all, is the John Barry penned theme tune to *The Persuaders*, with its fuzzy plangent opening chords played on an electric harpsichord, pipe organ and piano synth. To me, this is such exciting music. It suggests mystery, tension and menace. Something I don't hear in any of the pop music that comes my way.

And yet, although I am more than familiar with Simon Templar, John Steed and Jason King, I'd been oblivious to the existence of 007. James Bond didn't enter my life until last summer, when Mum took me to the Odeon Cinema in Blackburn, to see Roger Moore making his Bond debut in *Live and Let Die*. Although Moore's era would later see Bond entering the world of parody, at the time of *Live and Let Die*, the producers are still taking things seriously. And the additional elements of Blaxploitation and voodoo make for a heady cocktail.

From the first frame to the last, I am transfixed. Suddenly, everything else I've ever watched and enjoyed is revealed to have been kid's stuff. At nine years old I've glimpsed the future. The future is about being an adult, it's about action and danger and gorgeous girls and explosions. And, whilst I have no idea who Wings are, their recording of the theme song gives me goosebumps. In fact, the soundtrack – even though it's by George Martin rather than John Barry – is one of the things which excites me the most.

Once Bond enters my life, he doesn't leave much room for anything else. Even *Doctor Who* – my biggest passion since before I can remember – feels the squeeze. For my birthday, my Gran and Granddad give me a cassette album of Bond themes. I'm not interested in vinyl. I see cassettes as being much more futuristic. The cassette in question is *Roland Shaw's World of James Bond Adventure*, new recordings of a selection of John Barry's original themes and incidental cues. I don't care that it's not the original recordings. It's Bond music!

I listen to the cassette incessantly. I become intimately familiar with incidental music from Bond films I've not yet seen. I'm fixated on a track from *Thunderball* entitled 'Bond Below Disco Volanté' – composed to accompany an underwater sequence where Bond swims beneath a yacht owned by criminal mastermind Emilio Largo. Although, having not seen the film, I don't know this. The title leads me to assume Bond is checking out the basement of some nightclub.

'Bond Below Disco Volanté' begins with lots of dramatic pauses and silences. A wash of vibraphone is punctuated by low harp, strings and a muted trumpet, with menacing minor chords from a harpsichord. The whole thing builds into a dizzying crescendo of brass. I've never encountered a more mysterious, goose-pimple inducing piece of music.

Following on from the success of *Live and Let Die*, the earlier Bond films are re-released in a brace of double bills. Mum takes me to see them all. The first double bill we attend comprises *Thunderball* and *You Only Live Twice*. I recognise some of the pieces of incidental music that I know so well. If Roland Shaw's interpretations had sparked my passion, then hearing John Barry's original recordings blaring through a cinema sound system turns me into a full-blown devotee. At points, I'm so focused on the music cues I forget to listen to the dialogue and get momentarily lost in the plot. This is the most intoxicating afternoon of my life!

I save up my pocket money and buy the soundtrack to *You Only Live Twice*. From the moment the album is in the palm of my hand, I'm dazzled by it. The back half of the cassette case is bright orange plastic. Every other cassette case I've ever seen has been made from plain black plastic. And what about the contents? The sweepingly romantic theme tune sung by Nancy Sinatra hooks into my brain and won't leave. Whilst the suite of instrumentals which merge Barry's trademark brass arrangements and low slung guitars with delicate oriental instrumentation feels impossibly exotic.

Next, I save up for *Thunderball*. This is Barry's finest Bond soundtrack and it remains one of my most beloved albums. From the title track dominated by Tom Jones' over driven lead vocal, through to the spiralling strings of 'Search For Vulcan', and the deliriously cocksure swagger of 'Mr. Kiss Kiss Bang Bang', Barry creates a detailed and seductive soundworld.

In this time, long before the internet, before Blu-ray, before DVDs, before VHS recorders, a time even before any of the James Bond films have received their televisual premier, the soundtrack albums are the only way in which the experience can be replayed. And so that's exactly what I do. Over and over and over and over. I wear out one cassette recorder and move on to another. The music of John Barry is all the music I need. It's big and glossy and sexy and dramatic. In comparison, it makes pop music – The Osmonds and David Cassidys of this world – sound weedy and insubstantial. Like I say, pop music is for the stupid.

So how come I'm here, in the audience at King George's Hall, on a Friday evening in October, waiting for the start of a Cliff Richard concert?

I'm up in the balcony, near the front of the stage on the left hand side. With me are Mum, my Gran and my oldest sister Carolyn. She's 7 years old and she's the main reason we're here. She's a self confessed Cliff Richard fan. And me? Well, as a staunch opponent of pop, I'd had to be coerced into coming along. But really, now we're here, I'm intrigued.

A banner at the back of the stage announces the concert is a fundraiser for something called Tearfund. I don't think I've ever been in a room with this many people before. King George's Hall is packed. Whatever Tearfund is, they should do well out of this. Cliff is a proper star, a huge draw. In fact, he's one of the most famous people in the country. He was already famous well before I was born. And I'm ten.

Whilst rock musicians sometimes enjoy lengthy careers, the world of pop has always had a far more accelerated turnover of faces. Cliff's career kicked off all the way back in 1958. A time when, according to my understanding of things, the whole world was in black and white. And Cliff is alone in having been a ubiquitous fixture in the pop firmament ever since. By 1974, he has chalked up a staggering 84 hit singles and hit EPs in the UK top 40! Thirteen of those have been number ones. Thirteen!

Although Cliff's peak was undoubtedly in the early 1960s, when he appeared in a string of popular film musicals, his star still shows no sign of waning. Cliff is more than ubiquitous. He's inescapable. Aside from endless spins on the radio, appearances on *Top of The Pops* and guest spots on other people's programmes, for the last four years he's had his own BBC1 Saturday night prime time light entertainment show: *It's Cliff Richard*. It's a jumble of songs, comic monologues, sketches and guest singers. It's a bit like *The Morecambe and Wise Show*. Without Morecambe or Wise. But with Cliff Richard.

The brief but numerous comedy sketches feature Cliff alongside Shadows guitarist Hank Marvin. Neither of them is especially blessed with acting chops or comic timing and the writing is flat and predictable with little pretension to being anything other than lightweight between song filler. Even at my age, I know this is shoddy. Compared with the masterful Tony Hancock, Cliff's 'comedy' just doesn't cut it. His delivery is so unrehearsed and awkward it's like watching a well-meaning uncle just having a go.

There's also a dance troupe called Segment, who keep their routines energetic but strictly non-sensual, plus weekly appearances from Cliff's singing guests The Nolan Sisters. The Nolan Sisters wear matching primary coloured bri-nylon dresses and they certainly give Cliff a run for his money when it comes to smiling and being inoffensive. *It's Cliff Richard* is typical early 70s wholesome light entertainment fare, which appeals to grandparents and children. And anyone in between. As long as they have very undemanding tastes.

This is how Carolyn had developed her appreciation of Cliff. Although at first, aged five, she didn't know Cliff was called Cliff. She used to refer to him as 'Good News Bad News Man'. This was because in every episode, Cliff would do a comic monologue that began with him saying "This week, I've got some good news and I've got some bad news." So it wasn't just Cliff's singing which first fired her five year old imagination, rather it was his abilities as an all round entertainer.

Carolyn's Cliff addiction isn't quite as all consuming as my Bond addiction, but she still spends many a Sunday afternoon playing the same Cliff singles over and over again on her Dansette record player. One song in particular gets some extremely heavy rotation. It's a single called 'I Love You' released in 1960. It's one of his thirteen number ones. It opens with the line *"Your love means more to me, than all the apples hanging on a tree."* Not much of a compliment really. Unless you happen to be an orchard owner who depends entirely on the apple crop for your livelihood.

Carolyn is now already two years into her Cliff connoisseurship. Consequently, she is happy beyond measure to be sitting expectantly in King George's Hall tonight. Nevertheless, we do seem to have been sitting expectantly for an eternity. Finally, the lights dim, and there's a wave of applause and cheers. Someone steps up to the mic stand. It's difficult to make them out in the semi darkness, but it doesn't look like Cliff. It looks like a middle-aged woman in a dress. A bright spotlight comes up. It's a middle-aged woman in a dress.

She introduces herself as being from Tearfund. She talks about the important work they do. Tearfund are a charity organisation providing help for poverty stricken communities in Africa, whilst simultaneously spreading the word of Jesus. She then spreads the word herself. In fact, she spreads the word for nearly half an hour. "This is like being in church." I whisper to Carolyn. Except at least here, we're up in the balcony, away from any judgmental gaze. And we're eating Toblerones.

Finally, the middle-aged woman in a dress asks us to welcome to the stage Cliff Richard! Cliff bounds on, dressed in a black wide lapelled jacket and tight fitting white trousers. He looks every centimetre the star. The room erupts into applause.

Carolyn is thrilled; leaning forward in her seat, keen to soak up the view of Cliff. Mum smiles, pleased to see Carolyn so blissfully happy. I however, try to give the impression of someone who is completely bored by the whole thing. But secretly, I have to admit, deep down, even I'm pretty impressed. This is *the actual Cliff Richard.* The famous Cliff Richard, who's on television every week. Here. In the same room as us.

In a hall in Blackburn. It doesn't seem quite real.

Cliff goes into the first song. It turns out to be a long, slow dirge about Jesus. At the song's climax there's a burst of applause. Carolyn, Mum, Gran and I join in. "Thank you." Says Cliff. A voice in the crowd shouts out "Power to All Our Friends!" This is Cliff's most recent up-tempo top five single. It also came in third at last year's Eurovision Song Contest. The band start up, Cliff begins to sing. Unfortunately, he isn't singing 'Power to All Our Friends'. He's singing another long dirge about Jesus. It gradually dawns on me that this is what the entire evening is going to be like. Songs we don't know. Songs without hooks. Songs about faith, redemption and especially Jesus. The third song Cliff introduces is actually called 'Jesus'. And so it goes on. Tonight Cliff won't be singing his hits, tonight Cliff won't be gyrating around the stage like the English Elvis. No. Because tonight isn't about entertainment. Tonight is a gospel concert.

Up in the balcony, sitting with my legs crossed, staring off into space, I'm no longer pretending to be bored. I really am bored.

Now perhaps I should clarify what I mean when I use the word gospel. To some people, this will inevitably summon up images of soulful black singers belting out songs of devotion in an uninhibited display of celebration and excitation. This isn't that kind of gospel music. This is buttoned down, uptight and decidedly Caucasian. Cliff doesn't speak much between songs. But when he does speak, he tells us about Jesus. The other thing he tells us about is how important it is to tell people about Jesus. But there are a few pockets in the audience, who don't want to hear about Jesus.

They want to hear hit singles. And they keep shouting out for them. There's one woman in particular, who at the conclusion of every song calls out "Goodbye Sam!" in a broad Blackburn accent. 'Goodbye Sam, Hello Samantha' is another of Cliff's top ten pop hits from a few years back. It's a breezy, bouncy tune with an almost oompah feel. Its mood is significantly more upbeat than anything we've heard tonight. Cliff doesn't acknowledge any of the requests for his hits. Instead, he decides the best way to quell these voices is with another long dirge about Jesus.

Fifty minutes later, we walk out of King George's Hall into the dark night. "It's nearly half ten." Says Mum. I smile inwardly. Staying up this late is a rarity. And staying up late always feels like a real victory. But apart from anything else, it's clear that Carolyn has just had the best night of her life. And even a cynical ten year old like me can't deny how nice it is to see her looking so beatific.

The following Monday morning at Saint Bartholomew's Primary School, I say to my best friend Sean Connell "Hey, you'll never guess where I went on Friday night." He raises his eyebrows and looks blank. "To see Cliff Richard singing in Blackburn." Initially Sean doesn't believe me. But eventually I convince him that I did indeed see the actual Cliff Richard live on stage in a hall in Blackburn. "What were it like?" He asks. "Were it any good?" I shake my head. "No, it was shit. People who like music are stupid."

THE JAM

KING GEORGE'S HALL, BLACKBURN

MONDAY 12TH JUNE 1978

(AGE 14)

I've been back home from school for about an hour. My bedroom is up in the loft of the house and during the summer months it gets hot.

I've got the window open, but there's no breeze. I'm sitting on my bed, still in my school shirt and trousers, drawing in a sketch-pad. I hear the telephone ring downstairs and a moment later Mum calls up to me. "Graham, it's Peter." Pete Cowie has been my best friend for nearly three years. We're in the same form. He started talking to me in an English lesson in the second week of secondary school. He really made me laugh. Then I made him laugh. We've been making each other laugh ever since. We've become very close and even though we don't look remotely similar, people sometimes ask if we're brothers.

When I go down and pick up the receiver, Pete sounds excited. He tells me he's just phoned in to a competition on Radio Blackburn and won two tickets to go and see The Jam at King George's Hall that evening. "Do you wanna come with us?" "Yeah." I reply. "Pearlin'." Pearlin' is what we've started saying to denote that something is very good indeed.

Now *I'm* excited. We're going to see an actual punk band. Pete's been seriously into punk for forever. Well, for about 8 months. Since the tail end of 1977. Despite our close friendship and my trusting his judgment, I wasn't initially convinced by punk.

John Barry's dominance of my listening habits had lasted up until the summer of 1977. Then, at the age of 13, whilst on a holiday in

Scotland with my Gran, Granddad, Auntie Barbara and Uncle Brian, I hear The Beatles. Brian has a double cassette of *The Beatles 1967– 1970*. A greatest hits by another name, it covers the latter, psychedelic part of their career. We listen to it whilst driving through the Scottish countryside. 'Strawberry Fields Forever' and 'A Day in the Life' in particular sound so complicated I can't take them in on first listen. Or even second or third listen. There are some songs I'm less convinced by, like 'Fool on the Hill', but even when I'm not hooked by the songs themselves, the sounds and the arrangements still draw me in. I borrow the cassette and play it endlessly. The Beatles become my second big musical obsession after Mr. Barry.

Then, just three months ago, Pete and I managed to get in to see Nic Roeg's film *The Man Who Fell To Earth* at the Majestic Cinema in Blackburn. At 14 and 13 years of age respectively we are way, way too young to see an 'X' film, as movies classified suitable only for adults are known. Although apparently we are tall enough to be mistaken for 18 year olds, as, with our best deep voices, we purchase the tickets and slip inside.

The main reason we want to see the film is we'd heard there's quite a bit of sex in it. *The Man Who Fell To Earth* does not disappoint. There's a *lot* of sex and nudity in it. But, even if all those bits were cut out, it's still the best film I've ever seen. And that includes *Goldfinger*. It's a dazzling mosaic of a film, centring on several themes that I can't begin to untangle. And yet, despite the fact it's hard to understand – by which I mean I don't quite grasp who some of the characters are, what's driving them, how the narrative works, or what the whole thing means – it doesn't repel me, it bewitches me. But of course the most immediately engaging element of the film is Bowie's presence.

As alien visitor Thomas Jerome Newton, Bowie manages to radiate charisma, whilst maintaining a mood of utter detachment and otherworldly grace. Even though, apart from the odd song, I'm fairly oblivious to Bowie's music, I suddenly get why he's a big star, why some of the cool kids at school have his name written in magic marker on their exercise books and sports holdalls. So, like Carolyn, with her early appreciation of Cliff, my initial love of Bowie comes not from his music, but from his acting.

Within days of seeing the film, I buy *ChangesOneBowie* – a greatest hits by another name, it covers Bowie's career up to that point. So many hooks, so many quotable lines, so many ideas and characters, so many different voices. It's stunning. So here I am, ridiculously late to the party. As the rest of the world is being galvanised by punk I've finally woken up to Bowie and The Beatles!

Pete first got into punk via The Stranglers. He plays The Stranglers a lot. Personally, I struggle with The Stranglers. Even though I think a couple of their tracks are pretty cool – 'No More Heroes' and 'Dagenham Dave' to be precise – much of their stuff makes me feel uncomfortable. To be honest, with their sleazy and aggressive attitude and lyrics about sewers and shagging nubiles, I think they sound like the kind of lads I try to avoid at school. Put simply, The Stranglers sound like bullies.

My exposure to other punk bands is minimal. But then, one bright Saturday morning in February, I go around to Pete's house and he produces a seven inch single he's just bought by The Buzzcocks. It's called 'What Do I Get?'. The minimal green sleeve is immediately intriguing and when the needle drops onto the vinyl, I'm swept along in the rush of guitars and hyperactive drumming. Whilst The Stranglers frequently sound lumpy and turgid, The Buzzcocks are sleek and sharp.

"And you're not gonna believe this." Says Pete, flipping the single over to play the B-side: 'Oh Shit!'. It's terse, funny and it's all over in a minute and a half. It's so short we listen to it several times in a row. The thing that hits me hardest is the speed of the thing. "It's the fastest music I've ever heard." I tell him. "It's ace isn't it." He says. I nod in agreement. "Pearlin'." This is my moment of true conversion. Punk is where it's at. From now on, I hoover up anything I can find by and about The Buzzcocks, and investigate as many other punk bands as I can.

Our school is Norden County High. It's a big school, with maybe 1,200 kids and teenagers. But there's only one other lad we know who's into punk: Steve Dunn. He's not in our form, but he and I are in the same set for Science and Maths. He's voluble and cheeky with ash blond hair that seems naturally spiky. He looked like a punk, before he or we even knew what punks were. Even though my hair is still almost shoulder length, I'm secretly envious of Steve's hair. Although the less charitable might describe his haircut as being like a bog brush.

One day, Steve tells me about John Peel's late night Radio One show. "Some of the stuff he plays is shit." He says. "But he plays loads of punk." I keep forgetting to listen to it, but when I finally do remember to tune in, it's thrilling. So many bands I've never heard of but want to hear again. Although a lot of the music is harsh and serious, the show is fun too. Peel's voice is measured yet perky. He's witty and self deprecating. The show runs from 10pm to midnight and sometimes I fall asleep before the end of the show. Like countless other kids across the country I start taping choice cuts. The cassette is still king.

One morning, Pete turns up at school, having had his hair cropped into a short punk style. I'm a little bit shocked. He looks very different. "When are you having it done then?" He asks. He's really doubled the bet here. Almost all the cool lads at school have long shoulder length hair. I'm naturally shy and don't exactly welcome the attention that having short hair would bring. I dither for a while, then, on the Saturday morning, I go to the barbers and get my long hair cut right back. I'm disappointed with the result. For some reason, I can't get mine to spike, but it still looks severe compared to the long, fluffy hair of most of my contemporaries. "I think some punks put glue in it to get it to spike." Says Steve. This seems unlikely.

Our hairstyles are clearly seen as a provocative gesture. During school assembly the following Monday, Mr. Rushton the music teacher and deputy head, makes a disparaging reference to "so-called punk music" then instructs Pete and I to stand up, so our new haircuts can be seen by the entire school. "How much did you pay for those abortions?" He asks, in a voice verging on anger. Neither of us answers. This is embarrassing. I blush. There are a few sniggers in the hall, but the use of the word 'abortions' has made everybody feel uncomfortable.

Mr. Rushton himself is almost completely bald, a morbidly overweight Humpty Dumpty figure. This is a look that he accentuates by always wearing a pinstriped three-piece suit with a pocket watch and chain in his waistcoat. In fact, he's so big and round his nickname amongst us kids is Bubble. As we stand there, under his heavy glare, he advises any other boys who are thinking of butchering their hair to think again. "Sit down." He mutters and the assembly continues.

Afterwards, Pete and I compare notes. "That was so embarrassing." I say. "Yeah." Says Pete. "But it felt pretty cool as well didn't it?" Silly me, I was so busy blushing, I had forgotten to feel cool. But I know what he means. We stood up for what we believed in. Okay, we had to be told to stand up, by a teacher. And all we believed in was having short hair. But Pete was right. It had felt somehow significant.

Even at 14, I am aware of the irony that whilst a number of punk bands are working class and are articulating the frustrations of their limiting circumstances, Pete and I are from middle class families. My parents' house is in the part of town that is known locally as 'the jam butty end'. This is slang for 'the posh bit'. I've never understood why. I have a moment of doubt one afternoon at home. I'm listening to 'Career Opportunities' by The Clash, when I start to question if I have the right to call myself a punk. I realise that moment of existential crisis must have passed when I find myself dancing around my bedroom to 'Cheat'.

Music is now our entire lives. Neither Pete, Steve nor I have much money, but every penny is spent on records. The three of us buy different releases and lend them to each other, tape them, keep the music circulating. The Buzzcock's *Another Music in a Different Kitchen* and the debut albums by The Clash and The Adverts and of course *Never Mind The Bollocks Here's the Sex Pistols*. But albums are expensive, so our main passion is singles.

And so, after months of what might be called our punk apprenticeship, Pete and I are actually going to a real gig. Now I should mention that neither of us actually owns any records by The Jam. Not because we don't like them, just because we haven't got around to it yet. There are so many great records being released on a weekly basis it's impossible to buy or hear them all. Plus I'm still playing catch up on all the important releases from last year. The only Jam song I've heard is 'In The City'. But it doesn't matter. My thinking is, they're a punk band, so the concert is bound to be great. Nay pearlin'.

The bus pulls into Blackburn Boulevard and Pete and I make our way to King George's Hall. The venue doors aren't open yet and there's already a queue snaking around the corner. It's largely lads of our age or a bit older. Kids who don't know that not only is it not cool to turn up so early, it's actually completely unnecessary. Even though the tickets say *Doors open 7pm*, nothing is really going to happen until at least 9pm.

We spot Steve in the queue. Pete tells him about winning the tickets. "You jammy bastard." Says Steve. Another guy joins the queue. He's wearing flared velvet pants and a denim shirt. His shoulder length hair is light brown, but you can't see much of it, as he's also wearing one of those floppy hats made of patches of brown leather sewn together. He's stuck two short sandalwood joss sticks in the hatband, which send curlicues of smoke into the air. Two years earlier he would have appeared stylish – edgy even. But in this moment, standing in line with a gaggle of punk types, Jam copyists and schoolboys in jeans and tank tops, he couldn't look more anachronistic if he'd turned up sporting a doublet and a ruff.

There's a bit of excitement going on next to us. Steve gives Pete and I a nod, suggesting we turn around. We do so. Paul Weller is walking past the queue on his way into the venue, sharp featured and immaculately groomed in a narrow lapelled black suit, white shirt and black tie. I have absolutely no idea who he is.

"He's in the band." Mutters Steve, pointing to Weller's face on his Jam button badge. "He's *him*." Steve is the closest thing to a Jam fan we know and even he doesn't know the name of the singer. Weller is walking along with what I presume is his girlfriend, a hip and sexy brunette in a grey mackintosh. They both look very sophisticated. Weller is only 20, but from the perspective of a 14 year old school boy, he and the girl seem impossibly adult.

The doors must have finally opened, because the queue starts to shuffle forward. When we get inside it isn't how I expect at all. I thought there'd be rows and rows of seats. Like at the Cliff Richard show. There isn't. It's just a huge open space. What had seemed like a lengthy queue of people now seems like just a handful of lost souls. It feels like the hall is almost empty. The lights are already pretty dim and there's music coming through the sound system. It's a mixture of punk, reggae and pub rock. I hardly recognise any of the songs. On stage, there's two drum kits and numerous amps already set up.

Some of the older punters go through the double doors into the bar. It doesn't even occur to us to try and get inside. I'm not interested in alcohol anyway. Whilst some of our school friends have already developed serious smoking habits and tell tales of drinking half a bottle of their parents' Dubonnet or an entire can of Watneys Party Seven, I've never even tasted beer or wine. But we don't have any money with which to try and buy drinks anyway. We have our bus fares home and that's it. So we stand around chatting with Steve for nearly two hours.

Finally, the houselights dip further and brightly coloured lights come up on stage. Even now the hall is still only a third full. A band begins to assemble. There's three of them. They have short hair. They wear matching shiny suits. I assume it's The Jam. Steve assures me it's not The Jam. The singer steps up to the mike. "Good evening!" He shouts in a strong Scottish accent. "We're The Jolt!" This seems quite comical. Steve snorts.

The trio dive into their set, playing as if to a packed room. This is the first time I've ever heard live amplified rock music. It hits so hard. The effect is both physically and mentally extreme. The volume is such that there doesn't seem to be any room in my head for other thoughts. It takes my young ears a long while to adjust. I can hear the drums but everything else just seems to be a huge wedge of electricity with a sheet of trebly feedback hovering above it. When the singer comes in, I can tell he's singing something, but there's no way I can catch any of the words. The music is so loud I can *feel it* in my body.

Aside from their look and their name, I'd like to say The Jolt are a completely different proposition to The Jam. Except that I can't. They have clearly been ingesting a similar diet of The Who and The Small Faces and have developed an almost identical approach to songwriting as Weller.[1]

The Jolt leave the stage to pockets of applause. In truth, I'm feeling a bit shell shocked from the volume. I never knew live music was so different from recorded sound.

The hall is starting to fill up a little. There's maybe two hundred or so people here now. There are a handful of proper adults, but most of the audience seem to be young teens like ourselves. And, with a few exceptions, it's almost all male. As the lights come up on stage once more, The Jam step out, strapping on their guitars. There's applause and a lot of cheering. It seems slightly odd, that whilst a large portion of the audience are schoolboys, desperately trying to dress in a way which suggests they are both adult and rebellious, The Jam themselves are dressed in outfits which from a distance could be school uniforms.

There's no 'good evening' or announcing the song title, the band just tear straight into their first number: 'In The City'. The only Jam song I know. The Jolt had seemed noisy. But this is overwhelming. I've never heard anything so loud in my life. "I've never heard anything so loud in my life." I say to Pete. "What?" He asks. I'm not surprised he can't hear what I'm saying. *I* can't hear what I'm saying. In fact, I'm only guessing that he's saying "What?".

After 'In The City', they race through a set of songs that are completely unknown to me. And, it would seem, this is unknown territory, even for the serious The Jam fans in the audience. I realise much later that the majority of the set is comprised of the songs that will make up their third album *All Mod Cons*. But that won't be released for another five months. Much like the Cliff Richard concert, in between numbers there are frequent shouts for familiar songs. However, whereas

---

1. Some time later, I learn The Jolt are in fact signed to Polydor, just like The Jam. Their album is produced by Vic Coppersmith-Heaven, just like The Jam. It must have felt rather uncomfortable for Weller and co. to know their record label had another three piece Mod influenced new wave band sitting on the sub's bench just in case.

Cliff's response was to simply smile and glide serenely into another dirge about Jesus, Weller's reaction is to grab the mic and shout "Listen, we ain't no fuckin' jukebox alright!"

Within a couple of songs, the impact of the volume has become intoxicating. By now, we're standing right up at the front. The sheer amount of energy The Jam put into their performance is infectious. When the band is giving so much, it just isn't possible to simply stand and watch. As several people around us are pogoing, I join in. Now, the pogo has been described as the dance of the punk movement. This would seem to be over dignifying it somewhat. If you saw someone doing it unaccompanied by music, you would say they were jumping up and down. The addition of the music doesn't change the nature of what's going on. It's still jumping up and down. It's something I'd sniggered at when catching glimpses of people doing it on TV. But here tonight, in the tightly packed audience, caught in the full force of The Jam's sonic blast it makes perfect sense.

Speaking of jumping up and down, at various points in the evening, Bruce Foxton executes his trademark leap in the air, legs tucked underneath him. As iconic a move in its own way as Chuck Berry's duckwalk or Pete Townshend's windmilling guitar playing. Meanwhile, wedged against the front of the stage, and staring up at Weller, I notice that whilst he's singing, he's also constantly chewing gum. In fact, he does so throughout the entire gig. I marvel at how he can sing without swallowing or choking on it.

Weller introduces another number by saying "This next song is a love song. And we ain't ashamed of it." As a 14 year old who is still sorting out his emotions, this seems like a bold statement. It also speaks of the new orthodoxy which punk has put in place. A couple of years earlier, with a few notable exceptions, almost every song you heard on the radio would be some kind of love song. Now, in the aftermath of punk's scorched earth moment, it seems important that a song's subject matter has some wider relevance.

"This is gonna be our next single. And we hope you'll all go out and buy it." Says Weller, before the band launch into 'David Watts'. It's so punchy, so catchy, it immediately snares me. I've no idea that it's actually a cover version. I've no idea who The Kinks are. I've never heard of them. Hell, until tonight, I didn't really know who The Jam were. It's during this song that I move along the front of the stage in order to put my head right up against the stack of speakers. I'm curious to hear this blaring electric noise up close. The sound is all consuming. I laugh at the delirious assault on my senses.

Weller introduces the next song: 'Mr. Clean'. As it starts up, my first thought is it almost sounds like something that could be on The Beatles' *Revolver*. This surprises me, as in the world of punk, The Beatles are more or less forbidden. Even though I still listen to them at home, it's something I tend to keep quiet about. I know Pete doesn't really approve. As the song unfolds, the way Weller spits out the lines, he appears authentically angry. His is a bitterness that even Lennon may have struggled to summon. 'Mr. Clean' isn't just a critique of a certain character type, it's a clear statement that class is the ultimate divider and that, from Weller's perspective, the privileged will always deserve to be the object of scorn and antagonism. When he barks the line *"And if I get a chance, I'll fuck up your life!"* some people in the crowd cheer. Hearing swear words in song lyrics still seems quite a novelty and a good portion of the audience are young enough to feel unembarrassed about cheering profanity for its own sake.

Bruce Foxton's bass line is nimble and expressive and at points, it alone carries the melody. There seems to be lots of space within the song, yet it's packed with detail, each section with its own discreet melodic structure. Rick Buckler's drumming is robust but concise with whole portions of the song being driven just by his hi-hat. Buckler's use of cymbals is one of his greatest strengths and this song shows his skill at using them to add subtle colour. Weller's guitar work is deceptive. I don't quite understand how he's doing it, but his style is a mix of rhythm playing and lead lines.

By the end of the show, I've been jumping up and down for nearly an hour. This is the most exercise I've had all year. The band stride off stage to a huge roar of approval. I prepare to leave, but Steve assures me they will come back on. "It's called an encore." This is news to me. "So why do they go off then?" "Probably so they can have a piss." Says Pete.

Sure enough, after a few minutes of clapping, whistling and stamping, The Jam return to the stage to tear through another three songs. Afterwards, when the house lights come up, Pete, Steve and I are left standing, sweaty, breathless and thrilled. "That was ace!" Says Pete. I agree. "Pearlin'". The band played for around an hour and a quarter, and even though I only recognised one song, I've just had the best night of my life. I've just seen my first *punk gig*.

Except I haven't. This is June 1978. By now, punk's original fire and bile has long since dissipated. The Sex Pistols themselves split up in San Francisco back in January. Bizarrely I had been made aware of this by an announcement on *John Craven's Newsround* on BBC1 at tea time. The press and the radio now refer to bands like X-Ray Spex, The Buzzcocks and The Jam as New Wave. The word 'punk' actually feels a little out dated.

And of course The Jam were never really a punk band anyway. They had nothing to do with punk's 1976 year zero attitude. They had been feeling their way towards their signature sound since their first gig in 1973, when they played cover versions of early rock and roll tracks. But with Weller's youthful obsession with The Who and Mod culture in general, things slowly began to change. Gradually the band incorporated Motown and Stax covers into their sets. Whilst Weller's own compositions began to use the Mod worldview to help fashion a perspective that combined societal critique with the explicitly personal.

By 1976, the band had coalesced into the trio of Weller, Buckler and Foxton and they'd completely honed their sound. Not only that, they'd already nailed their instantly recognizable visual style. The band's attire standing in strict contrast to the quickly standardised punk look of garish colours, ripped and torn t-shirts held together by safety pins and so on. The Jam were neatly dressed in tailored sixties style suits and ties. Whilst many second division punk bands reveled in the abject and the moronic, The Jam looked smart and acted smart.

Nevertheless, the band benefitted from the movement's momentum and from both the public and the record industry's willingness to take on a stripped back, energetic sound. They also played on bills with many of the first generation punk bands, and had initially taken part in The Clash's 'White Riot' tour. But The Jam had never called themselves punks, nor seen themselves as having much in common with the trend itself. And yet, right here, right now, these subtleties are lost on me. I've just seen my first punk gig. And that's that.

We've missed the last bus. Pete phones his Dad. About twenty five minutes later we're being driven home. My ears are ringing and ringing. The feeling is disorienting. My hearing is muffled. It's like having earplugs in. Noisy, whistling ear plugs. Later, I lie in bed in the dark. The tinnitus is overpowering. It makes it difficult to think properly. The whistling combined with the excitement of seeing The Jam mean I find it impossible to sleep.

The next day at school, Pete and I are buzzing. And my ears are *still* ringing. "From now on." Says Pete. "We should go and see every punk band that plays Blackburn." I nod keenly. "Definitely."

A week later, I see a tiny advertisement on the second page of the Lancashire Evening Telegraph. It informs me The Clash will be playing at King George's Hall on 13th July. That's less than a month away! I ask Mum if she can buy me a ticket when she goes to Blackburn, saying I'll pay for it out of my pocket money. The next day at school, I inform Pete and Steve of the important news. Pete doesn't believe me at first. Steve of course already knew about it. Or at least claims he already knew about it.

The next step is obvious. We have to start our own band. Steve has a bass he's getting to grips with and his mate Mick Tunstall has an electric guitar. Pete's Dad buys him a drum kit and I start writing lyrics. We call ourselves Emergency. Then we learn there's already a band in Manchester called Emergency. So we become Emergency X. This is then contracted to Emergex. The fact this makes us sound like a kitchen scourer doesn't seem to deter us. In truth, it's irrelevant what we're called, as we never venture outside of Steve's bedroom.

Probably a good thing, as we sound uncannily like 14 year old boys who can't play or sing.

I embrace the new wave with a fervent passion. By the end of the year, I've been to see The Clash, Suicide, Siouxsie and the Banshees, Spizz Oil, Manicured Noise, 999, The Rezillos, Gang of Four, The Fall, Lene Lovich, John Cooper Clarke and local Blackburn new wave bands: The Accelerators, The Stiffs and IQ Zero. Increasing exposure to Peel sends me exploring down less obvious avenues. My taste expands. And yet, although by December 1978 my heroes are The Fall, Magazine and Gang of Four, I know it was The Jam gig that completely catalyzed my musical passion. However, there was one negative thing about that gig. The tinnitus.

Three days afterwards I still have the intense ringing in my ears. It doesn't seem to have decreased at all. I feel slightly nauseous all the time. I sit in lessons unable to focus on what's being said. I'm really worried that from now on the ringing will always be there. I feel so stupid for standing right up against the speakers.

I'm at home in the early evening, walking from the living room into the kitchen, when the tinnitus suddenly gets louder. And louder. Until it becomes deafening. I can't hear any sound other than the high-pitched whistle. I begin to lose my balance. I put my hand against the wall to steady myself. The whistling gets louder still. I black out.

I don't know how long I've been unconscious for, but when I come to, Mum and my sister Gillian are staring down at me looking worried. They help me into the kitchen. I sit down, feeling bewildered but somehow exhilarated. The tinnitus is still there but has gone down to a much quieter level. The next day, my Dad takes me to the Doctor to get my ears checked. The Doctor says everything is fine. And thankfully, by the end of the week my hearing has returned to normal.

* * * * *

2011. Thirty-three years later, after a lifetime of serious gig going, I've started sometimes wearing earplugs at concerts in order to preserve my hearing. I've developed long-term mild tinnitus in my right ear, so it's definitely worth taking the issue seriously. And yet, even though I know it's the sensible thing to do, wearing earplugs does feel somehow like cheating.

By this stage, I'm doing my dream job. Writing and acting in my own long running TV show. *Ideal* is a BBC sit-com about a lazy cannabis dealer called Moz, who deals to his circle of friends. The incomparable Johnny Vegas plays Moz, and the rest of the cast is none too shabby either. One of the great pleasures of the show has been selecting the soundtrack music. I've managed to get some great music on national television, including the kind of stuff you'd never normally hear coming through your TV set – Throbbing Gristle, Coil, Sleater-Kinney, Wire, late period Scott Walker and rather a lot of The Fall.

The combination of the soundtrack and the subject matter means the show has some cache amongst musicians. I haven't been slow to pick up on this and have invited a few cult musicians to play cameos. Mark E. Smith and Elena Poulou from The Fall, John Robb of the Membranes and Barry Adamson have all been gracious enough to play small roles in the show.

For the opening scene of the first episode of the seventh series, we want to film a fantasy sequence in which Moz describes his ideal night in. It turns out to be making out with glamorous TV actress Kara Tointon, whilst a famous rock star sits close by strumming an acoustic guitar and then offers to make them all a round of cheese on toast.

It's Johnny who first suggests getting Paul Weller involved. It sounds like a great idea. But when I ring Weller's assistant she seems very doubtful. "I'll ask." She says. "But I doubt he'll be up for it. Paul gets asked to do this kind of thing a lot." It strikes me as pretty unlikely that he's been asked to do anything *exactly* like this before, but I let that pass. Sensing this may be a dead end, I start drawing up a list of alternatives, but none of them have the attraction of Weller.

A few days later, his assistant rings back. "I'm really surprised." She says. "But Paul's said 'yes'. He's a big fan of Johnny and he really likes the show." I'm thrilled. Three weeks later, we shoot the scene at the BBC TV Centre on Oxford Road in Manchester. Weller arrives in a parka, and despite his silver hair, he looks youthful and lean. He also seems surprisingly quiet and shy.

It's an obvious thing to say, but acting is hard for non-actors. And perhaps the hardest thing of all is playing yourself. Trying to come over as you normally would, but delivering scripted lines is extremely tricky. Anybody who ever heard John Peel bravely playing himself during a guest spot on Radio 4's *The Archers* knows it can be a cringe inducing experience. And yet, when we shoot the scene in Moz's bedsit, Weller delivers his lines with subtlety and naturalism.

Afterwards, I'm talking with Weller in his dressing room, along with Johnny and the wonderful actor Ben Crompton. Johnny and Ben have brought in various albums and photos for him to autograph. I kick myself for not bringing along my creased copy of *All Mod Cons*. Johnny produces an old issue of the *NME* from 1978, featuring an interview with The Jam and asks him to sign it. "Look at that." Says Weller, pointing to the photograph of himself age 20. He shakes his head. "Just a little oik."

I tell him I saw The Jam that year. "I was 14. It was the first gig I ever went to." He doesn't need to know about Cliff. I tell him the story of the tinnitus. About how worried I was and how it made me black out three days later. Weller looks genuinely concerned. "Really? Oh, sorry about that mate." "It's alright." I say. "It didn't exactly put me off going to gigs."

THE SPECIALS, MADNESS & THE SELECTER

THE GOLDEN PALMS, BLACKBURN

TUESDAY 30TH OCTOBER 1979

(AGE 15)

It's the last day of October. This month has been the best month of my life. I'm in love. I'm head over heels in love. I couldn't be more in love.

Mind you, I don't have a girlfriend. I haven't even kissed a girl. I'm in love with music. Music is everything. It fills each and every waking moment. My interest in the more obvious pure punk or new wave bands has evolved into a fascination with the open-ended sounds of the emerging post-punk scene. Although I don't call it post-punk. Nobody does. That categorisation will come much later.

When people ask me what kind of music I'm into, like many music fans before me, who feel they are privy to something special, I refer to it as Underground. Most people then raise their eyebrows and look nonplussed. So then I go on to list the bands I like. Most people once again raise their eyebrows and look nonplussed.

I'm a complete junkie for new sounds. I save up pocket money and wash neighbours' cars at 40p a time in order to fund my habit. My most recent purchases have been The Fall's sophomore album *Dragnet*, which, despite its ultra lo-fidelity sound, is something of a masterpiece, as well as Cabaret Voltaire's spooky yet groovy *Silent Command* and the *About Time* EP by The Passage – a band whose sound is complex, propulsive and unique.

I've also recently bought The Slits' debut single 'Typical Girls'. To be honest, I already have this track, because it's included on their album *Cut* which came out a couple of weeks back. But I felt compelled to buy the 7" as it has a B-side I haven't heard. This is becoming a recurring feature of my record buying. A desire to hear *everything*. However, it turns out to have been a sound investment, as The Slits' version of Marvin Gaye's 'I Heard it Through The Grapevine' is a recording of raw fidgeting beauty.

But by far my most electrifying musical moments are experienced at gigs. Which is precisely why October 1979 has been the best month of my life. Because this month I've been to see Joy Division, The Buzzcocks, Stiff Little Fingers, The Donkeys, The Damned, The Ruts, IQ Zero, The Units, The Skids, Fingerprintz, UK Subs, Tiger Tails, The Killermeters and The Undertones. And tonight, just to round off October in style, I've come out to see three more bands.

Pete and I are queuing outside The Golden Palms nightclub on Mill Lane in Blackburn. This is an unusual venue for a gig. Almost all the touring bands that visit Blackburn play at the King George's Hall. The Golden Palms is a typical old-fashioned night-club. Opened in 1959 and formerly known as the Mecca – which many regulars still call it – it was the most popular dancehall in the area during the early 1960s. It enjoyed another boom, during the heyday of Northern Soul. Nowadays, it caters to the disco dating and mating crowd. Rock music is seldom heard here. On an average night, the DJ spins singles by The Bee Gees and a smooth covers band ladles out versions of 'Hopelessly Devoted to You' and 'If I Said You Had A Beautiful Body Would You Hold It Against Me'.

But tonight, The Golden Palms will be one of the ports of call on a 40-date tour, which the music press is comparing to an old-fashioned record label package tour. The label is Coventry's 2-Tone Records. And the so-called Ska Revival has been an instantaneous success.

The Specials' debut single 'Gangsters' was released back in May. Pete was an immediate convert to the cause. The day after John Peel first played 'Gangsters', Pete was buzzing with excitement about it. An enthusiastic Peel played it again that night and Pete taped it. The cassette is still king.

The following day after school, we sat on his bed, listening to the intro over and over, trying to figure out what Neville Staple shouts at the start of the track. We can hear the *"Don't argue!"* bit. But what does he say before that? Something about burning ropes? Burly rock guns? We just can't figure it out.[1]

Since this tour date was first announced, the 2-Tone movement has been gaining serious momentum. The Specials' first John Peel Session only went out on the 29th May, yet by August, they'd already established themselves as a top ten pop act. But this isn't just the sound of one band skanking. It's an entire movement. Jerry Dammers' fledgling label has also released debut 45s from Madness and The Selecter. Madness appeared on *Top of The Pops* for the first time last month. Performing their single 'The Prince', they looked for all the world like cheeky fresh faced schoolboys allowed to play out after their curfew.

Three weeks ago, The Specials released their second 45 – an up-tempo cover version of Dandy Livingstone's 'Rudy, A Message To You'. A week later, both The Specials and Madness released their debut albums. Both of which have been greeted with huge acclaim. That same week, The Selecter made their *Top of The Pops* debut with 'On My Radio', bouncing around the TV stage with more energy than

---

1. I had completely forgotten about this 'quest for knowledge' until 38 years later, when, during a conversation about The Specials with my friend and 2-Tone aficionado Paul Putner, he happened to mention that the phrase is *"Bernie Rhodes knows, don't argue!"* Bernie Rhodes had been The Clash's manager and was also briefly manager of The Specials. Perhaps more importantly, it was Rhodes who spotted the 19-year-old John Lydon walking down London's King's Road, wearing his self-modified 'I Hate Pink Floyd' T-shirt, and insisted the teenager meet Malcolm McLaren.

the rest of the show's acts combined. Last Monday, Peel presented The Selecter's first radio session, alongside a second session from The Specials. Then, on Thursday, both bands were back on *Top of The Pops* again.

Whilst this may not be Beatlemania, 2-Tone certainly seems to have tapped into a feverish need amongst Britain's youth for a sound that combines the power and drive of punk with danceable tunes.

Unsurprisingly, tonight's gig is now completely sold out. The queue is a long one, snaking right the way around the outside of the venue. There's a chattering excitability in the air. Were it a film depicting the era, the queue would be entirely made up of kids dressed in sharp examples of the 2-Tone style. Yet the reality of the scene in 1979 is very different. Sure, there are some teenagers dressed in the tight fitting tonics, skinny ties, crombies, pork pie hats and loafers which are now being advertised in the small ads in the back pages of *NME* and *Sounds*. But there are also lots of punks in jeans and straight leg trousers. Some with spiked hair, but most with merely short hair. There are plenty of straight looking lads too. And there's also several freshly hatched young Mods in squeaky clean parkas and off the peg suits.

The Jam's obsession with Mod culture has been sending out ripples. There are now a number of bands trying to cop the sound of 1966's blue-eyed soul bands. The musical puritan in me is immediately dismissive. Why go back to 1966? Why rake over old ground? To my 15 year old brain, focused on the forward pointing sounds of 1979, the mid 60s feel like ancient history.

The only Mod revival band I've witnessed in the flesh are Huddersfield's The Killermeters – who supported The Undertones two weeks ago at King George's Hall. Despite some mock guitar heroics, their sound was weak and, with lyrics that constantly referred to women as "baby" and "honey", they felt painfully anachronistic.

A couple of lads at school have declared themselves Mods and started dressing in the regulation gear. But to me, in essence, the whole thing feels like some kind of drag act. It reminds me of the three be-quiffed 20 year olds I sometimes see hanging around Accrington market.

They wear 1950s teddy boy suits and brothel creepers. Ultimately, the Mod revival is just another homage.[2]

There are also several girls in the queue tonight. This audience is definitely a little more mixed than many of the gigs I'm going to at the moment. Most of the girls are dressed in jeans and T-shirts, although two or three wear chic 1960s charity shop dresses. But, despite what the motion picture version of events might be expected to deliver, the audience seems exclusively Caucasian. In fact, as I continue to survey the growing queue, I spot several young lads who look wilfully Caucasian: skinheads.

This isn't necessarily a bad thing. The skinhead look has more than one connotation. Some skins are simply pared down stylists whose big passion is, in actual fact, black dance music – soul, ska and lovers rock. Just because these lads have shaven heads and wear Doc Martens, Fred Perrys and braces doesn't mean they are automatically right wing thugs. Then I notice the tallest of the skinheads has a swastika tattooed on the side of his neck. Oh well. Maybe they've just come to dance.

After queuing for an age, we are eventually allowed inside. The venue seems almost comically straight, with its tacky, brightly coloured carpets and mirrored panels on the red walls. As the tallest of the two of us, I go to the bar. "Can I get two halves of cider please?" Despite my asking in a nervous, quavering voice, the barman simply says "No." I'm blushing too much to argue. I wander back and join Pete. After five minutes, he goes off to the bar. I wait expectantly. He returns with two lemonades. I chuckle and we drink them. I'm still not really bothered about alcohol anyway.

Last summer, just a month after the Jam gig, Pete and I tripped on magic mushrooms for the first time. We were introduced to the concept by Steve and Emergex guitarist Mick both of whom had taken them before. So four 14 year olds drank a brew of mushroom tea, then

---

2. It took until the 1990s for the idea of tribute acts to really take off. But, back in the late 1970s, the nouveau Mods were seemingly operating as 'tribute fans'.

wandered around the parks of Gt. Harwood, marvelling at the colours of the floral displays and giggling like toddlers. The next time we tripped, I started to get a sense of the interconnectedness of the natural world and the plasticity of what we consider reality. Although I couldn't actually express it like that at the time. At the time I just said 'Wow' a lot. Following on from such mind expansion, the pleasures of alcohol seem pretty limited.

Emergex fizzled out in late April. Musical indifferences. Pete has now ditched the drums and taken up the guitar and I'm still writing lyrics. We are desperate to start a proper band. But we can't do it on our own. And there are no likely candidates amongst our friends. Then, at a school disco in Gt. Harwood in June, we meet John Blackett and Owen Brindle. They're a year older and have already left school. They live in the next town, Clayton-le-Moors. We start talking about music and discover we're all into more or less the same bands. John plays bass and Owen has a drum kit. To suddenly meet other lads with similar tastes – and instruments – feels like a lifeline.

We start rehearsing in the basement garage at Pete's parent's house. We sound a bit like Joy Division and Siouxsie and the Banshees. Or more accurately, we sound like lads who listen to an awful lot of Joy Division and Siouxsie and the Banshees. We call ourselves Seminal Effect. We're unsure why.

I simultaneously start developing ideas for a music fanzine, which I decide to call 'Hex'. I encourage Pete and other friends to write articles and reviews, but nobody else seems particularly inspired, so I set about writing the whole thing myself. And doing the photos and some collages. So, when I'm not listening to records, or going to gigs, I'm rehearsing or writing lyrics, or writing about other bands. Like I say, music fills every waking moment.

Suddenly, the lights dim and The Selecter take to the stage to much cheering. There are plenty of them. Seven in all, including two vocalists: Arthur Hendrickson and Pauline Black. Inevitably, in interviews and photo-shoots, it's Black who has been receiving the most attention. It's still rare to see a woman on stage in a music venue. And Black is a high energy presence too. Neither a demure vocalist nor a traditionally sexy one, with her skinny frame clad in a tight fitting black suit and her hair swept back under her 'stingy brim' hat, she strikes a distinctly androgynous note. Inevitably however, there are a few shouts of "Get your knickers off!" from some members of the audience. This is Blackburn after all. These requests are not dignified with a response.

Charley Bembridge lets off a roll on the snare as The Selecter spark their set with the only song the vast majority of the audience will know; their debut 'On My Radio', which is currently at number 21 in this week's national chart. This is a sassy move. Leading with an ace. It says The Selecter have got tunes to spare. It's also a smart ploy, in that it gets a good portion of the audience dancing straight away.

Oddly, the single isn't especially representative of the band's style. True, like the majority of their compositions, the verses skip along brightly, with a ska guitar line emphasizing the after-beat. However, when it comes to the chorus, there's a shift to something much more jerky, staccato and shrill. The repeated chorus of "It's just the same old show, on my radio" owes far more to the angular sound of the evolving new wave and wouldn't sound out of place on a song by XTC. Nevertheless, lead guitarist Neol Davies aside, The Selecter are the blackest band on the bill tonight. And at several points, their set feels closer to up tempo reggae than ska.

A lot of the current reggae I hear – by which I mean the roots reggae I hear on John Peel, as I don't know anybody who actually owns any reggae records – sounds like devotional music. It sings of Jah, it sings of redemption, it sings of righteousness and it definitely slows down the pace. The Selecter have taken a different tack. Their rhythms are all upbeat and often celebratory. Lyrically however, whilst their songs may not engage with the beliefs of Rastafarianism, they do address notions of pressure and strife. Just take a glance at their titles: 'Danger', 'Too Much Pressure', 'They Make Me Mad' and 'Murder'.

Next the band bound into 'Everyday'. Here again, the lyrics are distinctly downbeat and, with its chorus of "*Everyday, things are getting worse*", the outlook is bleak. And yet musically, the mood could hardly be more positive. Rhythm guitarist Compton Amanor keeps up an energetic flow, Charley Anderson skips on the spot and shakes his dreads, his bass line spacious and assured, whilst Desmond Brown's organ rolls could almost be coming from a fairground.

Above everything else, ska is a sound designed to be danced to. Many of my current heroes, such as Cabaret Voltaire, Public Image Ltd. and Gang of Four, frequently refer to disco or dub or funk in their interviews. But, when it comes to the music itself, the dance elements often feel stiff and uptight. Cabaret Voltaire use disco's repetition but not its pulse. Public Image Ltd. adopt dub's dread, but not its sensuality. Gang of Four deploy funk's rhythms but not its groove. Here, in the world of 2-Tone, there are no such conflicts of purpose. The Selecter are using ska and rock steady – the original building blocks of reggae – purely to get the audience up and moving. This isn't a sound influenced by black dance music. This *is* black dance music.

As the band start into 'Murder', Black is an endless battery of energy, darting around the stage and directing her voice with full force. Anderson's bass runs sound almost cartoonishly elasticated. The energy in the venue is increasing. I'm sweating now. Almost everybody's dancing. I glance around. Even the people standing back at the bar are vigorously bobbing their heads.

On stage, as the rest of The Selecter are cavorting, Davies stands calm and still. Playing guitar, wearing shades and chewing gum, he looks completely unruffled by the way his band are galvanizing the audience. At the opposite side of the stage, and the opposite end of the spectrum, Brown bounces about, jabbing at the keyboards with visible glee, a broad grin permanently on his face. The song concludes to a wave of applause. "They are so fucking good." Says Pete. He's right. The sound of their single hadn't prepared me for what a tight and vital live band they are.

Bembridge plays a series of lazy rolls as Hendrickson grabs the mic stand and leans over the edge of the stage. In his sharp grey suit, he's dripping with sweat, but somehow he still manages to look like the coolest, slickest guy imaginable. He fixes the audience with a piercing gaze then growls out "James Bond! The Killer!" Suddenly, the band launch into their version of the '007 Theme'. This sounds so fat and driving. I love it. Anderson pumps out an incredibly bouncy bass line, Black skips around hammering a cowbell and Davies executes the notorious 007 guitar line with lethal precision.

Hendrickson starts toasting over the urgent groove. His voice heavy with reverb, he interjects with the names of Bond villains. "*Do you expect me to talk?*" He asks, sounding like a menacing Prince Jazzbo. "*No, I expect you to die!*" Pete and I are dancing and grinning at each other. Ska and James Bond? Yes thank you![3]

'Missing Words' is the first real change of mood of the evening. Whilst many of their songs stick to a fairly obvious rock steady template, 'Missing Words' extends the band's melodic range. And it's one of the few moments in the band's set where a song's sentiments are matched by its setting. The lyrics describe a relationship breakup due to a lack of genuine communication. And, with Black's melancholic vocal, and Davies' grand, ringing chords, this has the classy gleam of The Pretenders. Nevertheless, the band are smart enough to make sure the whole endeavour is still driven along by the truly irresistible skank of Amanor's guitar.[4]

I suddenly remember I've got a small pocket notebook my Granddad gave me in my jacket. I take it out and make a note of the songs they've played so far. Now I've decided to write a fanzine, I realise I need to make regular notes for review purposes.

---

3. My own passionate love affair with James Bond had come to a screeching halt in a cinema in Llandudno in 1977. It was there, sitting in the darkness, with my Mum and my sisters, whilst watching Roger Moore smirk his way through *The Spy Who Loved Me*, that I decided Bond just didn't respect me any more. However, with the benefit of hindsight, I now realise Bond and I just needed some time apart.

4. Despite Neol Davies evolving serious skills as a songwriter, The Selecter were the first of the original 2-Tone bands to fade from media and public interest. Their ambitious second album, 1981's *Celebrate the Bullet*, is ripe for rediscovery.

Having opened with their hit single, they bookend their set with the only other song most people here will know, the B-side: 'Too Much Pressure'. This is one of their best songs and possibly their most high-energy number. And there's plenty of competition for that title. Hendrickson takes the lead vocal, telling of how much dissatisfaction and sadness he is suffering, whilst Black, Davies and Amanor repeatedly punctuate his woes with the chant of *"too much pressure"*. It's a driving and addictive piece of music and, by the time they hit the final note, the whole audience are in motion, the entire dance floor springing in time to the dancers. As Black shouts "Goodnight!" and the band wave and depart the stage, the crowd is unstinting in its applause and cheers.

The Selecter arrived the underdogs. And they left conquering heroes. They also came back on stage and did an encore. But I missed that, as I was queuing for a badly needed piss. I come out of the toilets and weave my way through the packed crowd to where Pete is standing.

We are excitable. Even though we're now both fairly seasoned gig goers, it still feels like each venture out to a venue is a sortie into the world of adulthood. We wouldn't be allowed to go into a pub. But we are granted access to dance halls, concert halls and clubs to see bands without question. As we chat, two roadies work away on the stage, adjusting mic stands and setting up another keyboard. Unlike just about every other man in the venue, the roadies have long hair and wear flared jeans. Despite the new wave's increasing dominance of the live music scene, some things are slow to change. The majority of roadies everywhere still sport long hair and wear flared jeans.

Moments after the roadies depart the stage, the lights dip and Madness step out to a building wave of applause and cheers. Each member of the band assumes a pose and stands stock still. Bizarrely, every one of them appears to be wearing a fez. A long, deep note comes from Lee Thompson's saxophone. It blares out of the sound system like a menacing fog-horn. It sounds again. Longer this time. The note stretches on and on. When it finally ends, Woody Woodgate plays a tight roll on the snare, the stage lights flash up and Madness burst into life like a choreographed party.

Aside from their unusual headgear, the whole band is dressed in suits and ties, with the exception of saxophonist Lee Thompson, who wears a suit-cut black leather jacket and jeans. Guitarist Chris 'Chrissy Boy' Foreman moves about the stage with a loose-limbed agility. Keyboardist Mike Barson has something of the mad professor about him, hammering the keys with a manic grin. Bassist Mark 'Bedders' Bedford is boyish and wide-eyed, whilst vocalist Graham 'Suggs' McPherson exudes a cocky self-assurance. When my Mum first saw him on *Top of The Pops*, she chuckled, saying "He's got such a cheeky face!" It's true. Madness in general, and Suggs in particular, definitely give off an air of impudent charm.

Right now, Suggs is singing, whilst simultaneously running on the spot. In fact, aside from Woodgate behind his kit, the entire band is running on the spot. Not only that, they are running in a stylish way, which makes it look like dancing. Christ, they look smart and self-assured. Madness already feel like proper pop stars. And they are an undeniably handsome bunch. I can't hear every word Suggs says, but he appears to be singing about the River Nile and monsoons. We are obviously a world away from the social realism of punk and the existential musings of the Underground. This is entertainment. This is fun.

Ska is often referred to as good time music, and yet, whilst both The Specials and The Selecter might provide danceable tunes, their lyrics offer a cynical and fatalistic appraisal of the world. Not so Madness.

Sharing centre stage with Suggs, is Chas Smash. Wearing a blue tonic suit, pork pie hat and wrap around sunglasses, with a razor sharp jaw line and razor sharp moves, Smash is Madness' special weapon. A member of the band whose primary function is to dance. And he does so with a cool precision. Smash is a bridgehead between the audience and the band. He may not play an instrument and might only provide very occasional backing vocals, but he does inject the majority of the songs with one of Madness' trademark sounds. At various points he hisses the *"chuck-a-chuck-chuck-a-chuck!"* rhythm into his mic. It's a noise that seems to urge the music on. Not that it requires much urging. There's so much energy coming off the stage, by the end of the opening number, over half the audience are dancing again.

Chuck-a-chuck-chuck-a-chuck!

The final notes of the song have barely finished ringing out, when Woodgate lets rip with a lengthy drum roll and the band drive straight into the next number: 'Land of Hope And Glory'. Suggs and Smash bound around acting out the song's narrative of borstal life. Although Madness give the impression that the playing of instruments is almost an incidental element to the fun that's being had on stage, they are consummate musicians and incredibly tightly drilled. Madness know their strengths. And these songs have been tailor made to show them off. Every nuance, every twist, every stop/start moment is inch perfect.

Chuck-a-chuck-chuck-a-chuck!

As the applause dies down, Suggs sings the line "*Buster, he sold the heat...*". But the next line is drowned out by a huge burst of cheering. Madness start into 'The Prince', their debut single that has only recently started to slide down the charts. After The Specials 'Gangsters', this is currently the ska revival's most instantly recognisable song. Perhaps the crucial line is "*This may not be uptown Jamaica, but we promise you a treat.*"

Chuck-a-chuck-chuck-a-chuck!

Like The Selecter, Madness are confident enough to toss out their big hit early on. The message to the audience is the same – you can have this now, because there's better to come. 'The Prince' is a tribute to one of the originators of the ska sound, Prince Buster. Born Cecil Bustamente Campbell, he released literally scores of singles, including 'Madness' (1963) and 'One Step Beyond' (1964). Versions of both of these songs will appear in Madness' set tonight. Buster also released the single 'Al Capone' (1964), which forms the basis of The Specials' 'Gangsters'. To say he is a major influence on the 2-Tone movement doesn't really cover it. Prince Buster is to 2-Tone as James Brown is to funk.

Chuck-a-chuck-chuck-a-chuck!

All around us, people are dancing. Many are trying to ape the moves of Chas Smash, although few come anywhere near capturing his graceful mania. This dancing, like the pogo, is as much about expending the maximum amount of energy as it is about celebrating the music. Pete is beaming from ear to ear. Right now, Madness are his favourite band and this performance is delivering in spades. In fact, from the response in the dancehall, I get the impression Madness are many people's favourite band. I've never before seen so many people grinning at a gig.

Chuck-a-chuck-chuck-a-chuck!

Their next offering is 'My Girl'. Musically this makes me feel slightly awkward. My Underground puritanism sniffs show business. This feels almost like a song from a musical. And yet, it's not a falling in love song, it's not a break up song, rather it's a song about the difficulties in a relationship when one person can't give the other a little space. Like The Selecter's 'Missing Words', it's about lack of communication. This is way beyond my experience. I'm not lucky enough to have a girlfriend to be uncommunicative with.

Chuck-a-chuck-chuck-a-chuck!

The biggest cheer of the set comes when Chas Smash steps up to the mic and shouts "*Hey you! Don't watch that! Watch this!*" It's the introduction to their new single, a cover of Prince Buster's 'One Step Beyond'. But it's already popular enough for portions of the audience to shout out the remainder of the song's intro with Smash. When the band dive into the tune, the dance floor jumps into renewed life. If Buster's vibrant original recording lollops along like a donkey that has just been whacked on the rump, Madness' version is like a racehorse full of stimulants, sprinting for the finish line the instant the race begins. And the audience loves them for it.

Chuck-a-chuck-chuck-a-chuck!

"This is a song about an old friend of ours." Says Suggs. "It's called 'Bed and Breakfast Man'". This is the one song I had hoped they'd play. A cool yet perky version of 'Bed and Breakfast Man' was on the band's Peel session earlier in the year. Driven along by Woodgate's supple, rhythmic playing and Barson's Jackie Mittoo style organ shuffle, it's the song that convinced me of their skills as songwriters. Barson's melodic and evocative keyboard lines are a big component of Madness' appeal. In fact, organ sounds are one of the defining elements of ska. Yet keyboards have largely been absent from the sound of punk, Dave Greenfield's showy flourishes with The Stranglers being a notable exception. As for synthesisers, they have been pretty much outlawed, due to their prog connotations. But what Barson and the other 2-Tone groups do is to take keyboards back to an earlier age – pre-punk, pre-prog, pre-rock.

Chuck-a-chuck-chuck-a-chuck!

There is no reason why Madness should be bound by punk's new orthodoxy. Whilst the influence of punk is clearly detectable in the music of both The Specials and The Selector, it is largely absent from the songs of Madness. Here, there's none of punk's fury. There might be disdain, there might be sarcasm and an occasional hint of bitterness. But there's no trace of anger. Ian Dury and the Blockheads are clearly Madness' closest cousins. They share the same streetwise patter, the same low rent theatrical charm. In fact, Madness are entertainers through and through. The whole time they are on stage, they are 'on'. They have paid careful attention to the details of their performance; the between song banter, the suits, the dance moves, the backing vocals.

Chuck-a-chuck-chuck-a-chuck!

But, if I'm honest, a part of me is actively resistant to the amount of show business in their performance. I've become fixated on authenticity. The Underground music I lionise doesn't seem to be about entertainment as such. It seems much more about the direct communication of ideas, attitudes and uncertainties. When I listen to a song, I want to believe what is lyrically being articulated is coming directly from the heart and the head. Whereas Madness often deal in irony, archness and characters. Also, despite the fact I love comedy, I feel suspicious of overt humour in music. And Madness style themselves as not just humorous, but 'nutty'. Cabaret Voltaire this isn't.

Chuck-a-chuck-chuck-a-chuck!

Live however, Madness' music has a dimension that the recorded versions can't capture. The rhythm section of Woodgate and Bedders has such muscularity it injects even their more lightweight songs with gravity. Besides which, of all the bands I've seen over the last year and a half, Madness are the ones who connect most directly with the audience.

Madness are not just a band. Madness are a gang. Madness are best mates. And they give the impression they could be your best mates too. Madness are a secret society which anybody can join. And, despite my antipathy to their honed entertainment skills, I want to join too.

Chuck-a-chuck-chuck-a-chuck!

It's only during the band's ska'd up version of Tchaikovsky's 'Swan Lake' that my attention really drops. Unlike The Selecter's take on the '007 Theme', Madness don't really bring anything special to the piece. And, unfortunately, it compares unfavourably with the recent Public Image Ltd. single 'Death Disco', which also uses elements of 'Swan Lake'. On that song, Keith Levene's guitar carves out the melody in a fervid and craggy manner. Madness' arrangement meanwhile, makes little pretence to being anything other than a novelty. Suggs and Smash face each other and launch into a bizarre dance, where they appear to be head butting one another in time to the music. This may be a dance craze too far.

Chuck-a-chuck-chuck-a-chuck!

As the song's final chords ring out, the cheering and applause are joyous. Clearly most folk here don't share my reservations. But as the applause fades, another sound becomes audible. About four or five men are chanting 'Sieg Heil'. Pete and I exchange a glance. Pete turns to me, and purses his lips. "That's bad class." I nod. 'Bad class' is what we've started saying, to indicate when something is really crass and misjudged. We can't tell whereabouts in the crowd the chanting is coming from. Suggs squints out into the audience. He can't locate where it's coming from either. He shakes his head. "You wanna knock that on the head, I tell yer!" He turns back toward the band. Woodgate clicks his sticks and the band go into the Kinks-like 'Razor Blade Alley'.

Chuck-a-chuck-chuck-a-chuck!

The National Front has had some kind of presence in Blackburn for as long as I can remember, with occasional marches through the town centre. NF skins have recently been on recruitment drives, attending punk and new wave gigs to stir up trouble and attract attention. In contrast, one of 2-Tone's main messages seems to be a call for racial unity. In fact, The Specials and The Selecter are living examples of racial integration. 2-Tone music is a triumph of hybridisation. Why fascists would be attracted to the gig is mystifying. At least I can't accuse them of preaching to the converted.

Chuck-a-chuck-chuck-a-chuck!

Madness conclude their set with their version of Prince Buster's 'Madness'. It's the B-side of their debut 'The Prince', but in most teenage bedrooms across the land, it's been receiving just as many spins as the flip. In fact, the recording could have easily been released as an A-side and scored a hit. Chrissy Boy skips on the spot as he chops out the rhythm, Bedders swings his hips as his deft fingers pluck the walking bass line and Suggs and Smash bounce around, seemingly determined to use up every last drop of energy. Portions of the audience sing along and greet the song's climax with cheers of devotion.

"We got time for one more?" Suggs shouts to the side of the stage. There is some brief debate between Thompson, Suggs and one of the roadies. "Sorry." Suggs gives the audience an exaggerated grimace. "We've run out of time." This sparks much forceful booing from the audience. Has anyone ever truthfully said "I've had enough fun now thanks"? We want more. A lot more. Nevertheless, it's time for Madness to leave. Suggs even gives several formal bows before he departs. He's doing it with a very cheeky grin. But it still feels like a genuine show biz gesture. Something I haven't seen at a music gig since Cliff Richard.

Long after Madness exit the stage the energy in the packed dancehall remains high. There are a lot of overexcited people here. There are also a lot of very drunken people here. Far more so than at other gigs I've attended over the last year. On several occasions, lads carrying beers collide with us, spilling the tops off their pints as they stagger back into the crowd to locate their mates.

I should perhaps at this point, make a confession. I don't actually own any 2-Tone records. Don't get me wrong – I've never heard a 2-Tone record I didn't like. But they are never at the top of my list when I'm out spending my precious car washing earnings. Mind you, I don't really need to own any, as I hear them constantly when I'm over at Pete's house. He's bought every 2-Tone record the instant it's come out. However, having experienced the full force of live performance, I've decided to remedy this situation.

As The Specials take to the stage, The Golden Palms is filled with the sound of hundreds of cheering fans. This band are simultaneously rebels, pop stars, folk heroes, fashion icons and everymen. With a shout of "One! Two! Three! Four!" they pile straight into 'Dawning of a New Era'. John Bradbury pounds out a thunderous beat on the toms, the combined might of Lynval Golding and Roddy Radiation's guitars twanging like an amped up Duane Eddy. They stand at opposite sides of the stage. Radiation is white, dressed in black sta-press trousers, a black long sleeve shirt with pearl buttons and a shiny pork pie hat. Golding is black, slender and nimble on his feet. He is also, without doubt, the most nattily attired man on stage tonight. And, in that he's clearly not without competition. The Specials are a band with true sartorial cohesion. But Golding's style is a little more flamboyant. He wears a broad lapelled black suit, a shiny silver grey tie, cream loafers and a jauntily angled broad black flat cap.

Jerry Dammers stands at his keyboards, dressed in tonic trousers and a sports jacket, with tacky white 60s sun glasses firmly in place. He's jabbing at the keys whilst hopping from foot to foot. Centre stage stand vocalists Terry Hall and Neville Staple. With his baritone voice and handsome leonine profile, Jamaican born Staple is a powerful presence. Originally, he had run a sound system in Coventry and worked as one of The Specials' roadies. However, the story goes that during a soundcheck at London's Music Machine, Staple plugged a microphone into the mixing desk and toasted along with a couple of the band's songs. After that, he was invited to become a permanent member. Now, bounding from left to right, dressed in two-tone trousers and a smart dress shirt, Staple looks like he owns the stage.

Next to him, and singing in a far higher register, is Terry Hall. He's wearing a black suit with a bright white shirt and a cravat. At just 20, he's easily the youngest member of the band. Skinny and doleful with heavy eyebrows and what can legitimately be described as a hangdog expression, Hall won't crack a smile throughout the entire evening. His demeanour has been compared to John Lydon. But whereas Lydon's glare is powered by frustration and anger, Hall's baleful stare seems to be fuelled by dissatisfaction and disdain. He looks like a man who only ever expects disappointment and has decided to save time by adopting the appropriate countenance in advance.

Just behind Hall and Staple, bassist Sir Horace Gentleman is pumping out the groove. He looks slightly underdressed compared to the rest of the band, wearing jeans and a black Fred Perry. This will turn out to be a smart decision, as the dancehall's temperature is about to soar. Whilst I may not have felt inclined to snap up their records, I can immediately appreciate that live, The Specials are indeed something very special.

'Dawning of a New Era' is an atypical Specials composition in that it's more indebted to rock and roll than to ska. It dates back to an earlier era of the band's evolution. For, whilst The Specials might seem to have suddenly materialised fully formed, their sound and style have been fermenting and maturing for two years.

They were formed in 1977 and originally went by the name The Coventry Automatics. At first, their sets had consisted of songs that often switched between punk and reggae rhythms. But, by the time they had scored the support slot on The Clash's 'On Parole' tour in the early summer of 1978, they had started to find their focus with their turbo-powered reinvention of ska. Now they've honed their style through innumerable live gigs. They are tight and supremely confident.

As 'Dawning of a New Era' powers on, Hall and Staple sing of violence, strife and poverty in a dystopian cityscape divided into distinct areas – "*In Area Six they throw bottles and bricks and kicks!*" Whilst the blokey sing-along chorus merely consists of the title repeated over and over. On the one hand, this serves as an ironic comment on difficult times. Just six months ago, the Conservative party led by Margaret Thatcher won the general election. Even as a school kid I sense this isn't going to end well. On the other hand, the dawning of a new era genuinely describes how the 2-Tone movement is suddenly sweeping the nation. Here, in this packed audience, skanking to the urgent beat, it really feels like we are part of something new and important. Something essential.

The Specials power to a precise halt and a huge cheer goes up. The atmosphere in the hall is truly celebratory. "This one's for all you rude boys here tonight!" Shouts Staple. And without a second's delay, the band bounce into 'Do the Dog'. I'm not entirely sure what a rude boy is. I presume it isn't simply a boy who interrupts his betters and elders and speaks with his mouth full. Or maybe it is. Despite the term's recent currency in the music press, it feels like something from black culture that I can't quite grasp.

Hall takes his mic from its stand and sings "*All you punks and all you Teds, National Front and Natty dreads, Mods, rockers, hippies and skinheads, Keep on fighting 'till you're dead!*" The message is clear – violence solves nothing. But when it comes to the chorus, I'm lost. Hall exhorts us to "*Do the dog*", whilst Staple clarifies with "*Not the donkey*". Is it a dance? A position within society? The energy flowing from the band renders such questions irrelevant. If Madness summon up the atmosphere of an on stage party, then The Specials are like a monochromatic carnival.

Next up is another cover version – the band's radical take on the Toots and the Maytals' single 'Monkey Man'. Curiously, whilst The Specials are seen as the most authentic and socially realist of the 2-Tone groups, it's noticeable that their set contains far more covers than either Madness or The Selecter. Like keyboards, covers have largely been absent during the rise of the new wave. The Specials' studio versions of Robert Thompson's 'Do The Dog', Toots Hibbert's 'Monkey Man', Dandy Livingstone's 'Rudy, A Message To You', Prince Buster's 'Too Hot' and Coxsone Dodd's 'You're Wondering Now' are faithful but not reverent. On almost all of these interpretations, The Specials up the tempo, making the originals feel distinctly languid in comparison. And live they kick up the pace even further.

The Specials' take on 'Monkey Man' is particularly energised. Bradbury, ever the band's engine room, plays with both strength and grace behind his bright green drum kit. The whole band are moving, skipping from foot to foot, whilst Staple swings the mic stand and Hall executes a dance which is like a semi-drunken stagger. The Specials abundant display of on-stage energy is a friendly but direct challenge to the audience. It says "We're giving 100%. What are you giving?" As I look around the dancehall, it's clear this audience is up to the challenge.

Then, as the applause for 'Monkey Man' dies down, Hall, Staple and Radiation begin to clap in time and repeatedly chant *"You're gonna get your fucking head kicked in!"* This is underscored by Bradbury pounding out a tribal pattern on the tom toms. A large portion of the audience join in with the chant. Some are doing it with a sense of irony. But from certain sectors of the dance hall, there's the sound of real aggression in the chanting. Suddenly the band launch into 'Concrete Jungle' and Staple smashes away at a tambourine as if it's his sworn enemy.

"I can't dress just the way I want" sings Hall. *"I'm being chased by the National Front"*. This is an on going problem for many of us. Whether punk, or ted, or mod, or whatever, our clothes mark us out, make us a target. Literally in the case of the mods.

Tonight, Pete is dressed in a late 60s suit originally belonging to his Dad, and I'm dressed in a late 60s suit originally belonging to my Dad. Despite this, there's nothing very mod about our appearance, as neither of the suits are an especially good fit and our hair is still spiked. Or rather Pete's is spiked and mine is muzzed. I also wear a thin yellow tie with black polka dots and some pointed leather shoes. It's not really punk attire, but apparently it's still enough to make people in the street stare.

It could of course be seen as an ill-judged act of rebellion to wear the clothes our Dads wore ten years ago. But in some way our clothes and our hair still seem to imply a challenge to society. And so society feels at liberty to strike back. Or at least drunken straights feel at liberty to strike back. On a number of occasions, Pete, John and I have found ourselves being threatened or chased through the streets. Fortunately, so far, we've avoided receiving a proper kicking.

But the threat isn't just from straights or the National Front any more. There are now so many different factions, so many different tribes. Teds want to beat up punks. Punks want to beat up skinheads. Skinheads want to beat up punks and teds and mods. In fact almost everyone seems to want to beat up mods. It must be the targets.

Aside from seeing the odd drunken scuffle, I've had no real experience of violence at actual gigs. Until that is, three weeks ago. Steve and I went to see Stiff Little Fingers at King George's Hall. Support act The Donkeys had jumped around delivering their guitar driven power pop to little response from the audience. Then Stiff Little Fingers arrived on stage, looking like The Clash's gawky nephews – leather jackets, white jeans, doc martens and rock 'n' roll rebel poses. The gig had been followed by a massive fight outside the venue. However, this wasn't a fight against the forces of oppression, it was a fight between Blackburn punks and Accrington punks. Feeling no affiliation with either group – and being very scared of physical violence – I remained a detached observer, watching from the steps of King George's Hall, Steve standing next to me.

I found the whole thing both unnerving and stupid. "Stiff Little Fingers' big message is don't let yourself get drawn into factions. Why are punks fighting other punks?" I asked Steve. "Because Accy punks have been taking the piss out of Blackburn punks." Ahh. He then headed off into the fray. Although, rather than diving into battle, he hung around the edges, kicking the legs of Accrington punks who were already locked in combat. Despite the fact the police station is quite literally right next door to the venue, it took the forces of oppression over ten minutes to arrive on the scene. Some of the kids immediately scattered, others felt it was more important to carry on thumping each other. Seeing the police, Steve immediately retreated back onto the steps of the venue. Then we snuck off to the bus station.[5]

Looking around the Golden Palms tonight, it seems like the music of 2-Tone might just have the potential to dissolve petty boundaries.

---

5. On the bus back to Great Harwood, I suggested to Steve that he review the mass fight for *Hex* fanzine. Sadly, he never got around to it.

Punks and skins and straights and what I can only assume are rude boys, are all dancing to 'Concrete Jungle'. But as the song concludes, whilst many are applauding and cheering, numerous men and boys in the audience once again start chanting "You're gonna get your fuckin' head kicked in!" This is Blackburn after all.

Staple tries to talk over the chanting. "Hear me now rude boys, hear me now!" He wipes his sweating brow with his sleeve. "It getting hot in here tonight. It getting too hot!" And with a roll from Bradbury, the band glide into 'Too Hot'. After the fury of 'Concrete Jungle', this sounds smooth and almost devotional. It's also the slowest song they will play tonight. But as Pete observes, "Even their slow songs feel fast."

Of all their many cover versions, The Specials' take on this Prince Buster cut is the most faithful. Like The Clash's interpretation of Toots and the Maytals' 'Pressure Drop', it emphasises the composition's solid musculature. Gentleman's bass playing has an easy flow and Bradbury's drumming is pin sharp. The version of 'Too Hot', on The Specials' debut album, gives prominence to Staple's more soulful vocal; live however, Hall's keening voice dominates proceedings.[6]

There's something slightly thin about Hall's vocals. To my ears, the only current vocalist with a similar tone is The Cure's Robert Smith. Yet the two performers are worlds apart. Smith's vocals, like his lyrics, are all about emotional extremes – alienation, euphoria and desperation. Hall has a more traditionally appealing voice, with a wider range and equally importantly, his voice is full of character and attitude. Although the words he sings are not his own, Hall's troubled tone and downbeat delivery give them a world weary authenticity. It's also a distinctly regional voice, and as such still a relative rarity on the music scene.

---

6. The Specials 1979 debut album was produced by Elvis Costello. It's a direct and unfussy affair that seizes the energy and vitality of the band's live sound. In fact, it's probably no exaggeration to say Costello displayed a similar élan to George Martin in his capturing of The Beatles on their 1963 debut.

Manchester, Leeds and Sheffield accents may have started to be audible over the last year or so, but the tones of the Midlands have largely remained absent.

"This next song is for all the schoolgirls in the audience tonight." Says Hall. "It's about what not to do." Staple nods. "S'right. Don't do too much, too young!" Bradbury executes a roll on the toms and the band slide into the cautionary tale that is 'Too Much Too Young'. Musically it's a brash and breezy knees up which is over and done in two minutes. But it's Dammers' lyrics which hit hardest.

This social commentary has particular resonance for Pete and I. There's a girl in our class at school called Julie. I was also at junior school with her. She's just 15. She's already got one baby and is now pregnant again. I can't begin to imagine what it's like being a parent. Hell, I can't even begin to imagine what it's like having sex. It apparently feels really good. Whereas being a parent apparently feels really boring. Speaking personally, I find the idea of that amount of responsibility, and all the restrictions it implies, terrifying. Although having said that, Julie obviously wasn't feeling so restricted and terrified that she couldn't go out and get pregnant a second time.

The song's conclusion is greeted by the best response of the set so far. But there is barely a pause before Staple shouts "One two!" and Radiation lets rip with a chiming riff which could have come straight off The Rolling Stones' *Sticky Fingers* album. This is 'Little Bitch', and its rocky sections are another hangover from The Coventry Automatics era.[7]

By this point, Pete and I have wheedled our way through the crowd, so we're now only about six feet away from the stage. The audience is tightly packed. All around us there are young men dancing and skanking. Next to me, there's a skinny lad pogoing. He wears a school

---

7. The opening of 'Little Bitch' does indeed recall The Rolling Stones – as does the title. However, listening to it now, the song's opening seems to have been grabbed wholesale by the Dandy Warhols, as the basis of their 2000 hit 'Bohemian Like You'.

blazer adorned with various button badges and several metal chains with sink plugs attached to his jacket by safety pins. Only a year ago, I was wearing something similar. I actually had a baby's patent leather shoe attached to a large kilt pin dangling from my lapel. Stylish, no? But his attire suddenly looks anachronistic. As does his attitude. During one of the song's Stonesy sections, the lad executes a high bounce and spits a wad of phlegm towards the stage. It hits Radiation on the trouser leg, although he doesn't seem to notice, as he's so busy channelling Keith Richards. Yet, for all its energy, 'Little Bitch' is another song that is done and dusted in just over two minutes.

The next song is yet another two minute wonder: 'Blank Expression'. The tune glides along on Dammers' Winston Wright-style organ work, punctuated by choppy guitar chords from Golding. Like many of Dammers' songs, its lyrics detail the pleasure and pain of urban nightlife. Whilst the chorus; "*Where did you get that blank expression on your face?*" sounds like something which must have been shouted at Hall on multiple occasions.

One thing that all three of the 2-Tone bands share is the fact their songs are not usually written by their lead singers. The Selecter's guitarist Neol Davies writes their songs, Madness' keyboardist Mike Barson writes the lion's share of their numbers, with Lee Thompson running him a close second. And of course Dammers is The Specials' mastermind. A former arts school graduate, and the son of a Coventry clergyman, he's a multitalented but relatively shy man who doesn't seek the limelight. Yet it's clear, despite The Specials' democratic front, Dammers is the driving force, not just of the band, but of the 2-Tone label itself.

'Blank Expression' climaxes with a double cymbal crash and the dance hall erupts with applause. However, it's at this point the sound of a handful of skin heads chanting "Sieg Heil" can be heard emanating from the back of the venue once more. Pete and I shake heads "Such bad class."

The chanting continues. It's only about five or six young blokes. But they are doing that low, sonorous voice that football fans do when they're trying to sound like more people. Terry Hall stands on the lip of the stage and berates them. "You have no idea how stupid you sound."

Hall addresses the rest of the room. "What do the rest of you think? Are they worth listening to? Or are they wankers?" "Wankers! Wankers!" shout hundreds of voices. Nearby there's a couple of skins, a boy and a girl, both probably around 16. They are also shouting "Wankers!"

Hall shakes his head then turns and nods to Staple who grabs the mic stand and leans into the audience before bawling out the introduction to 'Gangsters'. I still can't tell what he's saying at the start. But when he shouts the words *"Don't argue!"* he points to the chanting skins. As the band charge into the song's unmistakable descending opening, the audience roars with enthusiasm. The bass is pumping, the guitars are chopping, the dance floor is bouncing. The music drowns out the fascists.

* * * * *

Although I never saw any of the 2-Tone bands live again, I did have a very brief but uncomfortable encounter with Madness bassist Bedders.

1985. Six years after the gig. My girlfriend Natalia Whiteside is sharing a flat in Brighton with a girl called Cass. One afternoon, Natalia and I are making love in her bedroom, when we hear the front door of the flat open. It sounds like Cass is showing someone around the place. Natalia and I cool our passion and lie quietly under the duvet.

The bedroom door opens. Cass is standing there with Bedders. I suddenly remember her mentioning she and the bassist are friends. "This is Natalia's room." Says Cass. Then she spots us lying in the bed, looking flushed. "Oops! Sorry, I thought you were out." Bedders clears his throat. "Nice room." "Thanks." Says Natalia. He gives us a little wave then quietly closes the door. It's difficult to judge who is the most embarrassed.

Chuck-a-chuck-chuck-a-chuck!

KNEW NOISE ⎫ SEC
AFTERIMAGE ⎬
NO 1   ⎭ 25.
MY MOTHER ⎫ SIMON
RARED   ⎭

JAM   ⎫ ALAN
GIRLS DON'T ⎬
COUNT   ⎭

LOVE WILL ⎫ ALAN
TEAR US   ⎬
APART.   ⎭

DIGITAL ⎫ ALAN
EUROPO R ⎬ +SIMON
ETERNAL ⎭ IAN
                   CURTIS

JOY DIVISION

DERBY HALL, BURY

TUESDAY 8TH APRIL 1980

(AGE 15. 4 DAYS BEFORE MY 16TH BIRTHDAY)

I am a Long Mac. I have friends who are also Long Macs. I didn't realise that's what we were at first.

Like many clothing trends that originate amongst musical subcultures, it's a fashion that started out as an anti-fashion. Bands such as Joy Division, Cabaret Voltaire and Echo and the Bunnymen have frequently been photographed in the music press wearing long overcoats or mackintoshes in urban environments. This style is being picked up by members of their audience and the music press have now given these followers a name.

After the corrosive flamboyance of punk, the practicality of wearing an overcoat or mac seems like a strong statement. Punk fashions have often been about wearing your heart – and your bile duct – on your sleeve. Safety pins, chains, studs, armbands, bright colours, slogans. It all projects outwards. It says 'This is who I am, this what I think'. In contrast, the long mackintosh conceals. It covers up the rest of your clothing. It puts a barrier between you and the rest of the world. It signifies enigma. At least I hope it does. Without realising it, John and I ended up buying matching black mackintoshes from different stores on the same weekend. Pete jokes that we now look like The Thompson Twins from the Tin Tin books.

In defence of the long mac as a fashion item, I should point out that most of the bands and fans that have opted for this look do live in the

North of England. And in cities like Manchester, Leeds and Sheffield, the cold weather and heavy rainfall mean overcoats and mackintoshes are a very sensible option.

In addition to my mac, I wear late 1960s suits which I pick up from charity shops for as little as two or three pounds, black leather shoes and dark shirts, usually black, grey or blue. Most of the suits are a little too big. But I like that. More fabric between me and the world.

This coming Sunday, I'm going to be 16. Mind you, I haven't felt like a child for a long while. The number 16 will merely confirm what I already know; I am an adult with adult tastes and a level of sophistication most of my peers cannot even begin to comprehend. I listen to Joy Division with reverence. I obsess over a book on Surrealism that I keep borrowing from the library and I watch subtitled European films on BBC2 – even the ones that don't have any nudity in them. I couldn't *be* any more adult.

Admittedly my only source of 'income' is my pocket money and I still don't know my times tables. Oh, and I'm still a virgin. Although I have now kissed a girl: Diane. We kissed for about 20 minutes in the doorway at her parents' house one evening. Then I walked home in my long mac, grinning like a born again Christian. But when I saw Diane at school the following day she pretended it never happened. It definitely did though.

Today, despite being only early April, it's bright and warm, so I've opted to leave my long mac at home. Instead, I wear a black suit with a dark green tonic shirt. I'm on a coach going to Bury. With me is John – who has also left his long mac at home – and our friends the lanky James Wilson Ogden who has a very sharp mind and is usually known as Oggy, and Dale, a sweet guy who drums with the Accrington band Indefinite Article. Dale is accompanied by his mate Andy who is very small and shy and doesn't say a word. We're going to see Joy Division. My very favourite band.

I've been infatuated with them since I got my hands on the *Factory Sampler* double 7" EP back in January last year. It's like a various artists compilation album, but spread across two 7" EPs. I bought it from a record stall in Accrington Covered Market for a very reasonable 75p. To my young sensibilities, still feeling my way out of punk into broader vistas, the two tracks contributed by Joy Division, 'Digital' and 'Glass', sound like some futuristic vision of The Stooges, abetted by dub-wise studio effects. This is definitely not punk music, and yet both tracks have an undeniable brutality about them.

A few months later, I learn of the release of Joy Division's debut album *Unknown Pleasures* when TV journalist and director of Factory Records Tony Wilson shows a picture of the album cover during an edition of the news magazine programme *Granada Reports*. Quite what his superiors think about him plugging his own wares on their show, I don't know. I'm desperate to buy the album, but none of the local record stores stock it, so I have to order it from Reidy's Records in Blackburn, then wait two weeks for it to come in.

In the meantime, I read glowing reviews of the album in both *NME* and *Sounds* music papers. I finally pick it up on a Saturday morning in July then immediately catch the bus back home. I spend the rest of the day sitting in my bedroom, playing it over and over. Everything about it feels different. The black cover is thick and textured. There's no mention of the band's name or the album's title on the front cover. And no reference to the band members' names or instrumentation anywhere.

And then there's the music itself. Whilst the sound of most new wave bands is inevitably dominated by the guitar, Martin Hannett's production on *Unknown Pleasures* ensures each instrument is given equal prominence. Peter Hook's high, melodic bass lines, Stephen Morris' crisp drumming, augmented by synthetic percussion and Bernard Sumner's metallic and emotive guitar work, all of these are accorded acute attention and perfect placement within the soundfield. Despite the fact the band is making rock music, the mix seems more akin to the feel of reggae and dub.

Hannett clearly has a fascination with dub and is said to imbibe huge amounts of marijuana – a drug that enhances the effects of dub for both the music creator and the music consumer. Whilst the dub aesthetic may have felt alien to Joy Division, Hannett has wrapped *Unknown Pleasures* in its delays and reverberations if not its rhythms. Although Hook and Sumner will later claim the producer reduced Joy Division's power with his work, these inventive and precise studio interventions are a major component in the album's appeal.

For many, the idea has become fixed that Joy Division's music is bleak, depressing and gloomy. And, whilst there's no denying there's a genuine sadness to many of their songs, there are other emotions at play. There is power and grace here too. There is frailty and there is strength. Defiance even. I quickly reach the stage where I have immersed myself in Joy Division's music to such an extent that, although I still eagerly spin singles and EPs by Scritti Politti, Gang of Four, The Passage, The Mekons, The Human League, 2.3, The Fall, Cabaret Voltaire etc. nothing else comes close to summoning the same sense of excitement and awe as this Manchester quartet.

I saw Joy Division play live for the first time six months ago, supporting Buzzcocks at the King George's Hall. Buzzcocks play in Blackburn regularly and they always bring a solid Manchester support band with them. Bizarrely, I'd ended up going to the gig alone. John and Owen couldn't afford to go, Pete wasn't bothered, whilst Steve has become suspicious of anything that isn't straight up punk and so finds solace in the recently reformed Slaughter and the Dogs and The Damned.

Joy Division at Blackburn King George's Hall on 23rd October 1979 was the most keyed up I've ever been before a gig – a state of excitation made all the more potent by not having anybody to talk to. Joy Division weren't even mentioned on my green ticket. It just said "Buzzcocks With Guests". Although I'd heard the show was almost sold out, when the house lights dimmed for Joy Division's set, the hall was only about half full. The band walked out on stage, to be greeted by the sound of scattered clapping and just a few cheers. Ian Curtis stepped up to the mic. "We're Joy Division." Nothing more. Then, as they launched into the opening bars of 'Wilderness', I felt a wave of goose pimples run up my arms.

Drawing mainly from *Unknown Pleasures*, the set was powerful and tightly drilled with minimal audience interaction. They played their new single 'Transmission', during which Curtis danced his flailing arms dance to Morris' hectic fills. (I remember being disappointed upon first hearing the single version, that these drum fills had been omitted, in favour of a more linear beat.) They also played a song I'd never heard before, which transitioned from a slow, spacious and dislocated dub-scape into an almost Ramones-esque buzz-saw. My eyes never left the stage for a second. Following the interval, The Buzzcocks played brilliantly, but I hardly noticed. Afterwards, my Dad came to pick me up in his yellow Austin Maxi. As we drove back together I burbled away to him in a state of teenage over-excitement.

The second time I saw them was just a few weeks ago, when they headlined in Preston at the Warehouse. That was a frustrating gig. It couldn't have been more different to my previous encounter with the band. They had opened with a strident instrumental, Curtis chopping out a spiky riff on his white Vox Phantom guitar. But the evening was beset by equipment failure. An amp blew up and Bernard Sumner's synth packed in early on. The band consequently abandoned much of their intended set and asked the audience for requests. It was a ramshackle stop/start affair and the whole band was clearly infuriated, but it made for a perversely intense gig.

Afterwards, John, Oggy and I had not only been able to sneakily grab a couple of set lists off the stage, we'd also managed to insinuate our way backstage and chat briefly with Stephen Morris. Or more accurately, gush at Stephen Morris. Curtis had been sitting alone, eating some weird looking black noodles from a foil take-away container. "Of course!" I thought. "He doesn't eat ordinary food like the rest of us, he eats black food".

A couple of weeks later, I manage to locate a copy of *Earcom 2* in Accrington's Disc And Tape Exchange. *Earcom 2* is a 12" various artists mini-album on the Fast Product label. It contains two Joy Division out-takes from the *Unknown Pleasures* sessions. Namely 'Autosuggestion' and 'From Safety To Where…?'. Upon hearing this second track, I realise this is the one I heard them play when they supported The Buzzcocks – but in truth, on this outing, it sounds absolutely nothing like The Ramones. Both songs have a similar feel, the bass carrying the song's structure, the guitar often reduced to making muted and abstracted noises. If such a thing were possible, I am even further convinced of the band's genius.

I notice on the record's inner sleeve there's contact details for all three of the bands that contributed to the compilation. The information concerning The Thursdays and the oddly named Basczax (which looks like a Russian spelling of Buzzcocks) are of no interest. However, when I spy the phone number for Joy Division's management, I wonder if maybe I should phone them up and ask if the band would do an interview for my nascent fanzine. Then John hears the band is going to be playing a gig in Bury, just over 20 miles away. So, a few days before the gig, he and I bundle into a phone box near his house in Clayton-le-Moors and ring the number from the inner sleeve. After a few moments of nervous waiting, someone picks up.

Rob: "Hello?"

Graham: "Hi. Could I speak to the manager of Joy Division please?"

Rob: "Speaking."

Graham: "Are you Rob Gretton?"

Rob: "Speaking. What's it about?"

Graham: "My name's Graham Duff, I'm from *Hex* fanzine."

I say this as if *Hex* fanzine is something he might be familiar with. Whereas of course in reality, he couldn't possibly have heard of it. Because in reality, it doesn't yet exist. But saying it gives me a vague veneer of confidence in a situation that I am otherwise finding rather overwhelming.

Graham: "We're coming along to the gig in Bury and I wondered if we'd be able to do an interview with the band?"

Rob: "Yeah sure."

Graham: "Great. Thanks. What time should we come along?"

Rob: "I dunno. Just come and see us after the gig. It's not like we're gonna be hiding away in the dressing room."

Graham: "Erm, okay. Thanks."

Rob: "See yer."

Now, on the day of the gig, we are arriving in Bury, accompanied by Oggy, Dale and the silent Andy. I'm enthusiastic about going to see such a special band and feeling a little smug about the fact we're going to interview my heroes after the show. The five of us walk from the bus station to Vibes – a small independent record shop in Bury precinct. I step up to the counter. "Can I buy a ticket for Joy Division at the Derby Hall please?" The guy behind the counter doesn't even look up. "It's sold out." The five of us pull disappointed faces. It had never occurred to me that this might happen. Any band I've ever wanted to go and see, I've always been able to get a ticket.

I suddenly see my perfect day evaporating before me. We're not going to get to see the band, therefore I won't be able to interview them! "What should we do?" I ask the guy behind the counter. He shrugs. "The venue might still have some tickets. But I don't think their box office'll be open until this evening."

In a disconsolate mood, I flick through the record racks. I almost buy the *Elliptical Optimism* album by Spherical Objects. But then I set eyes on *The Visit*, a 12" EP by Ludus. I saw them supporting Buzzcocks in Blackburn last year and was extremely impressed, so I select this instead. I walk to the counter and pay for it. The man takes my money, then hands the 12" back to me inside a pink and white candy striped paper bag. To a shy teenage boy, this looks impossibly girlish. I ask if they have any other bags. "No." Says the guy. "We're out of our usual ones."

The five of us walk through the shopping centre, I feel awkward, as if all the other shoppers will see my large white and pink striped bag and make judgments about my sexuality.

We arrive at the venue. But sure enough, the box office is locked up and there's a handwritten sign sellotaped to the door that reads 'Joy Division – Sold Out'. Oggy suggests we might be able to get some 'returns'. This is a new concept to me, but I like it. It appeals to my sense of desperation. However, there's still nearly four hours to go before the doors open. Dale and Andy decide to give up and go back to the bus station. "Bye." Says Andy. It's the first thing I've heard him say.

John, Oggy and I hang around. And hang around. And hang around. Then, after a couple of hours, we see a car drive in the side entrance to the venue. Through the window, we catch a glimpse of Morris and Sumner. "They'll be coming to do a sound check." Says John. I nod. This is the extent of our knowledge of the situation. About half an hour later, we hear the sound of a band rumbling away inside. We try and guess what the song is. But the sound is so muffled it's impossible to tell if it's even Joy Division playing. Oggy nips off and returns with some cans of coke. We gulp them down. I haven't eaten since breakfast and the sudden sugar rush makes me giddy.

Then, John nudges me and points down the street. I turn to see Joy Division bassist Peter Hook standing about five yards away. Dressed in a dark green shirt and grey slacks, he's drinking from a bottle of beer. We egg one another on to talk to him. In the end, I take the initiative and go over to him, with John and Oggy trailing behind. I introduce myself. I explain how we've come all the way to see the band, but the gig is sold out. I tell him that it's particularly frustrating as we'd spoken with Rob a couple of days earlier and arranged to do an interview. The way I pitch it, it sounds like it's an extremely official arrangement, rather than a snatched 30 second phone call.

"I can put you on the guest list." Offers Hook without any prompting. "What are your names?" We tell him and he makes a note of them in a pocket notebook. I try to act as if this is the kind of thing that happens to me all the time. I turn to John and Oggy. They are doing the same, although John's eyes are bulging out of his head. I suspect mine are doing the same.

"Would it be OK to do the interview after the gig?" I ask. Hook nods. "We can do it now if you want. Where's your tape recorder?" This takes me by surprise. I'd been so excited by the prospect of the gig I'd completely forgotten to bring my tape recorder. "It's broken." I reply, surprising myself with how quickly the lie leaves my mouth. "It's okay." I continue. "I've got an amazingly good memory. And I can take plenty of notes." I pat my pockets. I locate a blue biro, but I don't seem to have any paper on me. I blush, realising that I'm not exactly giving the impression of being a hot-shot journalist. I lift up the candy striped paper bag containing the Ludus 12". "I'll write on this." I say. "What've you got in there?" Asks Hook. I show him the EP. "Do you know them?" I ask. He gives a noncommittal nod. The following 'interview' is a hesitant conversation in which my questions are far longer than the bassist's answers.

Graham: "There was a song you did on a Peel session last year called 'Exercise One', that hasn't been released yet, what's going to happen to it?"

Peter: "Nothing. It's gone."

Graham: "I was in Accrington a couple of months back and I met this guy who worked for RCA. He told me that about two years ago, Joy Division recorded a whole album for RCA but that it was never released. What happened?"

Peter: "That's bollocks."[1]

Graham: "Really?"

Peter: "Who was he?"

Graham: "I can't remember his name. He was wearing a woman's watch."[2]

Peter: "Well there you go then."

Graham: "When's your new album going to be coming out?"

Peter: "Wish I knew."

Graham: "What's it going to be called?"

Peter: "Dunno."

I stumble on in this manner for another few minutes. I begin to suspect Hook is mucking about. That he's not really taking me seriously. But then, is there really any reason why he should? I'm a 15 year old kid writing down an 'interview' on a candy striped paper bag. Eventually

---

1. Peter Hook wasn't being truthful here. Joy Division had indeed recorded an album for RCA in May 1978. But the deal fell through and the material remained unreleased.

2. I mentioned this, because the guy in question had been wearing a watch identical to the one my Mum wore.

he says he has to go back inside. "Can I interview the rest of the band after the show?" I ask. "Yeah, why not. See yer later lads." John, Oggy and I exchange glances. None of us really knows what to say. "Do you think he'll remember to put us on the list?" Asks Oggy. For the next twenty minutes or so, we debate whether or not we will actually be on the guest list and allowed inside.

Finally the venue doors open. As the queue of people head inside, the three of us hang back. We don't want to go in too soon. For some reason, we believe if we go inside a little bit later, we'll stand more chance of being on the guest list.

Eventually, we shuffle into the entrance. My stomach is lurching. I *know* we won't be on the guest list. In fact, as I say my name to the guy on the door, I blush. We won't really be allowed in. The guy checks the list, nods, crosses off my name and gestures for me to enter the concert hall. I look back at John and Oggy. They too are waved in. We are beaming at each other. "Fucking hell." Says John. All pretence of being detached evaporates and the three of us giggle. This is the coolest thing that could possibly happen. We're about to see Joy Division. We didn't even have to pay to get in! In fact Peter Hook put us on the guest list! "This is well good." Says John. 'Well good' is what we've started saying to indicate things are exceptionally fine.

The venue fills up fairly quickly. The first band on are Minny Pops – a Dutch five piece – tall, skinny men in drab, ill fitting clothes. They don't say anything to the audience they just walk on stage, plug in and play. They stand stock-still, it's one of the most non-rock performances I've ever seen. Their songs are built around staccato guitar lines, cool washes of synth and skeletal drum machine patterns. In 1980, it's still a novelty to hear a drum machine coming through a sound system. John, Oggy and myself are quite taken with the band, but generally the audience's response is muted.

During the gratifyingly short interval, we buy three more glasses of coke from the bar and briefly up our blood sugar. We return, weaving our way to the very front of the venue, right up against the edge of the stage. We want the best view possible.

Then, the house lights dim and Section 25 take to the stage. A recent Factory signing, they have yet to release a record. The chunky shaven headed figure of drummer Vinnie Cassidy starts up a rigid four to the floor beat, his open hi-hat hissing metronomically on the off-beats, as his older brother Larry repeats a sonorous yet truncated bass line. Guitarist Paul Wiggin stands, back to the audience, making adjustments to his amp as he sends out clusters of distortion. The track is 'Knew Noise'. It sounds dissonant, dubby and claustrophobic and Larry's primal vocals are shouted rather than sung. In fact, it's a sound that could have come straight from Public Image Ltd.'s *Metal Box* album.

"It's very Public Image!" Shouts John, upping his volume, so I can hear him over the band. Unfortunately, at the point he shouts this, the song stops dead. John's comment is left hanging, very audibly, in the air. Larry Cassidy glances down towards us with a sour expression. I get the distinct feeling this isn't the first time he's heard this observation. Oggy sniggers. "Good timing."

Section 25 plunge into their next number: 'After Image'. Whilst their sound doesn't vary much from song to song, here, Wiggin plays more discernible chords. But John is right, their style is undeniably very similar to Lydon's outfit. Another stark excursion follows. It's a bit indigestible initially, but I do warm to it. In fact there is definitely more applause and good will coming from the audience than there was for Minny Pops. Then, after their third song, as Wiggin tunes his guitar, the band is joined on stage by an additional member: Simon Topping of A Certain Ratio. This seems odd, as despite the fact both bands are on Factory Records, A Certain Ratio's funk inflected tunes are a world away from Section 25's bleached out dread.

The band start into another piece of music. Topping is singing, but there's so much reverb on his vocals it's impossible to tell what he's saying. The song goes on for a good while. Which is a shame, as it's by far the least engaging thing they've played so far. Then at the climax of that piece, another vocalist comes on to replace Topping.

He's a guy in jeans and a black shirt, with an odd hairstyle, close cropped yet still long at the back. Oggy leans over. "That's the bloke from Crispy Ambulance." I've never seen Crispy Ambulance, but I am aware of them, due to reviews in Manchester fanzines like *City Fun*. These reviews have all mentioned two things. 1) How daft their name is. A name that perhaps even eclipses Throbbing Gristle in the moronically memorable stakes. And 2) That their sound palette is very, very similar to Joy Division's, with vocalist Alan Hempsall essaying a similar haunted baritone to Curtis.

Section 25 then slide into 'Girls Don't Count' with Hempsall handling the vocals. It's probably the most upbeat thing they play yet it's still thick with heavy-duty unease. The song concludes in a blaze of guitar. Hempsall and the band wander off. But at the same time Peter Hook, Bernard Sumner and Stephen Morris come on stage. The trio looks slightly awkward and there's much on stage milling about as the audience cheer and applaud. Morris takes up his position at his kit and Sumner and Hook plug in their instruments. And, whilst Curtis fails to appear on stage, Hempsall is noticeable by his continued presence.

Suddenly, they start into 'Love Will Tear Us Apart'. Even though the song has not yet been released, I immediately recognise the clangourous strummed opening. Like many others in the audience tonight, I taped the song, along with three other new tunes, when Joy Division's second John Peel session was broadcast back in December. Over the past few months I've played it until I know the songs off by heart. The cassette is still king.

If I'm honest, when 'Love Will Tear Us Apart' is posthumously released as a single in June, like the studio version of 'Transmission', I find it faintly disappointing. The single has a palpable drive, and, like all of Hannett's productions, it feels like the details have been pored over. But the Peel session version, recorded in November 1979, has a far greater energy and bite. Curtis delivers the lyrics with a much more heartfelt imperative and Sumner's guitar break is alive with a lacerating frustration. I honestly don't think they could have bettered that performance.

They certainly don't tonight. Although Morris' drumming is tight and full of energy and Hook is giving it his all, Sumner's guitar is too dominant in the sound mix, with occasional squalls of feedback. And of course it's being sung, not by Ian Curtis, but by an Ian Curtis copyist.

"This is called 'Digital'." Says Hempsall as Simon Topping wanders back onto the stage. Hook carves out the muscular bass line with Sumner's lead following the same melody as the bass for the first four bars. Then, as Hook and Morris power on, Sumner begins to pick out fragments of sound. This song has been part of their live performances for nearly two years and the band know how to wring every last drop of tension from it. Hempsall and Topping tackle the vocal together, alternating lines on the chorus. It's an interesting performance, but as an audience, we still have no real idea what the hell is going on.

As the song concludes, Hempsall and Topping step away from their microphone stands and Ian Curtis finally wanders on stage. His manner is shy and awkward. And yet his appearance is greeted by a huge cheer from the audience. But then there's another frustrating pause whilst Sumner fiddles with his keyboard set up. I worry this is going to turn out like the Preston gig, with the keyboards refusing to join in. Apparently I'm not the only one with such concerns, as during this hiatus, somebody at the back shouts "Don't stop *now* for fuck's sake!"

Hook plays a short, mid paced bass figure and Morris marks out a beat on the kick drum. This is a relatively new addition to Joy Division's live performances. Tonight it's on the set list under the title 'Europop'. However, when it's eventually released in three months time, as the closing track on the band's *Closer* album, it will have been renamed 'Decades'. The later recorded version will sail out on a smooth and glassy synth riff. Tonight however, Sumner's keyboard sound is more queasy, distorted and off kilter, with a barely controlled edge of mania.

Curtis is leaning on the mic stand, singing with his eyes shut. Tonight he executes none of the frenetic dancing for which he has become known. Tonight he looks pale and washed out, his eyes hooded. And yet, despite his apparently frail state, vocally, Curtis still delivers.

His voice is deep and emotional. It's impressive how, in just a couple of years, his voice has grown in both strength and depth of expression. At points, he sounds like a modern day crooner.

When, in the song's final section, Morris moves from just kick drum and hi-hat to playing the full kit, the song blossoms into life. Curtis sings the *"Where have they been?"* refrain a couple more times, then, as the instrumental coda pumps from the sound system, he looks down towards the floor, his eyes still closed. The song's conclusion is met with the evening's first real full-bodied burst of applause and cheers. There's a strong sense of 'this is what we came for!' To see Joy Division proper. Not some freewheeling conglomeration.

Then they play my new favourite Joy Division song: 'The Eternal'. They played it in Preston a few weeks back. And since then it's been on my mind a lot. Sumner's synth releases a phasing rattlesnake sound and Hook begins to repeat a simple bass line. A funereally paced keyboard arrangement is then inched forward by the acidic splash of Morris' syndrum. The whole stage is bathed in washes of blue and green light. Next to me, a young lad with spiky blond hair and an electric blue mohair jumper is throwing himself around to the music. Or rather he's throwing himself around despite the music.

Over the years, 'The Eternal' is the Joy Division song I will return to with the greatest frequency. Mainly because it's one of their finest works – probably the saddest and most tender song in the band's catalogue in fact. Whilst most of Curtis' lyrics are situated either in urban spaces or mind states, 'The Eternal' summons up visions of the great outdoors, with references to gardens, trees, leaves, flowers and clouds. But what shines most clearly from the text is a deep sense of disconnection. The most heartbreaking couplet being *"Cry like a child, though these years make me older. With children my time is so wastefully spent."*

The other reason I return to 'The Eternal' in particular, is because it will be forever connected to *this moment*. Standing by the front of the stage, the slow motion beat of the syn-drum and the sweetly nagging keyboard line swimming through my mind, as I stare up at Curtis, caught in a shaft of green light. Out with my friends, days away from turning 16.

Feeling so certain that I am an adult. Yet able to look back and know I was a child.

Unexpectedly, as the last syn-drum splashes of 'The Eternal' fade, Curtis makes his way off the stage. As the applause starts up, I'm aware that around us, a number of people are also booing. Section 25 return to join the remainder of Joy Division on stage. Now I really don't have a clue what's going on. Suddenly, Sumner and Wiggin start grinding out the riff to 'Sister Ray'. Vinnie Cassidy thumps out the almost tribal beat. Larry grabs the mic and launches into the vocal. Topping and Hempsall join in on backing vocals. It's a mass jam, featuring everyone apart from Curtis. I still can't quite grasp what I'm watching, but it definitely feels unique.

John leans over and shouts in my ear "It's like a Factory supergroup!" I nod. "Well good." To be honest, my left field sensibilities are so purist at this point, that the very idea of a supergroup seems totally uncool. However, there is something undeniably special about seeing and hearing one of the most iconic of The Velvet Underground's songs being performed by members of Joy Division, A Certain Ratio and Section 25. Oh and the singer of Crispy Ambulance.

The song grinds on. I notice the lad next to me in the blue mohair jumper is far from happy. He's pointing up at Larry and angrily shouting something. Suddenly, a pint glass goes sailing above both our heads and crashes somewhere behind the drum kits. Oggy and I exchange concerned looks. A moment later and what looks like a coke bottle flies overhead and smashes against an amp. Another minute or so and the song begins to come apart. One by one the musicians leave the stage. I assume this is some pre-planned gesture. I saw The Fall do it at a gig last year. But as more projectiles fly overhead I begin to realise the musicians are actually fleeing the smashing bottles. Only Vinnie remains, but finally, even he abandons his kit and disappears.

I snatch a set list from behind a monitor. John grabs another one. "I didn't think I'd ever see anything like that." Says Oggy. John starts to say something, but his words are drowned out by booing, catcalls and stamping feet. This isn't the sound of an audience demanding an encore.

This is the noise of young men venting their frustration. The booing and shouting increases, more missiles come flying towards the stage.

Suddenly, a pint glass flies past us and shatters on the monitor near our heads. "Fuck!" Says John and we try to move away. Then, another glass hits the large, ornate chandelier overhead. Shards of glass shower down. In a matter of seconds, the whole room seems to erupt. People are throwing everything they can find at the stage. More slivers of chandelier are falling from above. Fights are breaking out between individual members of the audience. It's like one of those scenes in a western movie, when the entire bar room suddenly launches into a fight.

There are a handful of security personnel in attendance, but in the face of such violent chaos there's nothing they can do. John and I clamber up onto the stage and crouch down behind an amp. I've lost sight of Oggy, but presume he's found some other hiding place. A couple of skinheads seem determined to wrench one of the large monitors off the stage. However, Twinny, the band's no-nonsense roadie is having none of it. He's already got a gash on the side of his head, but is struggling bravely on. With a brash "Fuck off!" he swings a mic stand at them. The hard metal connects with one of their heads and the skinhead goes staggering backwards. Gretton – the band's equally no nonsense manager – is busily retrieving instruments from the stage. He turns to see John and I cowering behind the amp.

Rob: "Who are you?"

John: "We're just hiding."

Graham: "Are you Rob Gretton?"

He wisely ignores this and returns to the job of rescuing equipment, assisted by Larry Cassidy who pops out from behind the curtain at the back of the stage where he's apparently been concealed.

Suddenly, the bright house lights snap on. This seems to immediately alter the energy in the room. Within minutes the fighting and chucking seem to have calmed down and the audience are being ushered out. John and I are reunited with Oggy. The three of us are in shock. "I don't reckon you'll be doing that interview." Says Oggy. I nod. Despite

Gretton's assurance a few days earlier, the band did indeed end up hiding away in the dressing room.[3]

In the aftermath, the floor is littered with smashed bottles, glasses, broken chairs and bits of chandelier. We pick our way over the debris and out through the big wooden doors and down the stone stairs towards the venue entrance. As we do so, one of the doors opens and a man steps inside. It's an extremely stressed looking Tony Wilson, dressed in a long, black leather coat. He sees us walking towards him. He's probably assessing if we are rioters or observers. Although Oggy and I are both nearly 6 foot tall, I'm sure we must look fairly innocuous. Not skinheads, not violent punks, just teenage Long Macs dumbfounded by the turn of events. Wilson holds the door open for us. "Night lads." He says as we slip out into the cold evening air.

* * * * *

Five weeks on. Monday 19th May. It's about 10:30pm. I'm in the kitchen at my parents' house, pouring myself a bowl of Rice Krispies. I've got the radio on and I'm listening to John Peel's show. "There are few things I dislike more than being the bringer of bad news." He says. "But we heard during the day, that Ian Curtis of Joy Division has died." He says he has no more details, but that his thoughts are with Ian's family and friends. He then plays 'New Dawn Fades' from *Unknown Pleasures*. As the solemn and majestic music struggles to

---

3. *Hex* fanzine ran for one issue. It featured reviews of the gigs I'd seen over the last few months and interviews with Mick Duffy of Blackburn band IQ Zero and Paul Slack and Pete Davies, bassist and drummer respectively with the UK Subs. When I say *Hex* ran for one issue, what I actually mean is it ran to one copy. I finished all the content, but at the time I couldn't afford to get multiples photocopied. So the original sat on a shelf in my bedroom for a couple of weeks, until I spilled a cup of tea over it. And that was that.

force its way out of the tinny transistor, I sit, staring at my cereal. I can't take this in.

* * * * *

Three years later. The summer of 1983. I'm in an U-matic video editing suite in the basement of Tony Wilson's house in a cul-de-sac called Old Broadway off Wilmslow Road. Brian Nicholson and I are working for IKON – the video arm of Factory Records. Well, I say working – that sort of implies we're getting a wage. We aren't.

Brian is the audio/visual technician at Blackburn Technical College. He and I became friends whilst I was doing a two-year arts foundation course there. We have similar musical tastes, although being a couple of years older, his passions also include the more outré end of the prog spectrum. Arriving at the Technical College in late 1980, I was intrigued by the possibilities of video, both in terms of using it to create visual artworks and in creating backing videos for my band.

Brian is already making distinctive art videos of his own. It's inspiring to know there is someone thinking along similar lines. He allows me to book the video cameras and editing equipment as much as I like. Then in June 1982, he sends some of the videos to Claude Bessy at the recently opened Haçienda night club.

The response is very positive indeed. Brian joins IKON and starts shooting and editing promos for Factory artists such as Durutti Column and The Wake. I tag along to lug around video cameras and tripods and generally get in the way. We spend the late summer of 1983 shooting and editing a promotional video for Section 25's single 'Back To Wonder'. Being a typical Factory Records plan, it's all a bit higgledy-piggledy. There's no budget and the single has in fact already been released several weeks ago, so it's actually a bit late in the day to be making a promo.

By this stage, Paul Wiggin has left the band and Section 25 are now a genuine family concern, consisting of brothers and sisters Larry, Vinnie and Angela Cassidy and Larry's wife Jenny Ross on lead vocals and keyboards. They've just recorded their new album *From The Hip*, produced by New Order's Bernard Sumner. It's not been released yet, but Larry has provided us with cassettes.

Sonically Section 25 have moved way beyond their Public Image Ltd. style origins. They've developed a sound that is decidedly more electronic, melodic and dance oriented. Larry's rather dour vocals have largely been supplanted by Jenny's light and breathy voice, whilst Sumner's production is bright and sleek, giving the melodies space to shine. It is in fact a remarkably prescient album that predicts the sound of house and techno by several years.[4]

Naturally, I question the Cassidy brothers about the riot at the Bury gig. Despite the obvious stresses of the night, they recall it with an unlikely fondness. Then one afternoon, Sumner comes over to Tony's house to check out some of the footage we've been assembling. I try very hard not to be overawed. But I think I might still be coming across as overawed. Larry orders a Chinese take-away and we sit watching a rough cut of the 'Back To Wonder' promo eating ordinary coloured noodles. Just before Sumner leaves, I mention being at the Bury gig. He nods but doesn't make any comment. Larry shoots me a look. Obviously the subject isn't open for discussion.[5]

---

4. The Section 25 single 'Looking From A Hilltop', taken from *From The Hip*, became a surprise club hit in 1984. But perhaps the biggest surprise came in 2016, when Section 25 were sampled at length by Kanye West for his track 'FML'. However, he didn't sample *From The Hip* era Section 25, rather a track called 'Hit' from the first stage of the band's evolution, released in 1981. The recording appeared on the band's debut album *Always Now* and was produced by Martin Hannett and Ian Curtis.

5. The Bury Derby Hall gig is dramatised in Anton Corbijn's excellent film *Control*. However, in the film, we're given the impression that the decision to bring on Alan Hempsall was a last minute thing. Yet, the set list that I stole clearly shows it was planned from before the start of the gig who would sing which songs.

PSYCHIC TV

THE HAÇIENDA, MANCHESTER

MONDAY 5TH NOVEMBER 1984

(AGE 20)

1984 has been an absolutely miserable year. Although you couldn't really say we hadn't been warned. The clue was in the number.

Whilst the UK may not be under the jackboot of Orwell's all seeing totalitarian state, the nation has been experiencing a severe tightening of the screws. Margaret Thatcher's repressive Conservative government has positioned themselves as advocates of social control and opponents of sexual freedom.

Over the last year, there has been a growing feeling amongst certain sectors of society, that we now have a government that stands in direct opposition to the people. The Conservatives' monetarist policies have led to a serious economic downturn and subsequent mass unemployment. The government's lust for privatisation is matched only by Thatcher's desire to crush the trade unions. The miners' strike, which started back in March, has turned into a bitter and often violent struggle that shows no signs of being resolved any time soon.

And there's also the small matter of the so-called 'Troubles' in Northern Ireland. The government's policy decisions have led to entrenched sectarian divisions. The removal of Special Category Status for all paramilitary prisoners precipitated the Hunger Strikes of 1980/1981 during which ten hunger strikers died. Thatcher herself, the girl who graduated from Oxford with second-class honours and became Britain's first female Prime Minister, is now such a target of public hate, she's in danger of making the Yorkshire Ripper look like a national treasure.

Then, on 12th October, the rules of engagement change…

It's just before three o'clock in the morning and I'm fast asleep at my girlfriend Natalia's flat on Devonshire Place in Kemptown, Brighton. Suddenly, a deep boom shakes the ground, rattling every free-standing object in the room. We're both instantly wide awake. Tense and alert in the darkness. "What the *fuck* was that?"

We go and peer out of the second floor window. Although from our limited vantage point we can't see anything untoward, we can hear scores of car alarms going off. Also, every seagull in the city is now wide awake and bawling the odds. Moments later, we start to hear the sirens of emergency vehicles hurtling past the top of the road.

Eventually, we go back to bed, none the wiser. Mid morning, Natalia switches on the radio and we hear the news. The IRA has claimed responsibility for planting a bomb that has partially destroyed the Grand Hotel a couple of hundred yards down the road from us!

Thatcher, her husband Denis and other cabinet ministers and delegates have been staying at the hotel during the Conservative Party conference. When the announcer mentions that Thatcher was not injured during the explosion, I pull a face of disappointment. I fancy I'm far from the only person in the country pulling such a face. And yet the statistics are horrific. The final death toll will be 5, although the number of people seriously injured will rise to 31, with some disabled for life.

Natalia and I walk along to view the Grand Hotel. Despite the fact the whole road has been cordoned off, and there are crowds of people gathered against the barriers, it's still possible to get down onto the beach and see the massive black hole that has ripped through five floors of the Victorian sea front hotel. Thatcher meanwhile, is seemingly unruffled, as the Conservative conference apparently continued on schedule at 9:30am this morning. She will not be bowed by terrorism. And yet the IRA has just released a statement; "Today we were unlucky, but remember we only have to be lucky once – you will have to be lucky always."

You know how I said it's been an absolutely miserable year? Well, politically and societally that's 100% true. But speaking personally, I've been having a ball. I moved down from Lancashire to Brighton two years ago. I'm studying on a three year Polytechnic course in combined visual arts that goes by the excruciating title of Expressive Arts. This always strikes me as odd. Because let's face it, if there are any arts which can't be described as expressive, then they probably can't be described as arts either.

The course combines painting, printmaking, photography and videomaking with theatre, music and dance. Early in the first year, I start my own performance art group. Originally it's a duo, comprising myself and Tim Harrold, a bone-dry poet performer from Thurrock. We call ourselves Theatre of the Bleeding Obelisk. The unwieldy name is inspired by Tim's response to the traditionalist stuff we're being taught in our drama lessons; "Theatre of the bleedin' obvious!" We insert the word Obelisk to make it even more bizarre sounding.

After two chaotic improvised performances, we start creating more structured shows, when we're joined by three other friends from the course: film maker and performance artist Greg Pope, Dutch actress, illustrator and clarinettist Pol Wynberg and Julian Phillips, a gifted pianist and inventor of strange instruments. Later, after Tim's departure, we will be joined by the actress and painter Peta Taylor.

A self confessed surrealist group, we combine sketches, ritualistic acts, poems, strange songs and bizarre stage sets and installations. We play at a range of arts centres, comedy venues, theatres festivals and galleries. Sometimes we go down a storm and sometimes audiences truly hate us. We never perform the exact same show twice, so we're constantly writing, building props and rehearsing. And I love every minute of it.[1]

---

1. Between 1982 and 1987, Theatre of the Bleeding Obelisk performed 60 or so gigs, appearing at stand up clubs, arts centres, theatres and festivals as diverse as Elephant Fayre Cornwall, The ICA London and The Melkweg in Amsterdam. And yet a trawl of

I also love every minute I spend with Natalia. We started seeing each other back in July. An aspiring film maker, she's on the same course, in the year below me, even though she's a couple of years older. Natalia is clever and sophisticated and witty and petite and beautiful, with pale skin, light blonde hair, high cheekbones and blue cat like eyes. She's the kind of girlfriend I never thought I'd be allowed to have. Our first date was truly romantic. Thanks to her father acquiring some complementary tickets, we went to the Wimbledon tennis tournament, visited the enclosure, ate strawberries and cream, made each other laugh and fell in love.

1984 has been a very satisfying year for new music too. I've been incessantly playing Scott Walker's brooding 'comeback' *Climate of Hunter* (which despite popular opinion, I believe may be the best of his albums), as well as the nocturnal psychedelia of Siouxsie and the Banshees' *Hyena* (which despite popular opinion, I believe may be the best of their albums) and the Cocteau Twins' ornate *Treasure* (which despite popular opinion, and so on).

Other new releases receiving heavy rotation include Test Department's expansive debut *Beating The Retreat* and Coil's daring but uneven *Scatology*, as well as the murky and giddy *Nylon Coverin', Body Smotherin'*, a tape album credited to Nurse With Wound and Current 93, although it also features sizeable contributions from Jim Thirlwell aka Jim Foetus. These last three albums are indicative of the biggest development in my listening habits. Last year, I experienced Industrial enlightenment, courtesy of my ex-girlfriend Louise who bought me Psychic TV's second album *Dreams Less Sweet*. Since then I've gone back and absorbed all the Industrial artists I'd previously missed out on, such as Non, SPK and Monte Cazazza, as well as mopping up all of the original Throbbing Gristle albums.

---

the internet will produce virtually no evidence whatsoever of our existence. Somehow, I find that oddly reassuring.

I've become fascinated by Psychic TV. They were established in 1981, by former Throbbing Gristle members Genesis P. Orridge and Peter 'Sleazy' Christopherson, along with original Alternative TV guitarist Alex Fergusson. Together, they started to create a music that looked beyond the largely electronic soundworld of Throbbing Gristle. With assistance from contemporary orchestral composer Andrew Poppy, Soft Cell vocalist Marc Almond and jazz trumpeter Claude Deppa, they recorded PTV's debut album *Force The Hand of Chance* which incorporated conventional rock instrumentation, with acoustic instruments, string arrangements and a hint of 60s psychedelia. It's a striking album, but also a flawed one, which definitely sounds like a group finding its feet.

In contrast, 1983's *Dreams Less Sweet* is perfect. The album features an expanded line up, including P. Orridge's wife Paula P. Orridge (aka Alaura O'Dell), future Coil main man John Balance, future Current 93 main man David Tibet, future Mekon main man John Gosling and the return of composer Andrew Poppy. On a sizeable CBS budget, PTV created what is arguably the most ambitious, diverse and fully realised album produced by the UK underground during the early 1980s.[2]

Recorded using Zuccarelli Holophonics – a form of non binaural 3D sound recording, whereby the sonic information is channelled through a Perspex human skull no less – the album includes not only electric and electronic sounds, but acoustic instrumentation, lush orchestral and choral arrangements, early Emulator experiments, exotic instruments such as gongs and Tibetan thigh bones which are played as horns, as well as field recordings – including John Balance being tattooed, and the sound of a coffin being buried, recorded from inside the coffin itself.

---

2. Kate Bush's rightly celebrated album *The Hounds of Love* was released two years later in 1985. I may be wrong, but a number of the sounds, moods, textures and structures on that album seem to draw inspiration directly from Psychic TV's *Dreams Less Sweet*.

Some compositions – such as the gently flowing 'The Orchids' with its near medieval melody played on marimba and oboe – are beautiful. Whereas the tense electric scything of 'In The Nursery' is frightening in the extreme. It's an enormously imaginative album. In fact, if you're in the mood for a piece of crass reductionism, *Dreams Less Sweet* is Industrial music's *Sgt. Pepper*. There, I've said it. And instantly regretted it.

Psychic TV certainly never bettered the album. But then they never again had a major label recording budget to play with, and, probably more importantly, they were never again that uniquely diverse assembly of talents.

With the zeal of a fresh convert, during my second year at Brighton Polytechnic, I decide to do my final dissertation on Psychic TV. My Art History tutor Fenella Crichton doesn't try to dissuade me, but she does point out there's a dearth of documentation about the subject, so it may prove difficult to research. In these pre-internet days, research is a longwinded and laborious process, involving sitting in libraries, sifting through microfiche and trying to order books from other parts of the country. Luckily however, I have already amassed a sizeable number of fanzine articles and music press clippings. And I've pored over sleeve notes and bulletins from Thee Temple ov Psychick Youth.

PTV are putting themselves forward not as simply a band. In fact, in their press interviews and communiqués, P. Orridge often refers to PTV as being the propaganda wing of Thee Temple ov Psychick Youth. Whereas some artists have fan clubs, PTV have initiated an organization dedicated to the investigation of magickal experimentation and the development of what might be termed open ended post-discordian philosophies. Over time, Thee Temple ov Psychick Youth will spread out from its UK base, and spawn branches in North America, Australia and various points across mainland Europe.

It's this combination of radical music, combined with the global exchange of esoteric information which has attracted me to write about PTV and TOPY. But what I really need to do is speak with some members of the group. Which is why, tonight – bonfire night – I'm going to see PTV play at Manchester's Haçienda, and hopefully interview

Genesis P. Orridge himself. I travelled up from Brighton yesterday, on the back of my mate Trevor Wheelan's black Harley Davidson. Trevor is a dark haired, pale skinned architecture student from Essex who shares my fascination with PTV and has been helping out with some Obelisk shows.

We're sitting in the lounge at my parents' house in Great Harwood when the doorbell rings. It's Pete. We hug. We haven't seen each other for seven months. I introduce him to Trevor and moments later we're climbing into Pete's jeep. It's a Suzuki Vitara with a soft top. Which means the back portion is covered just with canvas. So for motorway journeys it's best to wrap up warm. Trevor produces three tabs of Red Heart LSD that have been concealed inside a fold in his broad black leather bracelet. Each one a vivid postbox red heart in a tiny square of transparent gelatin. The three of us chew on them as Pete starts the engine.

We have plenty of time to spare, so a few minutes later we stop in at The Game Cock, an old pub on the outskirts of Great Harwood. We buy drinks then wander through the back of the pub and out to an area of grassland by the car park. Here they've built a bonfire of tree branches and old wooden furniture. It's about 9 feet high and is already blazing away. Around the edge of the bonfire someone has laid down a walkway consisting of old wooden doors. The three of us stand on the doors, sipping beers and feeling the warmth of the fire on our cheeks.

By the time we're climbing back into the jeep about 50 minutes later, I'm starting to notice the first traces of the acid rippling through my system. I rub my fingertips together, there's an increased sensitivity. Light and colours are a little more pronounced. It's a slight change, but it's there and it's growing. For some reason – possibly the fact that I'm 20 – it doesn't occur to me that it might be a bad idea to take hallucinogens when intending to interview someone for your dissertation.

We drive to Blackburn, where we pick up Brian Nicholson and his girlfriend Alison. Brian loads some video equipment into the back of the jeep. He's still working as a cameraman and editor with IKON and he's going to be filming the gig tonight. We zip along the M66, spotting bonfires burning in peoples' gardens and on the hillsides, flaring like unstable jewels in the darkness. Pete and I have tripped many times and he's often driven us. Somehow I trust him and somehow he trusts himself. And somehow we've never had an accident.[3]

We arrive in Manchester and Pete parks up. The five of us walk up Whitworth Street West, towards the Haçienda. There are surprisingly few people in the queue. Well, it's surprising to me, as I'd naively assumed the whole of Manchester would want to be here to pay their respects to the magick of Psychic TV. Brian has made sure we're on the guest list, so we wander through into the darkened space. The sound of Kraftwerk's 'Airwaves' is coming through the sound system. My sensitized skin prickles slightly at the change of temperature.

The Haçienda opened just two and a half years ago. The former yacht showroom was re-designed by Ben Kelly and, whereas others might have tried to break up the space and disguise the industrial nature of the building, Kelly has the huge girders on full display. Some are painted with thick black and yellow stripes, others have red and white stripes. With its high ceiling and towering metal pillars, it still feels very much like a warehouse.

In a few years time, fuelled by the acid house explosion, the Haçienda will become *the place* to be. But right now, it's struggling to find an audience. It's just another live music venue, and Manchester is never short of those. Sometimes events sell out here. However, more often than not, like tonight in fact, the place is a third full at best. But then not only are PTV a thoroughly underground concern, tonight is of course bonfire night. And, as it's only three weeks since the most recent attempt to blow up the government, this year, for many, bonfire night will have an extra frisson of dangerous appeal.

We bump into Malcolm Whitehead, a clever and friendly man

---

3. Fuck knows how.

who has been working as one of the directors of IKON. He informs us we've just missed the support group: Ram Ram Kino. It turns out Ram Ram Kino are in fact Crispy Ambulance operating under a new identity. I giggle at the band's perverse Northern stubbornness. Having ditched what even Tony Wilson himself described as "the worst band name of all time", they have proceeded to saddle themselves with a new moniker which manages to be almost as irritating yet nowhere near as memorable.

Brian and Alison slip off with Malcolm to sort out the video cameras. Pete, Trevor and I go to the bar. As I sip the lager, I can't tell if it tastes good or not. My taste buds are picking up other elements to normal. Or, if you will, the flavour seems to have been arranged in a different order.

I stare up at the two huge video screens at the back of the stage. They're showing montages of material put together by Claude Bessy. Claude is a smart witted, playful and provocative Frenchman. He was a prominent figure in the original Los Angeles 1977 punk scene, launching the fanzine *Slash* and singing with his own band Catholic Discipline. And now he's the Haçienda's resident VJ or video jockey. The footage he selects includes sequences from low budget horror movies, titillating clips from bondage films and material plundered from 60s mondo features as well as 50s black and white documentaries and other less categorisable stuff.

Pete returns from the toilets, chuckling to himself. He tells us he was standing next to a six foot eight skinhead at the urinals when he glanced down to see the guy had a ring through the end of his cock about an inch wide. "I'm not sure how it'd feel to be on the receiving end of that." He says, grimacing.

Piercings of any kind other than earrings are still very rare. I only know three women who have their noses pierced. Tattoos are also still very much a minority interest. But Psychic TV and TOPY are in the vanguard of an unnamed cultural shift. Some individuals are employing tattoos, piercings and scarification as a way of reclaiming sovereignty over their bodies in an increasingly controlled world. Such markings and adornments could be seen to both reconnect people with their tribal past as well as indicating they wish to operate outside societally acceptable forms of beauty.[4]

I should mention at this point that I don't have any piercings. And I'm actually fairly comfortable with societally acceptable forms of beauty. I never even got around to having my ears pierced either. And I certainly don't have any tattoos. There are two reasons for this. Firstly they're so bloody permanent! It's like deciding you're going to wear the same pieces of jewellery every single day. Or deciding you're going to don the same coat every single day. I just can't make that kind of commitment. I mean what if I'd been sewn into my long mac back in 1980? I'd now be waiting for it to come back in fashion. And I'm not a patient man.

The second reason I don't want a tattoo is, given the choice, I'd rather not be repeatedly pricked with a sharp needle. In fact I can honestly say I've never ever volunteered for unnecessary pain. I am what the psychologists describe as 'a bit soft'.

The Haçienda has started to fill up a little, but the place is still under half capacity. The audience is predominantly male and aside from numerous indie types, there's a handful of spiky punks, as well as several serious looking men in their early 30s, standing around in army fatigues – this having been a component part of Throbbing Gristle's image. Some have adorned their camouflage gear with TG or PTV patches and button badges – but the implication is "we wear practical military clothes because we are engaged in cultural warfare". Never one for too much practicality, I'm dressed in a black demob suit and a red button collar shirt with my backcombed hair muzzed into a bird's nest of follicles.

---

4. As we approach the third decade of the 21st century, those mid 1980s signifiers of counter cultural difference and defiance, tattoos and piercings, have now become largely harmless mainstream lifestyle distractions.

But my hair is neither the biggest nor the most flamboyant on display here tonight. There are several young men and women wearing black clothing and dark eye make-up with artificially pale skin who have sculpted their hair into elaborate shapes. These are people whom I'm sure would have no qualms about identifying themselves as Goths.

Goth is Glam's dark twin. Goth is a narcissistic playground of ostentatious display. Goth is irritating. Like the New Romantics, Goths first manifested themselves at the dawn of the 1980s. A time when the line between rock music and hairdressing became strangely blurred.

Prior to the rise of the Goths, Siouxsie and the Banshees, Joy Division and The Cure had all produced work marked by a brooding otherworldly darkness. But crucially all three bands also possessed strong melodic skills and were not averse to deploying colours other than black in their soundworlds.

It was Bauhaus, with their stark theatricality and Max Factor menace, who opened the floodgates for a whole gaggle of Goth bands, including such stars of the dressing up box as Specimen and Sisters of Mercy. Despite their high dramatics and pretentions to existential horror, I find their music predictable and feeble. Then there's Alien Sex Fiend, a band who come over like the cast of *Night of the Living Dead* as played by the *Carry On* team.

The lights dim. A wave of expectation flushes through my body, amplified by the LSD. A black and white TV test card image is projected onto the large video screens; a series of black bars and grey scale spectrum charts. At the centre is an illustration of a human skull with a small psychic cross in the middle of its forehead. The group begins to assemble on stage to a building wave of applause. As the lights come up, we see a group of individuals, all wearing T-shirts of black, white or grey with different Psychic TV or TOPY symbols on them.

But there, standing centre stage, in jeans and a plaid shirt is Claude Bessy. He's a friend of P. Orridge's of many years standing, and tonight he appears to be serving as PTV's MC. Brian and I have worked with Claude through IKON and he's one of the most naturally funny people I've ever met. Unfortunately, it's impossible to tell how witty or otherwise he's being right now, as the mic keeps cutting out.

As Claude leaves the stage, the opening piece of music begins to take shape. Twenty-one year old John Gosling stands at a table with a tape deck and stack of cassette samples stacked before him. He's tall and toned, like a boxer, with a completely shaven head. Gosling presses play and a recording of a slowly ascending cello sample shivers through the sound system. The cassette is still king.

Another 21 year old, the pale, dark haired and elfin Paula P. Orridge stands at a keyboard, adding stark synth chords to the sound. Genesis P. Orridge strides about the stage in combat trousers and a white T-shirt with a red psychic cross emblazoned upon it. He's a youthful looking 34, with piercing eyes, his hair shaved extremely short with a couple of long braids coming from above the nape of his neck. A short and slight, but nonetheless charismatic figure, P. Orridge is putting his bass guitar through some kind of effects unit, using the instrument to create squalls of tense distortion.

Nearby, with his big eyes and straw blond side parting, stands the 32 year old Alex Fergusson. Fergusson is using *his* bass to pick out deep circling tones. Although he's a noted six-string stylist, tonight the Scotsman will almost exclusively be playing bass, whilst guitar duties are handled by the 25 year old, dark haired Paul Reeson. On this piece, Reeson plays a Roland GR-300 guitar synth, using it to create bursts of noise that could almost be the sound of a dentist's drill gone haywire. After several minutes, the tapes and other instruments drop away, until only the astringent drilling of the guitar synth remains.

Then, Gosling plays a tape of an orchestral loop. A sequence of deep moody chords. This is 'Enochian Calls', a staple of PTV's live shows at the moment. Enochian is a magickal alphabet, written of during the 16th century, in the journals of the occultist and spirit medium Edward Kelley and his colleague the mathematician, astronomer, astrologer and occult philosopher John Dee. Kelley and Dee claimed that the alphabet had been communicated to them by angels. Yet the sounds being created here sound more demonic than angelic.

As Paula stands, playing a sparse sequence of notes on the vibes, Gosling triggers another tape of what sounds like a monk intoning in a language bereft of recognisable words. 'Enochian Calls' is an unsettling piece which sounds like nothing else being produced by the British underground right now. This certainly isn't rock music. It's closer in tone to the avant garde experiments of Pierre Schaeffer or Gavin Bryars.

Behind the musicians, the large video screens show glowing images of wolves baying, their jaws wide open... A naked man, painted white is suspended by his ankles... the flickering pulse of Brion Gysin's dream machines... Meanwhile, to the side of the stage, there's an additional television monitor showing a different set of images.

I've seen a few groups experimenting with visuals in their live performances. Usually bands simply have films projected over them. And usually they opt for found material, as this is cheap and readily available. However, PTV are creating their own bespoke video footage. But these videos are not standard pop promo material. Strange, erotic and sometimes disturbing, with an emphasis on the psychedelic and the surreal, their videos are closest in tone to the Super 8 experiments of Derek Jarman, a noted PTV sympathiser.

The Velvet Underground are a major touchstone in terms of PTV's stage presentation. The New York band's early, partially improvised live performances had been augmented by Andy Warhol's multi-media enterprise The Exploding Plastic Inevitable. As The Velvets played, the stage would usually have two of Paul Morrissey's underground films projected side by side behind them, with light displays and oil light projections also playing across the band. As well as the musicians, there would be dancers on stage, along with the photographer Gerald Malanga, who would also be dancing and cavorting with a whip.

PTV have neither the budget, nor the extensive array of collaborators which were available to Warhol and Morrissey. Nevertheless their desire to create an 'overloading' experience goes way beyond what any other group is currently doing.[5]

'Information overload' is a much used counter cultural phrase in the early 1980s. There is a notion that we are living in a time of massive acceleration. That with the increasing number of news outlets and the domestic use of video cameras and recorders, the world is somehow shrinking, that we will soon have access to undreamed of amounts of information. PTV embraces this notion, believing they can juxtapose multiple televisual images in a bid to short circuit conditioned responses within the audience.[6]

As 'Enochian Calls' fades out with tapes of clattering chimes, the band plunge into 'I Like You'. It's the first thing they've played tonight which could be called a song. Paula stands, beating a strict rhythm on the roto-toms, Reeson's guitar synth grinds out a thick paste of granular noise, but Fergusson lifts the whole thing with his high, melodic Joy Division style bass line. I close my eyes and sway. The tug of the bass line and the swing of the drums are irresistible. *"I like you"* sings P. Orridge in his reedy voice. *"You're very nice."* Never have pleasantries sounded so unsettling.

I open my eyes and stare up at the video screens...

Two figures in blank grey masks entwine their legs around each other... A series of occult symbols fade in and out... Paula stands half naked in a hotel bedroom, a balcony window open behind her, the room

---

5. By the mid 1990s, with their 'Zoo TV' tour, U2 would take the idea of a band being backed by a huge bank of TV screens pumping out multiple images to the level of polished theatre. However, U2's strategy would be more about creating a dynamic spectacle visible to audiences at the back of huge arenas. Whereas Psychic TV usually appeared in much smaller venues, where the visuals could truly overload the audience.

6. Of course, when compared with the digital blizzard of information the internet now keeps in constant motion, the so-called 'information overload' of the 1980s resembles nothing so much as a solitary 1930s ticker tape.

flooded with light. She's slowly and carefully dressing in what look like a set of Edwardian undergarments…

For PTV, their work with video and visual image production shares an equal importance to the music. In fact, P. Orridge is keen to advance the idea that television and video are potentially magickal tools. TOPY also disseminate video-cassettes via their Temple mail order service. These cassettes comprise some of the images accompanying their musical performances, recordings of rituals and scarification, as well as interviews and what might be termed short lectures on self-empowerment.

And yet, even as PTV are making expanded use of video as a weapon of advanced artistic expression and direct communication, the video-cassette itself is being vilified. Due to the tabloid engineered moral hysteria about so-called 'video nasties', the Conservative government has been cracking down on horror and thriller films which until recently were freely available to hire from any number of video rental stores. Several stores have been raided and cassettes have been seized. By the end of this purge on civil liberties, 39 titles will have been successfully prosecuted in the British courts and deemed liable to deprave and corrupt. These include genre classics such as *The Driller Killer*, *I Spit on Your Grave* and *Zombie Flesh Eaters*.

The government has recently passed the Video Recordings Act 1984, which means from now on, every video release must be certificated. There is some considerable irony in the fact that the explosive device used in the Brighton bombing was fitted with a long-delay timer made from component parts of a videocassette recorder.

Back at the Haçienda, the video images are now carrying the majority of the show. Gosling is playing a tape of chanting monks. But there are huge intervals of silence, interrupting the sampled voices. You could charitably say this section of the performance is ultra minimal. But in truth, I get the impression the silences are unintentional. His voice riddled with sarcasm, P. Orridge says "Have you er, ever seen a mixing desk before?" Apparently the sound engineer isn't entirely sympathetic to the group's aesthetic.

The whole piece feels like it's on the verge of expiring completely, when suddenly a solid drum & piano loop slides in at full volume. This is the sound of PTV's recent single 'Unclean'. Paula plays the roto-toms over the top of the loop and Fergusson and Reeson begin to produce fertile layers of guitar scree. After a moment of near sonic extinction, the group clicks into a hard and spiky groove.

The sound palette on 'Unclean' is akin to that heard on the earliest Velvet Underground live bootlegs. Alex Fergusson's songwriting with Mark Perry in Alternative TV had long worn the influence of Lou Reed and Sterling Morrison, but within PTV's recent output, he has allowed his Velvets fetish to run riot. P. Orridge chants and rants over the looping sounds *"You may think you are holy, but you are unclean."*

On the video screens, a naked man smears himself in red paint... Another man in a restoration costume and tall white wig holds up what appears to be a large toy lion's head... a face behind a white jewel-encrusted mask crosses his eyes...

As P. Orridge straps on his bass, a skittering drum machine pattern fades in and the group start into a version of their recent single 'Roman P'. The studio cut, released as a 7" on the French Sordide Sentimental label, is probably one of the best songs of this period of the band's development. I've been spinning the single quite a lot at home. Initially it took me by surprise, as it was the first intimation that Psychic TV were now developing their sound in a more rock direction. What they play tonight is more skeletal in its construction. Fergusson picks out the Spartan bass line as Reeson plays high arpeggios on the guitar, Gosling thickens the plot with tapes of drones and Paula pounds out a beat like the sound of the drum in an ancient slave galley.

If Throbbing Gristle's lyrics often presented otherwise unpalatable subject matter with a near journalistic detachment, with Psychic TV, P. Orridge has decided to take a different tack. One of his current concerns seems to be using the raw material of the media to create modern day myths. 'Roman P.' takes as its subject the life and times of the film director Roman Polanski, including the death of his young wife Sharon

Tate at the hands of the Manson Family and Polanski's subsequent rape of the 13 year-old-girl Samantha Geimer. The lyrics suggest that Polanski is Roman by name, by nature and by destiny, implying the director's life has a narrative akin to that of a decadent and corrupt Roman Emperor.

Another big difference between Throbbing Gristle and Psychic TV is P. Orridge's vocals. With the former, P. Orridge was often more likely to chant, or talk the lyrics; with the latter he actually sings. Or does he? Whilst his performances on record sound convincing enough – possibly the result of multiple takes and in some cases multi-tracking – live P. Orridge sometimes struggles to hold notes or even hit the right ones in the first place. As a man who grew up in the punk era I have no problem with a lack of musical expertise, or instruments or vocals being off key or out of tune, but sometimes tonight P. Orridge ends up in some half way state where it doesn't feel like he's playing to his strengths.

This is the third occasion I've seen PTV live and this time around the energy feels a little low – both on stage and in the audience. With several improvised sections, the group dynamic is under pressure to gel and sometimes the sound just feels too sketchy and uncentred. I'm standing in the middle of the crowd at the Haçienda, I've travelled over 250 miles to be here and my head full of chemicals. I want this to be amazing. But it isn't amazing. It's just good. There are moments of excitement, but this isn't hitting the heights I know they can reach.

How can I tell? You might ask. How can I trust my judgment under the influence of LSD? Well, my dabbling with acid and music and combinations of the two has been numerous and varied, but the one thing I've always felt was that if something sounds good, acid only enhances it. If something sounds amazing, acid only enhances it. But if something sounds bland or uninteresting the acid is powerless to elevate it. Others may well tell you different tales. Of how they listened to Bananarama whilst tripping and it sounded as complex and profound as Ligeti. But my ears don't work like that.

Anyway, all of that aside, it turns out this is pretty weak acid. The feeling of increased sensitivity and receptiveness levelled out not long after we got here. Pete and Trevor confirm my assessment. We are alert and sensitized, but we are not out of our heads.

Gosling triggers what sounds like a field recording of a wolf howling at the moon. Slowly, further wolf howls become overlaid, until P. Orridge begins to join in, imitating the wolves. Reeson adds a layer of slide guitar, somehow managing to make it sound creepy in the extreme. Much later, I discover this song is called 'Southern Comfort', and, with its conjuring up of sinister swamplands the title makes perfect sense. Although, maybe 'Southern Discomfort' would have been even more appropriate.

Up on the video screens, a prepubescent girl in a white dress with a garland of flowers in her long blonde hair stands against a sky of boiling flames. It's a striking image that could have come from one of the hallucination sequences in Ken Russell's *Altered States*. It's the videos not the music that are exciting me tonight.

The next song is 'Godstar', a very recent addition to the group's repertoire. Although it appears tonight as a half formed work, its structure still fragile, it will evolve into PTV's best-known song. With its Keith Richards-esque guitar line and 60s style harmonies, 'Godstar's lyrics concern the life and suspicious death of original Rolling Stones guitarist Brian Jones. Poised somewhere between cautionary tale and hero worship, like P. Orridge's meditation on Polanski, it depicts its subject very much in mythic terms.

The song will go through various stages of development. Honed via numerous live performances, it will coalesce into probably the most 'rock' piece of music the band will attempt at this stage. Then, once taken into the studio, it will be transformed into a rather arch pop song that largely neuters the overdriven power of the live version, in favour of something far more bright and bouncy. When it is released as a single, in just over a year's time, it will mark the high watermark of P. Orridge and PTV's engagement with the pop mainstream. 'Godstar' will top the independent charts and also trouble the top 50 of the national charts. Although this by no means sets P. Orridge up amongst the Cliff Richards of this world, it does show just how much he has been able to reinvent himself.

Meanwhile, back on stage at the Haçienda, 'Godstar' concludes to a burst of applause. "I bet you didn't think we did rock 'n' roll did you." Says P. Orridge, obviously recognising the potential broader appeal of what has just been performed. But this flirtation with rock is a brief affair, as the group launch into a barrage of quivering and ascending synth tones and tribal drumming, accompanied by guitar scratching from Reeson and Fergusson. P. Orridge wails over the top *"In thee starlit mire… In thee starlit mire…"* It's murky and it's inchoate and it's mercifully brief.

The sound cuts, revealing a percussive loop. It sounds like African nyabinghi drumming, but it's been filtered to give it a more electronic feel. P. Orridge leans over the mic wailing like someone with a head injury, whilst Paula and Reeson exchange instruments. He pummels the roto-toms, as she strangles some brittle glassy notes from the guitar synth. This feels like an attempt to channel the group's remaining energies and frustrations into a true sonic bombardment. With its tightly shuffling rhythm and thick broth of synth tones, this sounds more like Throbbing Gristle. The piece lasts for nearly a quarter of an hour and it's definitely the highlight of the evening. I feel charged up as my head is bathed in the bristling noise. I turn to see Trevor beaming.

Suddenly, the cacophony drops away. All that remains are two loops of female opera singers, their voices constantly circling and ascending. Everyone on stage looks spent. As they begin to wander off, P. Orridge suddenly shouts into the mic "Why are you wearing those great big shoes!?" The target of these words remains unclear. Almost as an after thought, he politely adds "Thank you, goodnight." And then he too is gone. There's obviously going to be no encore. Such a gesture would be far too show biz. And tonight has been a long way from show biz.

As the audience applauds, I turn to Pete. He looks unconvinced. "Some of it was okay." He admits. "But it doesn't really feel like a proper band." I know what he means, despite some strong moments in the improvisatory sections the group's sound was sometimes much less than the sum of its parts. "I thought the videos were amazing though." I say. Trevor agrees. Of all of us, he seems the most impressed by the performance. "I loved it." He says. "It's not like anything else you're going to go out and see is it."

He's right. The combination of musical elements, along with the emphasis on distinctive and sensual video imagery and their commitment to channelling magickal forces and creating sensory maximalism definitely make PTV a very individual proposition. Although it suddenly occurs to me that the three of us are still tripping. So, as Brian weaves his way towards us through the rapidly dispersing crowd, I decide to get the opinion of the control subject. "It was *alright*." He says, emphasizing the word in that way that implies it was only so-so.

Deciding now's the time to make contact I walk behind the stage and bump into Paula P. Orridge. I introduce myself. She's so open and friendly I want to say how much I loved the gig. But I know it was only intermittently successful and, in the clammy grasp of the psychotropic experience, I don't feel able to lie. So I enthuse about the videos, which I absolutely did love.

Paula: "Thanks. Gen' put together most of them. Some of them were only finished late last night."

Graham: "Would it be okay to talk to him?"

Paula: "Sure. Go through if you want to. But he was up all night, finishing off editing the new videos. So don't be surprised if he tells you to fuck off."

Graham: "Okay, thanks. I'll give it a go."

I stride through the door to the backstage area. Having worked here on and off, I know my way about. This adds to my confidence. I push open the door to the green room (in reality just a grubby windowless space with a few chairs and piles of boxes). Some of the group is packing away equipment. P. Orridge is swigging from a large bottle of water. Sitting next to him is Reeson. The general atmosphere in the room is a little morose. I walk over and sit down next to them. Both Reeson and P.Orridge look at me with mild surprise.

Graham: "Excuse me, would you mind if I interviewed you about your work?"

GPO: (shrugs) "Okay. I suppose so."

I take out my dictaphone to show that I'm serious, proving that I'm not the sort of guy who would try and write down an interview in biro on a candy striped paper bag. Listening back to the tape later, I realise I neither introduce myself nor mention the fact I'm writing a dissertation about PTV. I think there's a good chance that I wouldn't have made these errors if I hadn't been tripping.

Graham: "What did you think of tonight's show?"

Reeson: "What 'show'?"

Graham: "Well, what you just did."

Reeson: "We did what we did. I don't want to comment on it."

GPO: "I thought the audience were very lazy."

Graham: "What were you expecting?"

GPO: "We thought they might react more. I thought they might take their clothes off and start having sex."

Graham: "But that's quite difficult in the context of a rock gig isn't it."

GPO: "Is it? Why?"

Graham: "Well, social conventions I suppose. Besides, if anybody did that, wouldn't they get thrown out?"

GPO: "Would they?"

Graham: "Yeah, I think they probably would."

GPO: "It's happened before."

Graham: "Really? Where?"

GPO: "Why are you questioning me?"

Graham: "Because it's an interview."

GPO: "Is it? What gives you the right to come in here and ask us what we think about what we're doing?"

Graham: "Sorry, it's just that I'm interested in Psychic TV and the ideas behind what you do."

At this point, GPO turns his back on me.

Graham: "Okay, I sense I'm just pissing you off. Would you like me to leave?"

GPO & Reeson: "Yes."

Graham: "Okay. Goodnight."

I stand up, exit and make my way back out to the stage area. I'm feeling crestfallen. I'm also feeling relief that the acid is so weak. Another couple of micrograms and I could have been sent into an emotional tailspin by the encounter. I step back out by the left of the stage. The Haçienda is nearly empty now. Pete, Trevor, Brian and Alison are hanging around by the entrance. "How'd it go?" Asks Pete. I shake my head. "They weren't really in the mood."

* * * * *

Whilst I take acid at quite a few more shows after the PTV Haçienda gig, I never again try to interview someone whilst under the influence of hallucinogenics.

Despite my unfortunate encounter with P. Orridge, I finish my dissertation on PTV and hand it in on time. Just. Not only that, but I go on to see the group perform another nine times over the next few years, as they evolve through various stages, from their ritualistic Velvets-like performances, to their hyperdelic pop-pomp, and on into their acid house incarnation. Some gigs, like that night at the Haçienda, will be awkward half formed affairs, whilst others will be transcendent.

One of the best was PTV's performance at Thee Fabulous Feast ov Flowering Light – a day-long festival which took place at London's Hammersmith Palais on 19th May 1985. The event was curated by PTV and featured a great line up of counter cultural artists, including US author Kathy Acker, The Virgin Prunes and Bjork's pre-Sugarcubes band Kukl. Although PTV's headlining set of songs was near identical to that performed at the Haçienda just six months earlier, the interpretations were light years away.

By this stage, Reeson had departed and Gosling was absent, so for this event, Alex Fergusson was back on lead guitar, and Genesis and Paula P. Orridge were augmented by Icelandic contemporary composer Hilmar Örn Hilmarsson on keyboards, Soft Cell's Dave Ball on synth and tapes, Strawberry Switchblade's Rose McDowall on guitar and vocals, Rema-Rema's Max (aka Dorothy Prior) on drums and Mouse (aka Sharon Beaumont) on drums. The sound was immeasurably richer and more varied and the group seemed to have realised their potential to become a post Velvets psychedelic powerhouse.

* * * * *

Twenty years after the PTV bonfire night gig, I'm staying in Manchester, shooting the first series of *Ideal*.

The Haçienda finally closed its doors in 1997. Problems with drug dealers and gang violence in and around the venue had been increasing for years. But in the end, what killed the club off was spiralling debt. The Haçienda was demolished two years ago and the site has now been turned into a residential block: 'The Haçienda Apartments'. And, as fate would have it, that's where the production company has put me up.

It feels weird being here. Yet inside, the flats look exactly the same as any of the other so called 'luxury apartments' which are springing up all over the city.

One evening, Brian Nicholson comes over to visit and we wander around the building, trying to reorient ourselves using the mental geography of the Haçienda's past. It's almost impossible. Until we take the lift down to the basement car park. Down here, with the black and yellow striped pillars and the concrete floor, it's like time has stood still and somebody has parked an awful lot of cars.

THE SHAMEN

THE ZAP CLUB, BRIGHTON

MONDAY 29ᵀᴴ NOVEMBER 1989

(AGE 25)

My girlfriend is pregnant. It wasn't planned.

And the reality of the situation hasn't sunk in. Mind you, the baby is due in just three months. It'd be good if it sank in soon. Maybe when they finally arrive it'll sink in then.

My relationship with Natalia lasted nearly two years. Right up until I stupidly destroyed it by having an affair. After that I had a couple of much shorter relationships, one of which left me heartbroken. Then I met Helen.

We've been seeing each other for just over a year. We're very different, but we've been having a lot of fun. She works as a sales assistant in a designer clothes shop and does voluntary work at the museum. She's attractive and funny and impulsive and stylish and sensual. She's also very optimistic and can always see the upside to any situation. The pregnancy was a complete surprise but we both decided that we'd just go with it and do our best and make it work.

Then, two months into the pregnancy, everything changed. Her optimistic nature evaporated. It's been replaced by a constant desire for conflict. This evening's argument flared up because when I moved all the furniture around in the living room as she'd asked, I'd done it wrong. She'd changed her mind about where the furniture should go. I should have *known* that.

"Don't worry." I say. "I'll shift it. It won't take a couple of minutes." Most days there's something wrong. She flies into a rage over the slightest thing. After a while, I begin to realise she's deliberately seeking out conflict. The spark is unimportant. What she wants is the fire.

I'm reminded of the argument we had yesterday afternoon. When she couldn't find a packet of biscuits in the kitchen and it was my fault. I found them for her. Apparently I'd put them in the wrong place. How could I expect her to find them on that shelf, in the food cupboard, next to the other biscuits? She's not a mind reader.

Last week, she came home early evening and there was no light on in the hallway. That made the house too dark and unwelcoming. What was I thinking!? She hates coming back into a dark house. "Just switch the light on." I say. "The switch is right by the front door." "That's not the point!" She shouts. I feel it must be at least *some* of the point.

Maybe this is what pregnancy is like. I've never spent any time with a pregnant woman before. Maybe all pregnant women are like this. What must it feel like to carry around another human being growing inside you? If I had to do it maybe it'd make me angry all the time. My insight is limited. I'm 25. I've only recently started to figure out what being a man is about. And now, suddenly, I'm going to be a father. And I'm not best placed to be a father.

I spent half an hour on the phone to Pete this afternoon, telling him about the situation. He listened patiently but didn't have any advice. He's never spent any time with a pregnant woman either. These days Pete and I talk on the phone about once a month. We talk about the music we're listening to, we talk about the films we've been to see, and we talk about our relationships. He's content. I'm nervous.

Since leaving college in 1985, I've been either on the dole or on the Enterprise Allowance Scheme. Over the last two years I've been developing creative ideas with my friend Malcolm Boyle. Since the cessation of Theatre of the Bleeding Obelisk in 1987, he and I have been performing as a comedy double act under the name Wax Cabinet and writing dark fringe theatre shows. However, away from Brighton's supportive environment, we have struggled to find an audience for our work. Although, with the benefit of hindsight, it's fairly easy to comprehend why our black comedy plays, infused with science fiction and incorporating shadowplay, violent slapstick and Burroughsian cut-ups haven't immediately set the theatre world alight. Wax Cabinet takes a lot of time and makes us virtually no money. And I get the distinct impression that being a father costs money.

I finish moving the armchairs and sofa and a bookcase. But, by now, where the furniture is positioned has become irrelevant. It's all just another example of how I don't want her to be happy. "You just go out and enjoy yourself!" She snaps in an accusatory voice. So I go. I leave the house, feeling tense and irritated by yet another needless burst of conflict.

I haven't been out to a gig for a good few months. I've been saving money. Saving for a future I have no way of picturing. But tonight, The Shamen are playing at Brighton club The Zap. I bought my ticket several weeks ago. Over the last couple of years, The Shamen have recorded what I consider to be some essential music. Indeed, they have become masters of a number of hybrid musical forms. And – whilst they are destined to become a highly successful chart act with a global appeal – at this point in their evolution, The Shamen are still very much a part of the counter culture.

The band was formed in Aberdeen in 1984. Originally they operated as Alone Again Or – a name taken from a song on Love's *Forever Changes* album. To begin they were an indie guitar band heavily influenced by 1960s freakbeat and psychedelia – advocates of mind expansion, but not just in terms of the psychedelic experience. There is political thought within some of their lyrics too.

Even when they changed their name to The Shamen and developed a more rigorous and hard-edged approach to songwriting, 60s psych remained their central inspiration. Their debut album, 1987's *Drop* (presumably as in 'drop a tab of acid') is a melodic and engaging listen. It contains well-crafted songs such as 'The Other Side' and 'Four Letter Girl'. Yet this is undeniably a sound that is looking back more often than it's looking forward.

However, by the time of the album's release, The Shamen had already started to feel the inexorable pull of black dance music. Namely the stripped down beats and collagistic possibilities of hip-hop and especially the looping squelchy rhythms of acid house. The Shamen are far from the only white Indie artists to experience a dance floor conversion during this era. But they were early to the party and they're doing it with more aplomb and devotion than most.

Discussions of this phenomenon – the moment Indie embraced the energy of dance music – tend to focus on Manchester's two most fêted ensembles of the era: Happy Mondays and The Stone Roses. Yet, despite an open musical mind and a natural sympathy for all things Mancunian, neither band touches me. I know this is heresy, but to my ears, they just sound like so-so support acts. Happy Mondays seem lumpy and uninspired, with far too much mediocre guitar noodling, and – despite Tony Wilson's outlandish claim that, as a wordsmith, Shaun Ryder is "on a par with W.B. Yeats" – lazy, half baked lyrics. Whilst The Stone Roses sound like a conglomeration of influences and nothing more. Both bands also seem to be fuelled by an overriding male energy that recalls the macho posturing of much mid 1970s rock. Something even an over abundance of 'E' can't quite hide.

I first saw The Shamen play live in Brighton at the Basement Club two years ago. They'd just released the single 'Knature of a Girl', possibly the best song of that era of the band's development. The gig had been very psychedelic, layering heavily treated guitars over earth shaking hip-hop drum patterns played by a live drummer. I attended on my own and returned home babbling enthusiastically to my flat mates Tony and Tamsin.

Since then, the band have moved from Scotland down to London and lost two members – reportedly because they didn't approve of the increasing prominence of dance elements in the band's sound. The Shamen have now settled on the nucleus of original vocalist and guitarist Colin Angus and bassist Will Sinnott (aka Will Sin), aided by various musicians, remixers and DJs.

Back in January of this year, they brought out their 'post conversion' album *In Gorbachev We Trust*. And I've played it to death. It sounds like a band with feet in multiple camps. Songs such as 'Jesus Loves Amerika', 'Adam Strange' and their cover of The Monkees' 'Sweet Young Thing' showcase melodic 60s psychedelia filtered through the bold production techniques of hip hop. Meanwhile, the title track, with its spliced news reports and shuffling electronics recalls the insistent Dada boogie of Cabaret Voltaire. Elsewhere, acid house tracks such as 'Raptyouare' and 'Transcendental' sound like a band attempting to exit their indie chrysalis entirely and emerge as a fully formed dance act.

But it's not just the sounds of the emerging dance culture that appeal to The Shamen. The band's embracing of the transformative potential of LSD and MDMA is unequivocal. I've taken MDMA a few times myself, both at gigs and clubs and once in the countryside. I get it. But it's not really the drug for me. Part of my reticence surrounds the very thing that, for many, gives Ecstasy its appeal, namely the way the drug engenders a feeling of commonality.

The 14 year old punk inside me will always remain suspicious of commonality. Although I will forever be convinced of LSD and psilocybin's ability to dissolve the ego and expand consciousness, I am mistrustful of MDMA's ability to create illusory bonds of unity. But my main problem with taking Ecstasy is the three days afterwards, where I find myself wading through a thick residue of anxiety, self-doubt and all purpose misery. After 6 or 7 such experiences I decide to give E the elbow.

The Shamen however, are obviously experiencing no such qualms. The track 'Synergy', which opens *In Gorbachev We Trust*, has a proselytizing chorus which leaves no room for misinterpretation;

> *MDMAzing... MDMAzing...*
> *MDMAzing... MDMAzing...*
> *We got the power...*
> *You and me... You and me...*
> *We are together in ecstasy.*

The freshly inspired Shamen are now operating at an accelerated rate. Barely four months after *In Gorbachev We Trust*, the band release the follow up – a mini album called *Phorward*. And in that short time, there have been considerable stylistic refinements. On the 10" *Phorward*, the four to the floor beats of house have now started to dominate, and almost all traces of rock have been erased. Personally, although I've played *Phorward* quite a bit, I definitely miss the psych and hip hop elements that have made the band such a unique proposition over the last two years. But obviously The Shamen can see where their future lies.

I've arranged to meet Malcolm outside The Zap around 8pm. I reach the seafront and lean over the railings, looking down, scanning the promenade. I can't see him. Malcolm is tall, articulate, authoritative, positive and playful. Originally, we had been in different Brighton based fringe groups. Me in Theatre of the Bleeding Obelisk and he in a company called Bright Red, who, as the name intimates, had a more political bent. We met through mutual friends at a party. Within minutes, we were making each other snort with laughter. Showing off basically. Doing daft voices and making surreal remarks. And no doubt irritating the other guests.

One of the levels on which we immediately connected was music. Our checklist of essential bands is very similar: Wire, The Fall, Captain Beefheart and so on. But there are differences too. He introduced me to several prog-rock bands I'd previously dismissed in my teenage years – largely due to them having long hair. He also introduced me to the world of hip-hop, a music I'd previously dismissed as sounding weedy. However, this was largely due to only hearing hip-hop coming through the radio. Then I heard Schoolly D's 'PSK What Does It Mean?' coming through a sound-system. Then I understood.

Meanwhile I inducted Malcolm into the labyrinth of industrial music and some of the lesser-known artists from the Manchester scene. He was also the first person I knew who was properly engaged with the sounds of acid house. I didn't quite get acid to begin with. I initially thought all acid tunes sounded like long introductions for songs that never arrived. I kept wondering where the rest of the track was. Then I heard Armando's 'Land of Confusion' coming through a club sound-system. Then I understood.

I walk down to the entrance of The Zap. Malcolm definitely isn't there. But punctuality hasn't ever really been his strong point. I check my watch; 19:56. Ah. The residual adrenaline from the argument has swept me down here in record time. I stand watching the sea rolling in under the night sky. I'm worried about the future. If there's so much conflict now, what will it be like after the baby's born?

The wind whips up, but I don't really feel the cold. I'm wearing baggy grey flannel trousers with a red and black plaid shirt and a black jacket. Oh and I've got dreadlocks. I know, I know. The ones at the back are over a foot long. I never really intended to grow them, it just happened. They started off very small. Not so much dreadlocks, more mild apprehension-locks. I've always been fastidious about washing my hair, but in the last five years or so, I've also been fastidious about muzzing it up. So inevitably it became tangled and matted together. Once the dreads took hold I decided to just go with it. Like I have with the whole having a baby thing.

"Alright sir?" I turn to see Malcolm approaching with a cheery expression. We hug then wander further down the beach, sit down on the always uncomfortable pebbles and smoke a couple of big pipes of hash.

The Zap club has existed in Brighton since 1982. It started out as a left field cabaret, performance art and underground music platform. Having had temporary homes at various venues in Brighton, The Zap finally built its own permanent residence inside a couple of the old King's Road arches on Brighton seafront. I performed there on the opening night in 1984 with Theatre of the Bleeding Obelisk. I can't remember any of the dialogue from the piece we presented, but I do clearly remember how Greg Pope and myself were dressed in suits and ties, wearing large flowery curtains as capes and I also wore a cow's pelvis bone as a mask. It wasn't one of our best shows.

I've seen many superb music gigs at The Zap, including early UK appearances from Sonic Youth and Big Black, as well as shows by 23

Skidoo, Meat Beat Manifesto, Bourbonese Qualk, NON, Alternative TV, The Moodists and multiple appearances from Psychic TV. The Zap has also hosted performance art pieces by Cosey Fanni Tutti and Ken Campbell and readings by Marc Almond, Kathy Acker and Lydia Lunch. In fact, for the past few years, for six nights a week, The Zap has showcased the cutting edge of everything. The club space has recently been overhauled and another two arches have been opened up, creating a wider stage and a much larger dance floor. And, as the big money is in the expanding dance culture, the performance art and left field music are being edged aside in favour of far more lucrative club nights.

Tonight we walk into The Zap to be greeted by the deep, squiggly sound of 'Touch My Lips' by The House Boys thumping from the speakers. The venue looks only about one third full so far. The crowd is made up of pasty-faced indie kids in jeans and leather jackets, some traveller types with dreads and bright, baggy just-back-from-Goa trousers. Plus there are a few ravers in bright, long sleeve T-shirts and stone washed jeans. And there are girls here too. The house scene has equal appeal to both genders. A few people are dancing, but most are just hanging around, drinking and smoking. There's not going to be a support band. Rather, in the spirit of the now, there's a couple of DJs playing house and electronic music.

With the ever-increasing influence of sampling and programming, the music press is now touting the death of the guitar band. This is utter bollocks. Just like back in 1982, when the death of the guitar band was apparently imminent, due to the rise of the synth-pop of The Human League, Soft Cell, Depeche Mode et al. Simultaneously of course, bands as diverse as Crass, The Fall and The Birthday Party were using guitars to devastating effect.

The same holds true now, in 1989. The rise of house is due to the power of groundbreaking tracks assembled using a Roland TB-303 and little else. Yet, even as The Shamen are adopting these techniques and utilizing sequencers and samples, bands as diverse as Napalm Death, Sonic Youth and Dub Sex are simultaneously using guitars in a manner which suggests six stringed forms of expression have not yet reached their limits.

Back in The Zap, dry ice envelopes the stage as sirens and echoing voices throb from the sound system. The Shamen step out. Angus and Sinnott stand side by side. Sinnott in a black track suit with silver flashes, Angus in a multicoloured T-shirt with dayglo patterns. He's also one of the few contemporary musicians who wears glasses – albeit the cool John Lennon kind. Behind Angus and Sinnott, there may well be a percussionist and a keyboard player. But there's still so much dry ice on stage it's impossible to be sure. They go straight into 'Synergy', a sequencer pounding out its deep, constantly modulating bass line, as Angus' guitar sends out sprays of electricity, accompanied by samples of the sliding doors of the USS Enterprise.

Although it's frequently seen as music of celebration and euphoria, true acid house isn't really about the climax. It's almost always about the plateau. A plateau of endlessly uncoiling possibilities. Like the motorik of Krautrock, the earliest acid house tracks – such as the clipped and spartan 'No Way Back' by Adonis, or Armando's ultra-wriggly 'Land Of Confusion' – are a journey not a destination. But The Shamen have now begun to use the beats and percolating 303 bass lines of house not as discreet forms, but as the spinal columns of their own songs. And, as I say, 'Synergy' is quite a statement of intent.

"MDMAzing... MDMAzing..."

There seems to have been more thought put into the lighting and presentation than is usual at most gigs I've seen recently. There are multiple films and slides being projected behind the band – ranging from animated abstract patterns and clips of cells and chromosomes, to dancing girls. UV strip lights stand upright at the side of the stage. At points, all the other lighting cuts and the various colours on the band's clothing and instruments are caught in the strange alternate reality of ultraviolet vision. This feels like a visually developed performance. Or, at the very least, it's an attempt to enlarge on the vibe of The Pink Floyd playing the UFO Club circa 1967.

Speaking of which, the band then go into their cover of The Monkees' 'Sweet Young Thing'. This is one of the highlights of the *In Gorbachev We Trust* album. This late 80s take on a mid 60s tune is a smart diversion. Whereas the original is focused on tight vocal harmonies, The Shamen's take lets the drums do the talking, with Angus adding occasional cascades of guitar.

By now, the venue has filled up considerably. Not a sell out by any means. But a decent sized crowd intent on enjoying themselves. As Sinnott puts his bass to one side and takes the mic from its stand, the drum pattern of 'Negation State' thunders in. This is the only track from *Phorward* that doesn't stick to the acid house template. On record it plays out like a kind of prickly Scottish hip-hop. Live however, it's a much more angry and untethered beast. It resembles the squat rocking sounds of World Domination Enterprises. Angus' guitar is far more raw and prominent than on record. Sinnott bites off the lyrics and spits them out in his terse Glaswegian accent. 'Negation State' is a textbook 'us and them' protest song, alive with acidic bile. It describes the UK as an 'altered state', that is a state under strict governmental control. Its aggressive drum pattern will prove a highlight of the evening. This song will also mark The Shamen's last blast of underdog anger and disdain. From here on in their career, 'E' powered positivity and unity will be their core message.

The volume is increasing with each song. In fact, it's starting to become overpowering. As 'Negation State' concludes, I pinch the tip of my nose with my fingers and blow to relieve the pressure on my eardrums. I suggest to Malcolm that we move up to the wide balcony. We weave through the crowd and up the stairs. "That was really full on." Says Malcolm. 'Full on' is what we've started saying to indicate when something is intense.

The latter part of the set is more squarely focused on the band's developing house obsession. 'Transcendental' is possibly the best of their early acid experiments. It was unceremoniously released last year on a 12" on the Desire label, in a trippy bright red snakeskin patterned sleeve. This was the first indication of just how deep into the realms of acid house the band were prepared to dive. It features a near ten minute version remixed by acid maestro Bam Bam, which takes the track through a number of evolutions. The interpretation the band performs tonight doesn't quite reach those heights, but its pulsing bass line certainly gets portions of the audience dancing frenetically and the track is followed by much applause.

The band launch into 'Raptyouare'. Here, Angus' lead line uses a modal Arabic scale, creating a melody with a Turkish accent and a strong, emotional tug. In contrast, the tightly sequenced drum pattern feels far more European, as it punches hard on the on beat, in the manner of Belgium's recently emerging New Beat scene. It's an incongruous concoction, which could only be The Shamen. Another hymn to transcendence, the song includes the repeated line *"Leave your body behind."*

Our friends Mark and Julia pass by. "We have to go!" Shouts Mark. I'm surprised. "You not into it!?" I shout back. "No, it's great!" Shouts Mark. "It's just too loud!" They head off downstairs, fingers in ears. It's true. This is the loudest gig I've attended in a long while. But I'm so thrilled to be here. To be away from the conflicts of home life. To be with a true friend who won't judge me. To be dancing. To be immersed in music I love. I'm prepared to risk a little more tinnitus.

Along the balcony, just a few feet away from us, Primal Scream main man Bobby Gillespie is standing with a mate. We have a couple of mutual friends, but I don't feel confident enough to go up and introduce myself. Looking skinny and effortlessly cool, Gillespie is leaning against the balcony, dressed in denims and nodding along keenly. Especially when The Shamen glide into a cover version of The 13th Floor Elevators' song 'Slip Inside This House'. Despite the fact that The 13th Floor Elevators, like The Shamen, were devoted cosmonauts of inner space, this seems an unusual choice for a cover version. I shout as much into Malcolm's ear. He nods. "Maybe it's the word 'house' in the title that made them do it!" He shouts back. And yet, as the tune unfolds, it becomes apparent the band are using the burble of an acid synth line to mimic the sound of Tommy Jones' electric jug playing on The 13th Floor Elevators' original recording. The song provides a bridgehead between the earlier psych-influenced Shamen and their current incarnation as dance floor interlopers.

Two years later, Primal Scream will release their take on 'Slip Inside This House', as part of the *Screamadelica* album. It would be easy for me to try and spin a theory about how it is in this moment, as Gillespie watches The Shamen perform their acid enhanced version of the track, that he decides to nab the idea for his own band. However, the man is an acknowledged devotee of music of a psychedelic stripe and he would have doubtless already been well aware of the track. Oddly, The Shamen's own version will not see the light of day until 1992, when it is tucked away as an extra B-side on a 12" single. And sadly the mix is not exactly what you would call full on.

Back in The Zap, the song's conclusion is greeted with applause and cheers. It's the only piece they will perform tonight which isn't taken from either *Phorward* or *In Gorbachev We Trust*. This is a decisive time for The Shamen. This is the point in their evolution when they are shedding the remaining vestiges of their past.

"Who wants to get funky?" Asks Sinnott. "Because we've got a new version of 'You Me & Everything' which is just a shade funky." The phrase "just a shade funky" really makes me laugh. And it's noticeable that although Angus is The Shamen's sole original member, lead singer and de facto front man, he's a relatively reserved figure compared to the vocal and voluble Sinnott.

The new version of 'You Me & Everything' turns out to be several shades of funky. Angus executes another Arabic inflected lead line with unexpected chromatic shifts. Meanwhile, the fat, squelchy synth bass line has a mid 70s Herbie Hancock feel, whilst the string sample sounds like the ghost of a Philly floor filler.

And yet here, in The Shamen's work, the sounds of house are still trapped within discreet song forms. Unlike being at a rave, where the tunes blend into each other in a seamless composite of rhythm and sound, here the songs come to a natural conclusion and there's a pause as guitars are tuned, samples are loaded and the next song is introduced. This works against the atmosphere of sustained euphoria The Shamen are reaching for. Something the band seems acutely aware of. "Sorry about the gaps." Apologises Sinnott. "If anybody wants to buy us another sequencer? Then we don't ever need to stop."

It's also noticeable how cluttered their acid tracks sound in comparison to the spacious minimalism of original house cuts by the likes of Adonis, Marshall Jefferson and DJ Pierre. Yet, although I love those, I'm no purist. Hybridisation and mutation are frequently the phenomena that lead to advancement. For me, part of the Shamen's appeal at this point is they are capturing the essence of house, without being slavish to the genre's template, or excluding other influences.

As Angus puts aside his guitar, the band closes the set with 'Phorward'. The studio version is a pulsing, juddering instrumental, which opens with the sampled sound of the HAL computer from *2001: A Space Odyssey* saying *"My mind is going"*. Live however, the song has become a more determined proposition, with the driving acidic synth motif insistent on the root note.

The studio version also contains a sample of a man's voice repeatedly asking *"Can you pass the acid test?"*. On stage, this is transformed into a vocal line, with Angus and Sinnott chanting the phrase with raw enthusiasm. This is not just a call to entheogenic excess, it can also be read as The Shamen challenging their audience – at least half of whom are still primarily an indie crowd. It's a band asking its fans if they are brave enough to move from the confines of rock into the world of rave. Looking at the audience here tonight, I'd say it was about 50/50.

As the band down their instruments and leave the stage, the DJ immediately starts playing a house tune I don't recognise. Whilst this serves to create the seamless night of music The Shamen desire, it does rob the audience of the chance to show their appreciation for the band. Malcolm and I compare notes. He's enjoyed it but he seems less keen than I. "It's almost there isn't it." He says. "Some great tunes, but some of the subtlety is missing." I'm suddenly feeling knackered. A sense of depletion after dancing off the adrenaline built up during the evening's argument. I tell Malcolm I have to go. We hug. Then Spanky's 'Acid Bass' begins to pound through the sound system. I'm not leaving just yet.

* * * * *

Bizarrely, as 1990 unfolds, the best of The Zap's club nights happen on a Monday of all nights. This is when the place is taken over by Tonka Sound System. DJs Choci, Harvey and Rev play contemporary house as well as sometimes throwing in the most bizarre of curve balls such as Nirvana or even Supertramp. The nights are always rammed, and, when the club closes at 2am, the sound system moves a mile or so down the road to Black Rock, for a free all night party on the beach, with sets from Markie Mark, Para and other names lost to time. I go to Tonka a few times, but only once make it down to Black Rock and on into the next day. On that occasion, I rationalize that as a new parent, I'll be having quite a few sleepless nights soon anyway, so it's good to get some practice in.

My son Misha is born in March. He's tiny and handsome and he soon starts smiling. He's a joy to be around. Unfortunately however, my relationship with his mother is on a terminal slide. Lack of sleep and lack of money only make matters worse.

I can't really afford to buy music this year. Well, I make the occasional exception: Wire's *Manscape*, Mazzy Star's *She Hangs Brightly* and the next Shamen single 'Pro-gen' (aka 'Move Any Mountain'). It's a full on house track with a propulsive four to the floor drum pattern and an irresistibly catchy synth line. With this release, their transformation from indie group into amorphous dance act is complete. The Shamen are riding a wave that is sweeping across contemporary music.

I'm so certain they're on the right track, I buy their next single 'Make It Mine', without even hearing it. It's dreadful. It's got a tired rap metal style riff at its heart and it all feels very second hand. Which is what it becomes, when I take it back and exchange it for a copy of My Bloody Valentine's sublime *Glider* EP.

I hear the following Shamen album *En-Tact* around at my friend Daniel's house. It has some good moments. But everything has become very smooth and glossy and streamlined and it doesn't really hold my attention. But hey, what does my opinion matter? As Angus' frequently existential lyrics are supplanted by the cartoon like positivity raps of Mr. C, The Shamen become the country's most successful dance act.

Tragically, Sinnott doesn't live to see the rewards for the years of hard work. On 23rd May 1991, following a video promo shoot in Tenerife for a re-release of 'Pro-gen', he drowns whilst swimming off the coast of La Gomera.

Just a couple of months earlier, he had started working on a side project called Elsi Curry. He and an unnamed female vocalist recorded a shiny, optimistic piece of dance floor gold called 'U Make Me Feel'. Despite 12" promos having been pressed up, the song will never see a proper release. Whilst musically 'U Make Me Feel' would have provided a classy memorial for Sinnott, it seems likely the problem lies with the lyrics. The opening lines of the first verse are *"Come on in, swim, don't wait to be invited"*.

Malcolm leaves Brighton and moves up to London. We keep in regular contact and continue to develop loose writing projects, but the period of close collaboration comes to an end. Mind you, as parenthood and arguing are taking up most of my time, I don't really have the opportunity to collaborate with *anybody*. So, in my few brief moments of calm and solitude, I start thinking about writing a one-man show. Oh, and I cut off my dreadlocks.

PRIMAL SCREAM

GLASTONBURY FESTIVAL

FRIDAY 26TH JUNE 1992

(AGE 28)

It's dark. It's noisy. It's ten at night.

We're outside, walking through hundreds of people. Well, we're not walking. We're wedged. All of us are wedged. We're at a stand still. On the threshold of a field.

A portion of the audience who've been watching The Orb on the Glastonbury *NME* Stage, are now attempting to leave. Simultaneously, hundreds of festivalgoers are arriving, keen to see Primal Scream on the same stage. Nobody is going anywhere.

There's a mass cheer from the distant audience. The deep sound of a kick drum begins to reverberate through the ground. About an hour ago, I ate a hash space cake, so now I'm feeling every beat.

I'm really keen to get to see Primal Scream's set. And the thudding rising up from the earth suggests they've just started. I'm holding hands with my girlfriend Sarah. We don't want to suddenly lose each other in this huge mass of people. Sarah is short, petite and fine boned. I worry about her getting squashed. I, on the other hand, am tall, chunky and coarse boned. But I worry about me, because I have mild claustrophobia. Being confined like this is making me edgy. And the space cake is starting to enlarge my senses.

This is the first time either of us has been to Glastonbury Festival. The scale and topography of the site are difficult to grasp. At points, the number of people is bewildering. And even in 1992 the amount of tie-dye is sickening. I still possess a strong streak of post-punk puritanism, so anything overtly hippie causes me to switch to auto-suspicious. Glastonbury Festival – a place where I can count more than five stalls selling tie-dye baby grows – is a true test of my mettle.

The festival feels like a meeting of many different tribes. Students are here in sub-sets. From the cautious ones who haven't even been camping before, never mind attended a festival, to the pilled up party animals swigging cider from plastic demijohns. There are couples in their 30s and 40s who used to be rebels, but who now want their 'rebellion' in bite size weekends. There are those whom have been unkindly dubbed crusties; young travellers who have side stepped society's fixed channels in order to live a life of no fixed abode or direction. There are also aging traveller types who are probably wandering around Glastonbury feeling the uncomfortable stirrings of commodification that are destined to swamp and ultimately repurpose the festival in later years. There's even a few Goths. I find the notion of Goths going camping delightfully daft.

Sarah and I frequently miscalculate how long it will take to walk from one part of the site to another, so we inevitably end up missing the start of some bands' sets. Sometimes, like now, we find ourselves trapped in a kind of gridlock, stuck in a huge wedge of festivalgoers, unable to move forwards or backwards.

Although we have a number of mutual friends, Sarah and I talked properly for the first time just over a year ago. That was at another music festival – the Brighton Urban Free Festival, where a few local bands and poets performed to a meagre audience. I'd split up from Misha's Mum just three months earlier and I was emotionally bruised and living a hermetic life. I was renting a flat down on the seafront near the Marina. Misha was staying with me three days a week and the rest of the time I was furiously writing three full-length radio scripts that I expectantly sent off to Radio 4 one after the other. I then received three rejection letters one after the other.

Sarah is charming and funny and self deprecating. And, with her dark Chinese eyes, her olive skin and her dyed platinum blonde cut into a thick bob she is head-turningly beautiful. I chose my opening line very carefully. It's the kind of phrase that some women find irresistible; "Would you like anything from the off license?" To my delight, she did. Three months later we were living together.

Misha is now two years and five months old. He's bright and chatty and sophisticated. Half the week he lives with Sarah and I, the rest of the time he's with his mother. Sarah works at the art college library and has a painting studio where she quietly produces canvases of brooding night skies and constellations. I'm still on the dole, but I earn a tiny bit of extra cash writing a column for a local listings magazine. So that's £40 a month I don't need to find anywhere else.

I've also written my own one-man show, *Burroughs*, about the life and times of notorious beat author William S. Burroughs. I've been absorbed by the writer and his ideas since the age of 19, when I read his 1981 masterpiece *Cities of the Red Night*.

Malcolm directed the show with infinite patience and I premiered it last month at the Brighton Festival. Now I'm booked to perform it at various arts centres and theatres around the country for the next year. The gigs average out at about two a month, so it's not exactly cost effective. Or a career. I'm giving three performances of *Burroughs* at this year's Glastonbury. So that keeps me busy for an hour of each day. But the rest of the time, Sarah and I are free to wander around, check out different areas of the site, bump into friends, get lost and watch a variety of groups.

Blur – a band I've seen once before and will go on to see several more times – pump out one of their most high energy performances, with Graham Coxon going into effects pedal overdrive, as Damon Albarn clambers up the scaffolding at the side of the *NME* stage, hangs apelike from the bars and sings several songs through a megaphone.

I have to leave before the end, as over on the Pyramid Stage, The Fall perform a bold and concise set, including a soaring version of the lead track from their new EP: *Ed's Babe*. Naturally enough, Mark E. Smith can't miss the opportunity to slag off the festival: "We've been banned from fuckin' Glastonbury for ten years. They invited us back and we're supporting The Levellers. Marvellous innit?"

We catch the last three songs of Curve's set and I'm immediately converted to their distortion soaked brand of melodic shoegaze. Yes they use a lot of effects, but they also have a mature sense of song craft. One afternoon, I happen upon another band I've never heard of before: Ocean Colour Scene. Although, in years to come, their name will become a short hand for retro-dad-rock, at this stage in their development, they're an inventive and psychedelic live band. Their song 'My Brother Sarah' is a touching meditation on transgender anxieties, stashed away as a B-side on their *Sway* EP, and to me, it's one of the finest songs of the 1990s. I urge you to abandon any prejudice you may have and listen to it. I should also warn you, I shall be mentioning the song again a little later, in a bid to increase the likelihood of you tracking it down.

Sarah and I also watch Jah Wobble's Invaders of the Heart, who, despite some good moments, frequently descend into a polite and largely anonymous blend of world music. The Shamen are playing too, but, whereas three years ago, their name on a gig poster would guarantee my attention and attendance, these days they're purveying the kind of glib dance pop that ensures my absence. We'd much rather go back to our tent, make love, then wander off to the comedy marquee to enjoy the manic charm of Charlie Chuck.

But right now, all we want to do is get to see Primal Scream. I can still only see the very side of the stage. It's taken us two minutes to move about a yard. I'm keeping an eye on my breathing. It's okay. I can just about keep the claustrophobia at bay. As the kick drum thuds, a bass throbs and synth tones fire off like shop alarms. It's a version of The 13th Floor Elevators' 'Slip Inside This House'. The Shamen may have covered it first, but Primal Scream's take on this slice of cult US psychedelia is the real winner. The rhythm is a nimble shuffle, as Denise Johnson's rich vocals swim out across the air and Andrew Innes and Rob Young's guitars add a metallic groove. Martin Duffy's piano playing suggests the lyrical uplift of Italo house. And, in a sharp nod to the hallucinogenic tastes of the times, Gillespie has reaffirmed the original lyrics' intentions by changing the chorus to *"Trip inside this house"*.

I still have Sarah's hand in mine. Everyone is so tightly packed we can't dance, but the beat is so pervasive, the entire wedged crowd begins to gently sway in time to the music. Some people are giggling. It's a sweet moment that relaxes my nerves.

A couple of years back, I would have been in no real rush to see Primal Scream. Their 1987 debut album *Sonic Flower Groove* delivered a competent but unremarkable 60s flecked indie, whilst their self titled follow up added a heavy but louche 70s Rolling Stones vibe. Yet what I heard didn't make me especially hungry to hear it again.

However, on their third album, those retro stylings have been blended with elements of soul, country, gospel and genuine psychedelia. And, perhaps more unexpectedly, Primal Scream have also been experimenting with the architecture of house music.

After seeing Bobby Gillespie at The Shamen's Brighton gig, I'd noticed him again, at the bar and on the dance floor of The Zap, for a few of the Tonka Sound System parties in early 1990. The singer once told an interviewer that as a teen, he'd bought The Sex Pistols' 'Pretty Vacant' and Donna Summer's 'I Feel Love' on the same day.

But the first indication that Primal Scream were starting to really evolve came in the shape of the single 'Loaded'. The track may have originated on the band's sophomore album, under the title 'I'm Losing More Than I'll Ever Have', but the mastermind behind the revitalised 'Loaded' is DJ Andrew Weatherall who has remixed it beyond recognition.

I initially become aware of the song, when I see a brief interview with Gillespie and a screening of the promo video on BBC2's *Snub TV* – a wonderful but short lived left field music series featuring some of the most thrilling bands of the era, including The Fall, Butthole Surfers, Ultra Vivid Scene, Wire, Napalm Death and Galaxie 500. Although the video for 'Loaded' is nothing special, the music immediately snares me. More than anything, I'm seduced by Robert Young's simple yet gorgeous slide guitar motif. As soon as I hear 'Loaded', I want to hear it again. And again. And if possible again. And then some more.

Having dispensed with the track's original drum pattern and all of Gillespie's vocal (with the exception of one impassioned *"Oh yeah!"*) but retained elements of Innes and Young's guitar parts as well as the song's distinctive and uplifting horn arrangement, Weatherall added a vocal sample from the chorus of The Emotions' 1976 disco B-side 'I Don't Wanna Lose Your Love', plus a snippet of Gillespie singing *"I'm gonna get deep down"* – a line extemporised from blues originator Robert Johnson's song 'Terraplane Blues'.

Weatherall then proceeded to rebuild the whole track, based around a loose and lazy drum loop, sampled from a 1989 Italian bootleg 12" remix of Edie Brickell & The New Bohemians' bland pop single 'What I Am'. However, the actual beat itself had originated on the song 'Keep On Movin'' by Soul II Soul.

Yet perhaps 'Loaded's most well known component isn't a musical one. Rather it's the song's opening exchange of dialogue, sampled from Roger Corman's 1966 exploitation film *The Wild Angels*. Frank Maxwell plays a preacher who struggles to understand the hedonistic motivations of a San Pedro motorcycle gang led by a young man known as Heavenly Blues played by Peter Fonda. *"Just what is it you want to do?"* asks Maxwell. Fonda's answer, slightly edited down from the original dialogue, is direct. *"We wanna be free. We wanna be free to do what we wanna do. And we wanna get loaded. And we wanna have a good time. And that's what we're gonna do. We're gonna have a good time. We're gonna have a party!"* This speech, simplistic though it might be, has captured the mood of Ecstasy fuelled hedonism which has spread from illegal raves, through clubland and out onto the streets and football terraces.[1]

Since its release back in February 1990, 'Loaded' has become ubiquitous. The song has transformed Primal Scream from a minority

---

1. This celebration of hedonism as an end in itself would devolve into an increasingly reductionist worldview. *Loaded* magazine was launched in 1994, and with it came lad culture, and the acceptable face of sexism.

concern, operating on the fringes of indiedom to a globally recognised chart act. In many ways, 'Loaded' represents the whole of *Screamadelica* in microcosm. Primal Scream's masterpiece, like Roxy Music's debut album, is an act of collage. A collage assembled by connoisseurs of multiple genres, a sound concocted from disparate sources, some electric, some acoustic, some electronic. The samples employed across the album span numerous genres. From Can to Dr. John, from Sly and the Family Stone to Brian Eno, from the jazz of Young-Holt Unlimited to the reggae of Tommy McCook and the Aggrovators.

The album is the work of many hands. The Orb produced one version of 'Higher Than the Sun', whilst Jah Wobble plays bass on a second version. Manchester based Hypnotone did initial production on 'Slip Inside This House', but the majority of the album is co-produced by Weatherall with Hugo Nicolson, who had previously worked with Julian Cope. Meanwhile, 'Damaged' and 'Movin' on Up' are Rolling Stones styled country blues tunes, so why not get Jimmy Miller to produce those? After all, he produced the Stones' *Sticky Fingers* and *Exile on Main Street* albums.

Screamadelica is as much about curation as it is about individual creativity. Again like *Roxy Music*, or say *Never Mind the Bollocks Here's The Sex Pistols*, or Scott Walker's *Scott 4*, or The Congos' *Heart of The Congos*, it's an album which, whilst sounding like a coherent set of songs, simultaneously feels like a greatest hits collection. Having reached number eight in the album charts and soundtracked thousands of parties and late night sessions over the past nine months, for many it has become a lodestone for the times. Wherever we walk at this year's festival, we see people wearing bright red happy faced *Screamadelica* T-shirts.[2]

---

2. There are several points in the early to mid 90s, when for certain artists the journey from the underground to the mainstream is a sudden, unexpected and swift one. It happens with Bjork's *Debut* (1993), Portishead's *Dummy* (1994) and DJ Shadow's *Endtroducing* (1996). All three albums are initially seen as strange and mysterious

There's very little movement in the clotted mass of people trying to get into the *NME* field. Largely due to the clotted mass of people trying to get *out* of the *NME* field. I can still only see the side of the stage. Sarah can't see anything. But we can hear the opening chords of 'Movin' On Up'. It's an uptempo rocker with the same kind of funky flare the Stones brought to 'Gimme Shelter'. If it was 'Loaded' which broke Primal Scream in the UK, it was 'Movin' On Up' which launched the band in the USA. Sections of the audience sing along, not just to the chorus, but to the whole lyric.

Then the crowd unknots ever so slightly. I let out a long, slow lungful of air. Now there is movement, I feel my whole being lighten. We're almost inside the *NME* field now. A high-pitched chirruping sound starts up, piercing the night. The noise is greeted with shrieks of elation from the audience. The chirrup is the central motif of 'Don't Fight It, Feel It'. And, like all the best modern dance floor hooks, it straddles the borderline between irresistible and irritating. The tightly sequenced hi-hat pattern comes in accompanied by a solid yet sinuous bass line. This is the closest Primal Scream get to pure house. Again the massive wedge of festival goers begin to sway to the music. Johnson takes the lead vocal, although it's the synths and keyboards that carry most of the emotion.

The first half of the lyric "*Rama lama lama fa fa fa, Gonna get high 'til the day I die.*" is 'borrowed' from The MC5's song 'Rocket Reducer No. 62 (Rama Lama Fa Fa Fa)' from their epochal debut *Kick Out The Jams*. Another example of *Screamadelica's* wide ranging cut and paste aesthetic. On the surface, 'Don't Fight It, Feel It' sounds like it's been born of the feel good vibe of 1988's 'second summer of love', and yet it's adorned with a lyric by a band who embody the most incendiary and confrontational aspects of rock circa 1968.

Suddenly we're moving, walking forward. I breath deeper. I can see Sarah again, rather than just feel her hand. The band start into the

soundworlds. Yet, within a couple of months, they are being dismissed as middle class dinner party music.

slow, mournful blues of 'I'm Losing More Than I'll Ever Have'. Despite its undeniable qualities, it's a testament to Andrew Weatherall's skill and inventiveness that there is so little evidence of the all conquering 'Loaded' to be heard in this iteration.

We edge into the field proper and weave our way through the crowd so as to get a better view of the stage. We can see now, but we're a long way back. The group are distant figures. This is probably the furthest I've ever been from the band at a show. Yet I can see Gillespie, a master of rock star postures, striking arresting shapes, the light bouncing off his bright white shirt.

At six foot two I've never had much of a problem with site lines at gigs. Sarah however is five foot two. So she can't really see anything much. Apart from the backs of the people in front of her. I'm standing behind her. I put my arms around her and kiss the top of her head. Coincidentally, like me Sarah's first rock gig had also been The Jam. At Crawley Leisure Centre in 1980, age 13. Although, with her view of the stage almost completely obscured, she says her main memory is of looking upwards and watching the shadow of a back-lit Rick Buckler playing across the venue's ceiling. Here of course there is no ceiling. Just the night sky. And the backs of the people in front of us.

Robert Young picks out the opening notes of 'Damaged' on an acoustic guitar. Again, this is instantly recognised and applauded by swathes of the audience who have had *Screamadelica* on repeat play over recent months. It's a downbeat tale of lost love and redemption through treasured memories. A classically structured country blues, this is Primal Scream at their most Stones-like. In fact, with its closing, repeating refrain of *"Stone in love wit chew"* it could be straight out of the Jagger/Richards songbook circa 1973's *Goats Head Soup*. Yet it's still something of a risk in the middle of the set, as it takes the energy down several notches. But, glancing around, I see the crowd is largely into it. A few people are even holding their lighters aloft, the yellow blue flames quivering in the night air. This seems like a gesture from another age. And I can't tell if it's being done ironically or not. Again my post-punk hackles rise at this display of indulgent 70s-styled appreciation.

A honkytonk piano announces the start of 'Call on Me'. This is the only new tune they play tonight, and, with the exception of 'I'm Losing More Than I'll Ever Have', it's the only song not taken from *Screamadelica*. With its bluesy strut and strident riff, the Stones are once again the prime influence. Yet despite the band's swagger, the crowd is noticeably less responsive to this. For many, *Screamadelica* is the be all and end all of Primal Scream and anything outside its parameters isn't going to hold their attention. This is a shame, as whilst 'Call on Me' could be said to offer nothing new, it still offers it with power and panache.

'Come Together' is another deftly judged assemblage, proving again how the band is able to make the second hand sound startlingly fresh. The title itself has of course already been taken by The Beatles. Whilst the song's seductive groove is built up from a sample of 'The Dub Station' by reggae producer Bunny Lee's in-house band The Aggrovators. The opening of the recorded version also features a lengthy sample of a speech given by US Baptist minister and civil rights activist Jesse Jackson. He talks of unity and togetherness. Yet perhaps the key line is *"You will hear gospel, and rhythm and blues and jazz. All of those are just labels. We know that music is music."* This could easily be Primal Scream's current mission statement.[3]

Tonight however the band don't deploy the Jackson sample. Instead, they go straight into the chorus. This is where the band's gospel influence shines strongest. With its soulful lift and its spirit of unity, 'Come Together' is a perfect festival song. In fact, right now, Primal Scream are *the* perfect festival band. Their collagist approach means they cover all the major festival bases –

---

3. A number of UK indie bands will follow in the wake of *Screamadelica*, attempting to weld psychedelic rock to dance floor grooves. But most will only conjure up a pale imitation. Take a bow The Farm, The Soup Dragons and Flowered Up.

energetic dance numbers, hard driving rock songs and blissed out nod-alongs.

Speaking of which, a sound somewhere between an alpine horn and a lowing cow begins to echo across the site as a reggae flavoured drum pattern starts up. From where we're positioned, I can't tell if it's a sample or if Toby Tomanov is playing it live. It sounds like it could be the opening to a track by African Head Charge or Dub Syndicate. The drums roll on in a hypnotic cycle, and a celestial organ chord resonates across the field. I realise the band are gliding into a version of 'Higher Than the Sun'. It's a sensual and hazy sound. Sarah and I stand in a hug, swaying to the rhythm.

Gillespie, Innes, Young and company continue to add to the patchwork of genres as they suddenly slip into several bars of Led Zeppelin's 'Whole Lotta Love', and Johnson belts out the lyric with real soul power. The space cake has now engorged my perception of sound. The spaces between the notes and beats have an equal if not greater importance. The groove is everything.

As the opening dialogue sample of 'Loaded' is triggered, the cheer from the crowd is jubilant. The sample itself has been looped. *"Just what is it you want to do?"* and *"We wanna get loaded"* repeat over and over, over and over. Bright shafts of red and white light criss-cross the stage. As the drum loop slides in, the entire audience locks into one languorous rhythm. This is the song everyone has been waiting for. This is the *moment* everyone has been waiting for. A moment of celebration in a ram packed field on a warm summer night.

The music cuts down to just bass and drums, as Gillespie – who is largely absent from the single version – drops in a portion of the lyric from Bo Diddley's caustic R 'n' B song 'Who Do You Love?' – perhaps the ultimate declaration of outsider cool; *"I walk forty seven miles of barb wire, I got a cobra snake for a necktie."* It's an unlikely yet perfect fit.

The whole crowd is in motion. Some are holding their arms up high as they sway. Huge clusters of the audience are singing along with Johnson, as she lets out the heartfelt *"I don't wanna lose your love"*.

Maybe it's the power of the space cake. Maybe it's the love I feel for Sarah. Maybe it's the sheer volume of the music. Maybe it's the sheer volume of people. Maybe it's all these things. But I find myself embracing the feeling of commonality I used to be so suspicious of in the MDMA experience.

Being here, at this moment, dancing to this song, with my girlfriend, with all these people, suddenly feels binding. It feels significant. It feels important. 'Loaded' continues for maybe eight minutes or more. But it doesn't feel anywhere near long enough. We want to extend this moment. We want to dance on and on and on.

* * * * *

It's two weeks later. It's dark. It's two in the morning.

I'm on a sleeper train. We're travelling through France. I'm breathing heavily. I've just had a panic attack. Claustrophobia.

I was in a top bunk in one of the sleeper cabins. I became overwhelmed by the confined space. Now I'm standing in the corridor that runs along one side of the train. I have a small window open. I'm drawing in air as slowly as I can. In reality I want to gulp down huge great lungfuls of the stuff. But that will only make matters worse.

Claustrophobia is a hard one to explain. Sometimes people say "What is there to worry about? Nothing's going to *happen*." For me, an attack of claustrophobia is an indication that something has *already* happened. I've allowed myself to get into a space where I cannot easily stand up, or leave swiftly, or defend myself. I think it's partly some kind of survival instinct.

I'm clutching my Walkman, listening to a mix-tape I've made of some recent favourites… Rising High Collective's 'Fever Called Love'… Aphex Twin's 'Schottkey 7th Path'… Coil's 'Dark River'… Blur's 'Badgeman Brown'… The Telescopes' 'Flying'… Julian Cope's deeply addictive 'Heed: Of Penetration And The City Dweller'… Ocean Colour Scene's 'My Brother Sarah'… The cassette is still king. I'm starting to calm down.

About ten minutes later, Sarah awakens from a nightmare in which she sees the shadow of an axeman advancing on her bunk. Her scream wakes the people in the other bunks. None of us is destined to sleep through this journey. I stand peering out at the passing French countryside. Long shadows under a bright moon. By the time Primal Scream's 'Come Together' is pumping through the headphones, my breathing is back to normal.

THE VELVET UNDERGROUND

GLASTONBURY FESTIVAL

FRIDAY 25TH JUNE 1993

(AGE 29)

We've got the hang of Glastonbury this year. We understand the distances involved. We've worked out the geography.

Well, Sarah has worked out the geography. Even with a map of the site clutched in my hand I still get lost. Luckily, like last year, we're camping in the performers' compound, where it's a little bit calmer. Which is good when you need somewhere a little bit calmer. And there are showers. And proper toilets. Which is very good. Because the improper toilets are quite scary.

I'm doing a performance each day in the theatre tent. It's a one-man dramatisation of Russian author Nikolai Gogol's 1836 short story 'Diary of a Madman'. I gave my first performance earlier this afternoon. The tent was about a quarter full. People were constantly drifting in and out. In the end I just about got away with it.

Sarah not only designed some of the costumes and props for the show, she's also operating the lighting. She's so capable and practical and adaptable. It's humbling. Especially to someone like me, who frequently feels like I'm not even particularly good at the things I'm particularly good at. My son Misha is three years old and lives with us half the week. But right now, he's at his Mum's house. Some people take their kids to festivals. But it never occurred to me to bring a three year old with me.

This year's musical highlights come courtesy of the jazzy hip hop of Digable Planets, the grandiose grind and drone of Spiritualized and a brash and energetic mid afternoon set from Belly. But the main thing that has been at the forefront of my mind for the last few months is this evening's performance by The Velvet Underground. This is the most enthusiastic I've felt about seeing a band in a couple of years. I mean, come on. It's The Velvet Underground for Christ's sake!

I first encountered The Velvets in February 1980 at the impressionable age of 15. I'd heard Slaughter and the Dogs' cover of 'I'm Waiting For The Man'. Which is a lively stomp, but as is true of the majority of music, nowhere near as good as The Velvet Underground. And I'd seen both the band and Lou Reed frequently referenced in so many music press interviews and articles, that in the end I felt compelled to investigate. None of my friends owned any Velvets records, so I went to W.H. Smiths in Blackburn precinct and bought the band's 1967 debut *The Velvet Underground & Nico*. I had no real idea what to expect.

Yet in the time that elapsed between the gentle chimes of John Cale's celeste which open 'Sunday Morning', and the final reverberations of Sterling Morrison's guitar which close 'European Son', I had fallen deeply in love.

It was a moment of epiphany in fact. I experienced a sudden change of perspective on so much of the music I'd been drawn to over the last couple of years: Joy Division, The Fall, Siouxsie and the Banshees, Magazine, The Raincoats. I realised that in different ways, they all owed an undeniable debt to what The Velvets had been doing a decade earlier. I played the album to Pete, causing him to immediately go out and buy the double album *Andy Warhol's Velvet Underground With Nico*. A compilation comprising cuts from the first three VU long players, it provided our young minds with further proof that this was indeed an incredibly exciting and important band.

The Velvet Underground may well have struggled to find acceptance and achieve credible record sales in the late 1960s and early 70s, but the patronage of art world superstar Andy Warhol, the involvement of beautiful chanteuse, model and actress Nico, and their role at the heart of music's first multimedia shows with the Exploding Plastic Inevitable, are all elements which have helped them go on to achieve a mythic status.

Then there are the band's recordings. Four studio albums, all with their own separate identities. *The Velvet Underground & Nico* is a treasure trove of unearthly delights, matching the savage droning art rock of 'Black Angel's Death Song' with the folk-like delicacy of songs such as 'Femme Fatale'. It's arguably the finest debut album of all time. And unarguably one of the most influential.

After that, with its recording needles pushing well into the red, 1968's hectic and nihilistic *White Light/White Heat* saw the band extending their experimentation, incorporating noise, dissonance and spoken word into the rock form. The Burroughsian 'Lady Godiva's Operation' sounds like nothing which came before or since, whilst 'Sister Ray' is 17 minutes of pummelling discordant excitability. For generation after generation of parents, it's an archetypal "Turn that bloody noise off!" song.

1969's *The Velvet Underground* is a reflective and tender set of songs of hope and bruised love. Sonically it's far more stripped back and less experimental, reflecting the involvement of Doug Yule following Reed's sacking of the more avant garde minded Cale. Here, songs such as 'Pale Blue Eyes' and 'Jesus' evince a shimmering intimacy and fragile optimism. This is the band's late night album.

1970's polished and rocking *Loaded* sees the band offering up a stash of classics including 'Sweet Jane', 'New Age' and 'Rock and Roll'. These could be called signature songs. But in reality, *every* Velvet Underground song is a signature song. There are no minor works in their catalogue.

Except perhaps for those found on their fifth and final studio album, 1973's *Squeeze*. By this time, Reed himself was long gone, and the LP is only of interest to those with a morbid curiosity. At the other end of the spectrum, the band's legacy was furthered by the release in the early 1980s of *Another View* and *VU*, two compilation albums of studio out-takes from both the Cale and Yule eras – many of which had been previously circulating only on inferior quality bootlegs. But these are no mere collections of unloved offcuts. Songs such as 'Temptation Inside Your Heart' and 'Guess I'm Falling in Love' are indispensable.

The retrospectively released double concert album *1969: The Velvet Underground Live* is an essential document of the post-Cale Velvets at their live peak. It includes at least one example of incandescent musical alchemy. Namely a near nine minute version of 'What Goes On'. Reed's vocal is urgent and direct, arch-minimalist Maureen Tucker makes every drumbeat count, whilst Yule's constantly roiling organ work out is thrilling in its audacity. But, at the heart of it all, is the dialogue between the rhythm guitars of Reed and Morrison. In fact this recording may possibly be the definitive example of rhythm guitar riff as artistic statement.

The first time I heard this recording of 'What Goes On', I could scarcely believe that something so perfect could have been created. Let alone created live. As someone once so acutely observed, the only problem with this version, is it ends. It's an exuberant, self-confident outpouring of pure exhilaration and whenever I listen to it, for those nine minutes nothing else matters.

And so, like so many others, since my first discovery of the Velvets, I have listened to them religiously ever after. Indeed, they have got me through some difficult times.

* * * * *

November 1981. Age 17. I'm besotted with a girl named Jackie on my Foundation Arts course at Blackburn Technical College. But she's not interested in me "in that way". I'm curled up in bed in the foetal position listening to 'Candy Says', crying until my eyes burn.

* * * * *

April 1983. Age 19. I'm falling behind on my art history studies at Brighton Polytechnic. I've handed in an essay on 'Sculptural Approaches in Contemporary Painting'. My tutor Fenella has handed it back, saying it makes very little sense. She also says I should write a new essay from scratch. I decide the best way to deal with this is to wait until the evening before it's due in, then do a couple of lines of speed and stay up all night writing it off the top of my head, whilst listening to the first two Velvet Underground albums on repeat. I will not be the first student, nor the last, to adopt this strategy.

As dawn breaks, I finally finish the essay. I can't tell if it's any good or not. It probably isn't. I need to grab a couple of hours sleep before I go and hand it in. To try and ease myself out of work mode and into sleep mode, I change the soundtrack from *White Light/White Heat* to Lou Reed's *Legendary Hearts*. It's like suddenly switching from high-grade cocaine to street Bovril.

* * * * *

April 1991. Age 27. I've split up with Misha's Mum and found a nice flat down on the seafront near the Marina. I've just moved in. There are piles of boxes everywhere. I stand in the second floor living room, staring out of the window, watching sunlight glittering on the sea. I experience a surge of relief. To finally be away from the constant conflict is intoxicating. The first thing I do is set up the cot in Misha's room. The second thing I do is set up the hi-fi in the living room. There's so much more unpacking to do. This is a job for The Velvets. I put on 'Foggy Notion' and turn up the volume.

I start unpacking, but this devolves into dancing around and singing along. There's a knock at my door. It's the neighbour from the flat upstairs; a woman of about 60. With a stern expression she says "If you don't turn that music down and stop singing about calamine lotion I'm going to phone the landlord." I turn the music down and stop singing about calamine lotion.

* * * * *

The Velvet Underground's original recordings are an inexhaustible wellspring of inspiration. And yet, the idea that I might one day get to see the band play live had never even entered my head.

I mean, why would they reform? Nico tragically passed away five years ago, whilst Reed and Cale are both still enjoying long established and successful solo careers. The notorious acrimony between the pair has always seemed to be an insurmountable stumbling block. And yet, against all the odds, in 1990, the band had reconvened for a brief performance at a Warhol retrospective in France. Then Reed and Cale collaborated on the album *Songs For Drella* – a well-intentioned yet patchy affair, which honours the memory of Warhol. To the approval of long-term fans around the globe, this has opened the way for a proper reunion.

The Velvets played the first gig of their tour just two weeks ago in Edinburgh. Since then, the band have appeared at Wembley Arena, then on to Amsterdam, Rotterdam, Hamburg, Prague in the Czech Republic, Paris, Berlin, Strasbourg and now... Pilton.

Sarah and I arrive in front of the Glastonbury Pyramid Stage around six thirty, in what we assume will be plenty of time to find a good vantage point. After all, the act prior to The Velvets was Rolf Harris. I mean who in God's name would bother going to see a former children's entertainer and presenter of *Animal Hospital* singing twee novelty songs from 20 odd years ago? A good few thousand people it turns out.[1]

Harris left the stage moments before we arrive, and we can immediately see he has been a huge draw. According to numerous reports, he completely won over the audience with his wobble board version of Led Zeppelin's 'Stairway to Heaven'. Jesus!! Personally speaking I can't think of anything I'd like to listen to less. Except perhaps 'Bohemian Rhapsody' played on the didgeridoo – which, for all I know, may well have also featured on Harris' set list.

---

1. The previous year, Tom Jones had been a surprise special guest at Glastonbury. Like the booking of Harris in 1993, this signalled the start of a tradition for including ironic, mainstream and unfashionable guests in the Festival line up. However, who could have predicted quite how 'unfashionable' Harris was destined to become? And indeed who could have predicted that by 2017 the festival line up would be almost entirely made up of mainstream acts.

We are quite a way back from the stage. We make an attempt to weave our way closer to the front, but the audience is densely packed and there are several clusters of people sitting down which makes it even harder to progress through the crowd. We decide to give up and stand sipping our cans of Red Stripe.

There are bands that never experience any recognition for their work. There are bands that enjoy recognition in their own time and are then forgotten. There are bands that go unrecognised during their own time but are discovered by a later generation. But The Velvet Underground are perhaps the ultimate example of a band who were ignored during their own time, but have gone on to become a towering and compelling force for later generations.

The Velvet Underground's influence is splattered all across contemporary music culture. And crucially, they have inspired artists who themselves have become hugely pervasive influences – Can, Roxy Music, David Bowie, Throbbing Gristle, Joy Division, R.E.M. etc.[2]

And so, as Reed, Tucker, Cale and Morrison emerge blinking into the sunlight, they have plenty to live up to. However, there is as they say, a lot of love in the field.

As the cheers and applause swell, Cale straps on a Fender jazz bass. He wears a black suit and shirt, looking slender and smart with his floppy side parting. Across the other side of the stage, Morrison is in jeans and a green cotton shirt, looking like a lean and casual middle-aged woodsman who's just been handed a Stratocaster. Reed is centre stage, short, compact and focused, dressed, as ever, in jeans and a sleeveless black T-shirt, a black headless guitar around his neck. Behind them, Tucker stands at her white drum kit – just upright bass drum, tom-tom, two large floor toms and a couple of cymbals. Wearing a white shirt and a grey cardigan, she looks like a practical mom, who won't be taking any shit today.

---

2. It's probable that the majority of the bands whose gigs are covered in this book would recognise The Velvet Underground as an influence. Although I'm guessing Cliff would most likely prefer to be left off that particular list.

And then, suddenly, I'm watching The Velvet Underground performing 'Sweet Jane'. At least the *band* is playing 'Sweet Jane'. Reed appears to be singing the words with a very different melody. When The Velvets slide into the chorus, huge portions of the audience begin to sing along. It's a celebratory moment, a moment of vindication for a group who sold so poorly during their original lifetime, and a moment of adoration for an audience who have used The Velvets to soundtrack their lives. Personally speaking I can scarcely believe I'm watching *the actual Velvet Underground.*

However, if I'm completely honest with myself, the band initially don't sound so good. There's no real power to what they're doing. Also, there's something deeply incongruous about watching the band play during daylight hours. And in a field too. The Velvets are, after all, a band closely associated with urban space and the darkness, distractions and dangers of the night. And they're not exactly a festival band either. For all their influence, The Velvet Underground exist in isolation.

Today they aren't competing with the other bands in the Glastonbury line up. In terms of cultural importance and reach, who else on this year's bill could claim anything comparable? The Kinks and Van Morrison seem like the only possible contenders. But in truth, The Velvets have the clear advantage. Today The Velvet Underground are not competing with other acts, they are competing with their own legacy.

Cale puts his bass to one side and sits down at the electric piano. In his buttoned down attire, with his beaky profile, he looks almost like an illustration of a public school music teacher. The band start into 'Some Kind of Love'. Morrison and Reed's guitars chug, as Cale punches out a bluesy piano line. Throughout the whole song, Tucker plays only the cowbell. And yet it's this hard, piercing *clack-clack-clack-clack*, which both defines the song and propels it forward.

'Some Kind of Love' may not be The Velvet's most celebrated song, yet it does contain two of Reed's standout lines of the era. *"No kinds of love, are better than others"* could seem like a statement of the obvious. Yet in 1969, its sentiments would have verged on the confrontational. Meanwhile, the phrase *"Between thought and expression lies a lifetime"* is a mordant observation artfully arranged, showing how Lou Reed at his best – that is to say Lou Reed in his mid 20s – had a true mastery of matter of fact poetry.

Unfortunately, after a couple of minutes, the song drifts into a section where Cale hammers out a manic yet so-so piano solo, whilst Reed simultaneously turns in an histrionic yet so-so guitar solo. This goes on for far longer than it should. There's a sense that neither Reed nor Cale want to be outdone. But it's an early diversion in the set that doesn't really deliver. However, as the song concludes, the audience's applause is still vehement. I mean, come on! Look who it is!

Reed plays the first bar of 'All Tomorrow's Parties' then Tucker begins to mark out the linear primal beat. This is greeted with more cheers of recognition. Cale plays the rolling piano line and takes the lead vocal originally essayed by Nico. This is starting to feel better. It's the best interpretation they've played so far, yet it all still feels a little pale and inchoate. Somehow the band seems less than the sum of its parts. Maybe they haven't rehearsed enough. Or maybe they've rehearsed too much. Either way this feels distinctly underwhelming.

The opening of 'Venus in Furs' is almost drowned out by the audience's cheers of recognition. Like I say, there are no minor works in their catalogue, so the opening notes of each and every song are greeted with applause and cheers. We love this band! We love these songs! This music is hard wired into our psyche. In fact, The Velvet Underground's songbook contains the majority of the building blocks of contemporary left field rock.

And yet… And yet… And yet… That's exactly what it feels like we're listening to right now; building blocks. Nothing is really gelling. The overriding impression is not of a band, but of four separate musicians occupying the same sonic space. There seems to be no genuine chemistry here. And, at one point, Reed is so busy trying to reinvent the melody of 'Venus in Furs', that he actually forgets the words.

This meddling with the song's top lines will be an ongoing issue. It's something Reed has frequently done with his songs in performance over the years. But this evening, he seems to be more wilful than ever. He alters the timing and cadence of pretty much every lyric he sings.

Reed is a noted contrarian and it's highly possible he's taken the attitude that although he's agreed to revisit the past, he's not going to simply retread the same ground.

As a general rule I would say, artistically it's best not to repeat yourself. It's good to keep overhauling your working practice, to push forward and stay out of your comfort zone. But for fuck's sake Reed! You're taking melodies that are recognised as masterpieces and adored by millions, and overwriting them with half sung, half spoken throw-aways. The gesture plays out as a perverse statement of ownership.

It's only with their fifth number the band seems to really lock together. 'Beginning to See the Light' is delivered as a direct and uncluttered sliver of rock and roll, as sprightly as Buddy Holly and the Crickets. Tucker's rhythm is perfect and Cale and Morrison's backing vocals are sweet and cool. Unfortunately Reed has once again abandoned the song's distinctive top line for something much more staccato. But that aside, this feels good. This sounds like I'm listening to the actual Velvet Underground playing live. And that makes me very happy.

Then they slide into the opening of 'Heroin'. More cheers and much applause. On its original release, the song would have been viewed by many as a daring and depraved exercise and it remains a challenging and at times, brutal piece of work. Tucker's pounding floor toms, Cale's searing viola drones, Morrison's strangulated guitar assault and Reed's largely monosyllabic lyrics – with their straight talking Beat generation tone and allusion to the smack high as a near religious experience – all add up to a composition of startling intensity.

Easily the most lyrically transgressive of their earliest songs, it's also structurally atypical with its deployment of extended feedback and multiple changes of tempi – the points of acceleration mirroring the narcotic rush, the decelerations echoing the come down. And it's also a landmark composition in that it was almost certainly the first song to talk about heroin in a non-metaphorical manner. If the band had only ever recorded this one song they would probably still have been assured a place in the musical history books. Sadly however, today 'Heroin' sounds like it could fall apart at any point. With Cale playing the viola, there's no bass to hold things down. The piece is so disengaged it's almost a relief when it's over.

This is followed by 'Hey Mr. Rain'. While Morrison etches out the riff and Tucker hammers at her toms, Reed and Cale engage in another lengthy guitar and viola solo-off. It's the closest they've come to articulating the noisy art rock that is a huge part of their legacy. It's also the closest they've come to being quite boring. On record, the song exudes an abstracted folk melancholy. But this isn't like that. As with much of what they've played today, this is lumpen and slightly awkward. Once again I sense that Reed and Cale, rather than combining their sonic assaults, are trying to out do each other. It's showy and, despite the heavy-duty discord, it's ultimately bland. I so wanted this to be a life affirming experience. But it isn't. It's plain frustrating.

As the applause dies down, Tucker walks out front to sing 'After Hours' accompanied by Cale on the piano. This serves as a sweet interlude. Tucker's voice is gentle and reedy, but her pitch is excellent. Although the song could easily come across as a mere party piece, it's actually touching and, for fans of the recorded version, for once we are listening to the original melody.

Cale switches back to bass and it's straight into 'White Light/White Heat'. But it's a smooth and bloodless rendition. All the mania, all the euphoria, all the exultant paranoia seems to have been leeched out of it. Here, as elsewhere, it's as if The Velvet Underground have become their own tribute band. Sarah turns to me "This isn't very good is it. Shall we go?" I shake my head. "I can't." She laughs. I feel the need to elaborate. "I know it's a bit ropey. But it's *The Velvet Underground*. I can't just leave. I need to be here." She understands. "They probably won't be on much longer anyway." I can't believe I'm saying this. I've been looking forward to this for months. And now I'm wishing it away.

Next up it's 'Rock and Roll'. One of the highlights of the *Loaded* album, it's typical of some of the more linear structures favoured by Reed during the band's latter period. Lyrically it's a meditation on how music can serve as a balm in a troubled life. In fact, the song's key line – *"She started shakin' to that fine, fine music, you know her life was saved by rock 'n' roll"* – could have cropped up in any number of early songs recorded by say Jerry Lee Lewis, Chuck Berry or Little Richard.

It's a simple and potentially meaningless phrase. And yet, how many in this huge audience might say their life had been saved by The Velvet Underground? How many here, during some time of deep personal desolation, found solace in, or in some way felt ourselves healed by the music and words of this New York ensemble? How many have felt our sense of alienation softened by the company of 'Head Held High' or 'That's The Story Of My Life'? How many have felt our fury and frustrations being syphoned off by leaping around to 'Black Angel's Death Song' or 'I Heard Her Call My Name'? How many have had our broken hearts mollified by 'Pale Blue Eyes' or 'Sunday Morning'? How many of us have stayed up late into the night, playing the Velvets over and over? Because, when we are at our most vulnerable, our most excitable, our most addled, few other bands come as close to capturing the vagaries of the human spirit.

Which makes it all the sadder that this evening the Velvet Underground seem capable of summoning up only intermittent flashes of that genius. As 'Rock and Roll' progresses, Morrison takes the solo. Whereas Reed's solos dominate proceedings by sitting on top of the songs, here, Morrison's solo swims *through* the song, picking out flecks of the main tune and shaping them into new melodies. The band's performance seems to have acquired some passion and the audience's response at its close is one of both enthusiasm and relief.

As the applause dies down, Cale sits at his keyboard set up and proceeds to play something nobody here is expecting. It certainly doesn't sound like it was composed in the 60s or early 70s. In fact, it doesn't sound remotely like The Velvets at all. Played on a synth with a string setting, Cale essays a short mournful piece, which seems more in the 19th century romantic orchestral tradition, with echoes of Bruckner or even Liszt. But, as the last note fades, Tucker starts playing her bass drum with a stick, like it's a snare. She keeps up a constant and insistent beat, as Reed and Morrison slide into the opening of 'I'm Waiting for the Man'.

Cale begins to jab at the electric piano, mirroring Tucker's drumming by producing a series of staccato monotone semiquavers. On the original 1967 studio cut, Cale's piano is buried deep in the mix, but here it takes centre stage, full of urgency and stabbing with a convulsive mania. Surprisingly, Cale also takes charge of the vocals, his nuanced baritone delivering the lyric with real confidence. Yet this still doesn't mean we get to hear the original top line. But for once, I don't care.

This doesn't resemble the original version on their debut, nor any of the various interpretations on the countless VU live bootlegs I've heard. This is something else again. Something new, with a real edge to it. And, more importantly, this sounds like a real integrated band, not an assembly of talents. And it contains the true experimental spirit of The Velvets circa 1966. Here, at long last, we are listening to thrilling music. As the song uncoils for a punchy instrumental coda, Cale's violent piano playing recalls the intensity of David Bowie's favoured keyboard collaborator Mike Garson. It becomes increasingly polytonal, until eventually he's hitting most of the keys within the octave. It's so energized, so vibrant – a moment of true exegesis.

I stand, eyes closed, nodding my head hard in time to the delicious monomania of the rhythm. I can feel the muscles in my throat contracting with emotion. This feels *so fucking good*! Why can't the rest of the performance be up to this standard? Suddenly the group smack to a perfect halt. The song receives the best response of the set. We love this band! We love these songs!

Although, having said that, due to the low impact of the majority of the performance, a few hundred people have drifted off. Consequently Sarah and I have managed to move considerably closer to the stage.

Cale straps his bass back on and the band plunge into the rockabilly rhythm of 'I Can't Stand it'. Tucker's drumming is so exuberant and Morrison's playing so wiry and bright that even Reed jettisoning another timeless vocal melody can't derail this one. Here again, Reed inserts a gnarly guitar solo. However, this time it works. Finally the band seems to have hit their stride.

But suddenly they are taking off their guitars. That's it. It's over. No 'What Goes On'. No new songs. And precious little real chemistry, apart from the last ten minutes or so.

The band stand in a row and bow. There is cheering and applause. We still love this band. We still love these songs. But there is markedly less love in the field than there was 50 minutes ago. Sarah and I turn to look at each other with raised eyebrows. They say you should never meet your heroes. Maybe you shouldn't see them reform either.

* * * * *

A few months later, back at home I watch a TV recording of the reformed Velvets playing live in Paris. Whilst it's a pretty uninspiring showing, it is head and shoulders and chest and probably groin above their Glastonbury appearance.

They also play a new song: 'Coyote'. The best that can be said about it, is it's okay. Its tentative melody hardly makes it an earworm and its simple and repetitive lyrics don't suggest great insights. As an indicator of where the reformed quartet might be heading, it doesn't exactly set my pulse racing. Maybe I'm being a bit tough on it. But 'Coyote' is amongst some fairly august company. And even the most ardent Velvet Underground devotee would be hard pressed to claim the song could stand tall next to 'White Light/White Heat' or 'All Tomorrow's Parties'. Finally the Velvet Underground's original line up has created a minor work.

In the end, the reunification doesn't last long. Cale and Reed fall out once more and The Velvet Underground become part of history again.

Personally, I leave my second Glastonbury feeling like I've cracked performing at a festival. I am so very wrong. I return in 1994 with *The Self-Help Roadshow*. I play Doctor Devlin, a former US astronaut turned porn star, turned self-help guru. My Friday night show in the theatre tent is scheduled so late it's actually on Saturday morning. By which time the majority of the audience are asleep and treat my show as an unwelcome early alarm call and respond by either trying to get back to sleep or by verbally hitting the snooze button. By which I mean shouting "fuck off!"

My Saturday show is on much earlier in the evening and the audience is wide awake. So wide awake in fact that they boo me off stage. In between my performances, I take musical solace from Orbital, Dub Syndicate and Suns of Arqa.

In stark contrast, my Sunday evening show goes down really well. Until that is, twenty minutes from the end, when the stage is invaded by a man in a full biohazard suit who is tripping so hard he can't speak using words. Yet that doesn't stop him from trying to communicate with me at considerable volume. I make some capital out of it for a while, responding to the chaos with a few reasonably snappy ad libs. But, try as I might I can't guide the guy off stage. And no security personnel come to remove him. So I struggle through the remainder of my act accompanied by what looks like an astronaut who has lost the power of speech.

The following year I return to Glastonbury with my good friend the comedian and writer James Poulter. We've teamed up to write and present *The A-Z of Drugs,* a show which combines factual information, comic improvisation and the testing of legal highs on audience members. James describes it as 'infomedy' and it's a show that is definitely festival ready. We do three boisterous and enjoyable performances.

Unfortunately, not long after we arrive, Sarah comes down with some kind of virus and spends a lot of time in the tent trying to sleep. We're camping next to dub maestro Mad Professor, who keeps a constant flow of roots reggae pumping from a small sound system outside his tent. One day, Sarah is feeling so ill she goes to ask Mad Professor to turn down his music. To his credit, he does.

I spend a lot of time wandering around the festival on my own and frequently find myself in the new Dance Tent, enjoying Mixmaster Morris, the Massive Attack Sound System and Higher Intelligence Agency.

Two months later, James and I take *The A-Z of Drugs* to the Edinburgh Fringe Festival. We have a blast. We present a run of sell out shows, get signed up by a talent agency and receive an invitation to undertake a nine week residency in Melbourne. It's almost something you could call a career.

A few days after the end of the Edinburgh Fringe Festival, Sarah and I are on a plane about to fly off on holiday. I'm feeling a bit burnt out. Doing the *A-Z of Drugs* shows is draining – constant on stage improvisation, constantly dealing with audience members. This is what it's going to be like for the best part of three years. We'll tour and tour, notch up almost three hundred gigs and meet some amazing people. We'll be interviewed by the press. We'll be interviewed on the radio. We'll be interviewed on TV. And we'll be interviewed by the police. Twice. And we'll both end up giving evidence in Lewes Crown Court. But that's a separate story. For now, I'm just looking forward to spending some time lying unconscious on a sun lounger.

As the plane takes off from Gatwick, I'm skimming through a copy of *The Independent*. I glance at the obituaries. Shit! *Holmes Sterling Morrison (1942 – 1995)*. My heart drops an inch. He passed away on 30th August, the day after his 53rd birthday. Poor Sterl.

Usually, when people talk about 'guitar heroes', they are referring to lead guitarists. The showmen, the peacocks, the attention junkies. But Morrison was none of these. He was primarily a rhythm guitarist, although he was also an excellent bass guitarist, as can be heard on recordings such as 'Sunday Morning' or 'Lady Godiva's Operation'. Morrison was unshowy, his style paired down and spare. Yet he was a powerhouse. The very heart of The Velvet Underground.

I think about the hundreds of hours I've spent listening to his music, and of how it's helped me get through difficult times. Tears begin to form in the corners of my eyes, but I wipe them away.

I think of Morrison on stage at The Matrix in San Francisco in November 1969. He's 27, lean, long haired and doe eyed. The Velvets are performing that magnificent nine-minute version of 'What Goes On'. The song is in full flow, a skittering headlong rush. With a cry of *"You know it'll work alright!"* Reed steps away from the mic and chops out the guitar riff with renewed vigour. From here on, the instruments will do all the talking. Tucker is beating the snare with metronomic power,

Doug Yule's organ playing edges toward delirium. Morrison stands with his head to one side, thrumming his red Gibson guitar. He's hitting the same chord progression over and over and over. His face is calm, his fingers a blur, the song rushes ever onward. Nothing else matters.

Melting Vinyl presents from Olympia, WA. USA

Sleater—Kinney

Plus Marine Research
And Turbocat

Friday 23 April
The Pavilion Theatre
New Road • Brighton
Tickets • £6 Advance
(Rounder/ Edgeworld)
£7 on the door
C/C Rounder 01273 325440

SLEATER-KINNEY

PAVILION THEATRE, BRIGHTON

FRIDAY 23RD APRIL 1999

(AGE 35)

The thick buzzing synth tones of 'Revenge of the Black Regent' by Add N To (X) are oozing from the monitors in the radio studio.

The volume is up high. I'm sitting with Mike Bradshaw. It's 11 o'clock at night. There isn't another soul in the whole station. The studio mics are off, but we are just listening to the music. It sounds so dense and satisfying. Hosting a late night new music show on local radio has made my obsessive-compulsive music habit seem fairly acceptable. That's what I tell myself.

Thanks to presenting *Totally Wired* on Surf 107, I've managed to wheedle my way onto an awful lot of music mailing lists. More and more pre-releases arrive every day. From indie to electronica, to house, to hip-hop, to drum and bass, to experimental drones, to things which have no name. Each week 30 to 40 albums, singles, CDs and cassettes are delivered to my door. Does this satisfy the music junkie in me? Not really. I still seem to spend an inordinate amount of time in record shops flicking through the racks. The more music you listen to, the more music you want to listen to. And when I say you, I mean me.

After I started working on *Totally Wired*, I discovered to my childish enchantment I could get onto the majority of Brighton gig guest lists. Consequently I'm going out to see bands two or three nights a week. I've been privileged to see the likes of Add N to (X), Stereolab, Pole and Broadcast playing Brighton dates as part of national tours, but I've also had fantastic nights out watching early gigs by local bands such as Feltro Media, Electrelane, Eeyore and Clearlake.

The last time I was in a position to absorb this much live music was 20 years ago, in 1979. Then I was 15 and had no responsibilities. Then I went out to see as many gigs as possible. Now I'm 35 and due to my 'work', I'm convinced that my main responsibility is to go out and see as many gigs as possible. The human brain is a remarkably subtle thing.

Radio has always fascinated me, both musical and speech based shows. *Stereonation* – my first BBC radio comedy series – was broadcast on Radio 4 last year. It was an attempt to fuse both these interests, with me playing a different music obsessive in each episode. Malcolm also appeared in several supporting roles, as did the gifted comedienne Jackie Clune. The show got great reviews and great listening figures. What it didn't get was a second series. So I wrote and recorded a pilot for a new show: *The Audio Mall* – a satire of shopping channels. That didn't even get a first series.

I'm now developing further programme ideas for TV and radio, whilst compering a fortnightly comedy cabaret night and presenting *Totally Wired*. What with that and all the gig going, I have virtually no free time. And yet this has stopped feeling like something you could call a career. However, in Sarah, I have a partner who supports my vision and my ambition and keeps the household flourishing. She is the reason I'm able to focus on my art. And she never ever suggests that maybe I should get a proper job. Which is good, because as someone who has spent their entire adult life listening to music and thinking up stories and jokes I'm not exactly bristling with transferable skills.

Surf 107 was launched in Brighton in March of last year. Set up by Eugene Perera and my good friend Daniel Nathan, another true music enthusiast and a man who has dedicated his life to radio and nurturing the talents of others. During the day, the DJs and the songs are more mainstream, but at nights and weekends, the specialists come out to play. The excellent *Beats to the Rhyme* is a hip-hop show put together by twin brothers Simon and Curtis James, Kish and a man who prefers to be known as Scratchy Muffin. *AfroBase* is the velvet voiced John Warr's home of world music, whilst *Skint on Sunday* focuses on big beat, with J.C. and Damian Harris (aka Skint Records' Midfield General).

But *Totally Wired* isn't a specialist show. It covers a whole spectrum of left field musics. Mike Bradshaw is one of the best music radio DJs I've ever heard. He's also one of the most eclectic. He has a reverence for the music of the past, a passion for the music of the present and a thirst for the music of the future. He has, as they say, a great set of ears, and his mix-tapes are compendia of unexplored pleasures. His extensive record collection is a thing to be respected and feared, but Mike himself is a charming, gentle and self-deprecating man, and exceptionally fine company.

We first met in 1984, when Theatre of the Bleeding Obelisk did a radio session for *Turn It Up* on BBC Radio Sussex. Mike was one of a number of presenters on a show that played and reported on the best underground and emerging music of the era. Later, in 1993 Daniel suggested we team up to present a programme on Festival Radio, a station that ran for the duration of the Brighton Festival. The end result was *The Agony And the Ecstasy* – a late night phone-in show with me in the guise of unfeeling US agony uncle Dr. Devlin, fielding questions from callers whilst Mike spun 60s and 70s mondo film soundtracks and perverse novelty records. It was a solid hoot, and we've been firm friends ever since.

One of the great things that happens when you form a friendship with another music obsessive is you inevitably turn each other on to things you've missed out on. And it turns out I've been missing out on rather a lot. Mike's cross genre knowledge is astonishing. Aside from all the stuff we share an interest in, he also has an understanding of the subtleties within musical forms which are beyond my frame of reference; rockabilly, surf, musique concrète, be-bop and so on. I thought I'd been swimming through a sea of music. But apparently I'd been paddling in the shallows.

Our friendship blossomed at the point I had become deeply enamoured of 1960s UK psychedelia. I was delighted to discover that

Mike had a sizable vault of the stuff. Soon he was introducing me to several recordings that have become all time favourites. Glorious early pop-psych singles by bands such as The Mirage, The State of Mickey and Tommy, The Pretty Things and The Shy Limbs.

Best of all is a blissed out single from 1969: 'Try a Little Sunshine' by The Factory. It sounds as if The Who have joined forces with Joy Division in an LSD free fall, as John Pantry's high, angelic voice sings *"Try a little sunshine and you'll be right back"*. This is not the kind of thing I say lightly. But if you don't like this single you are a massive berk.

Totally Wired goes out seven nights a week. Mike presents three shows, with the other presenters being the smart and knowledgeable Sally Oakenfold and Melita Dennett who rival Mike in their cross genre mastery. Then there's me. I present a solo show on Friday, but the most fun I have is on the Sunday night show, which Mike and I co-present.

Right now, we're both trying to decide what to play next. I look through the contents of the heavy shoulder bag of new and pre-releases I've lugged down to the studio: Rob Swift's *The Ablist*, Mogwai's *Come on Die Young*, Hydroplane's 'International Exiles', Smog's *Knock Knock*, Volume All*Star's 'Sergeant Bumbledillopig', Pole's *Pole 2*, Roots Manuva's *Brand New Second Hand*, Avrocar's *Cinematography*, Drexciya's *Neptune's Lair*, Slipstream's 'Everything and Anything', Company Flow's *Little Johnny From the Hospital*, Chris Carter's *Small Moon*, Wheat's 'Raised Ranch Revolution'…

"I've got something you might like." Says Mike with a smile. He produces a CD album: *The Hot Rock,* by a band I've never heard of called Sleater-Kinney. "In fact, I think we'll put them in to bat next." He takes out the disc, slips it into one of the players and cues it up. I stare at the cover. It's a colour photograph of three women in their 20s standing in a street, dressed in practical clothes, seemingly in the act of hailing a cab. One of them is holding a guitar case, but none of them are looking at the camera and it feels very un-rock'n'roll. It's a photograph of people who are on their way somewhere else. There's something throwaway about

the image, but it's that couldn't care less attitude which gives it its appeal.

As the clamour of Add N To (X) begins to fade, Mike presses play on the CD deck and a clipped and sparky guitar riff emanates from the studio monitors. "Wait 'til you hear the vocals." Says Mike. We sit and listen to the Sleater-Kinney track unfold. It's a sharp and unpredictable tune, melodically austere, with a post-punk angularity. Although the component parts feel vaguely familiar, the overall sound is strikingly individual. And Mike's right, the high-pitched vocals are definitely grabbing my attention. After a couple of minutes, I say "Wow…". It seems the only appropriate response. "Can I borrow it?" Mike smiles and shakes his head. "I think I need to listen to this when I get home tonight." Fair enough.

"How long have they been going?" I ask. But the end of the track is coming up, so Mike hands me the press release and puts his headphones back on. "Sleater-Kinney and 'Banned from the End of the World' from their new album *The Hot Rock*. And we'll be playing another track from that, later on tonight I shouldn't wonder." As Mike goes on to introduce the next record, I study the press release.

Like most press releases, when it comes down to it, it contains a lot of opinion and very little real information. So for the time being, all I can glean is *a)* the band formed in Olympia, Washington USA in 1994, *b)* they are a trio consisting of guitarists Corin Tucker and Carrie Brownstein and drummer Janet Weiss, and *c) The Hot Rock* is their fourth album. Wait. What!? Their *fourth* album? How come I've missed out on this band? I thought I had my finger somewhere reasonably near the pulse!

Aside from my mailing list bounty, I read *Wire*, *Select* and *DJ Magazine,* and still occasionally pick up a copy of the *NME*, although its content is now relatively slight.[1] I still listen to John Peel's show. Not

---

1. From 1978 to 1989 I read the *NME* pretty much every week. Although I didn't like all the groups covered, the writing of journalists such as Ian Penman, Lucy O'Brien and Paul Morley was, at points, almost as inspiring as the music itself. Aside from informing me about a wide range of bands, it was in the pages of the *NME* that I first

religiously as I did in my teens and early 20s. Now I'll only tune in four or five times a month, but I always hear something new and intriguing. And I still tape choice selections. The cassette is still king.

My conversations with Mike, Malcolm and Pete and other friends usually include an exchange of new musical discoveries and obsessions. And yet, in spite of my keen vigilance, there are always so many excellent groups and artists who slip undetected under the radar. Not only have I never heard Sleater-Kinney before, I've never even heard *of* them. This is, in actual fact, one of the endlessly pleasing things about a life spent immersed in music. There is always more.

Back in the radio studio, I play 'Warp in My Dreams', a recent 7" by Southall Riot. They're one of my favourite bands right now and this tune is an uplifting fuzzy clatter of a record. Not to be outdone, Mike follows this up with 'Riot on Sunset Strip' – a 1967 single by US garage band The Standells, its truculent vocal riding out on a sawn-off guitar riff. As the track fades, Mike speaks into the mic. "That's The Standells with a classic song of teenage rebellion in which they complain about being 'hassled by the man' with that chorus of *'It just doesn't seem fair to bug you coz you got long hair'*. Graham of course never gets bugged, because he is completely bald." I laugh. "I should mention this is self inflicted baldness. Each dawn I shave afresh".

When I was a kid I never thought about my hair. It was just on my head and that was that. The only time I ever gave it any consideration was when Mum or Dad said "I'm going to take you for a haircut."

---

read of Gilbert & George, feminism, post-modernism, CND, J.G. Ballard and George Bataille. But over the years, the publication would go through multiple changes and reductions, until it became little more than a glossy pamphlet that was being given away for free. Within its scant pages you could find snippets of information about four or five bands, as well as reading about hair styling products and what complete strangers in the street were listening to on their ipods. By the time the plug was finally pulled on the print version of the *NME* in March 2018, it couldn't have felt more like a mercy killing.

And I'd think "Boring!" Then in 1978, in line with our punk epiphany, Pete and I had our hair cut brutally short. Suddenly it seemed like the hair on your head was a weapon, a spiky weapon. Although of course I couldn't actually get my hair to spike. So *my* head was more of a blunt instrument.

After being told to stand up in front of the entire school to be reprimanded by the Deputy Head Teacher for our short hair, Pete and I made a pact. "If we ever start to get bald patches." Said Pete. "We should shave our heads." I nodded in keen agreement. This was clearly a pearlin' idea. So we shook hands on it.

By the mid 80s I was consciously muzzing up my hair into a thick bird's nest of follicles. This was the gateway into dreadlocks. But then, once parenthood arrived in 1990, the dreadlocks were gone. Not because I wanted to look like a respectable dad, I just didn't have the spare time that dreadlock maintenance requires. After that my hair settled into a more relaxed side parting and I discovered that I'd developed a minor wave. Then, around the age of 30, I acquired a tiny bald patch. It was so small you could have covered it with a one pence piece. However, within just a couple of years you would have needed a fifty pence piece. I could see exactly where this kind of inflation was leading.

I didn't like the style of haircut that my increasingly confident bald patch was tricking me into having. Then I remembered the pact I'd made with Pete 19 years earlier. So, in December 1997, having first bought myself a hat, I went to the barbers and had my head completely shaved. And that's the way it's stayed. Pete of course still has a full head of hair, with no hint of a bald patch. He also has a lucrative career as a hairdresser.

During the last half hour of the radio show, Mike plays a second track from *The Hot Rock*. It's another superb slice of angular and angry rock. I am now completely convinced of Sleater-Kinney's power and significance.

The next morning, I phone up one of the pluggers at Mutanté Promotions and ask him if he can send me a copy of the album. I suspect my enthusiasm and desire for information about the band may be giving me a stalker-ish air. Nevertheless, now I've discovered them, I'm determined to find out more.

Corin Tucker and Carrie Brownstein originally started Sleater-Kinney as a side project, whilst they were performing in separate bands. Brownstein was guitarist and vocalist with Excuse 17, who brought out 2 albums of unruly and often undistinguished punk rock. Tucker meanwhile, was playing with drummer Tracy Sawyer in the riot grrl duo Heavens to Betsy, who released a passionate and fierce album by the name of *Calculated*. But, as so often happens, the side project was destined to become the main event. Heavens to Betsy and Excuse 17 both eventually disbanded, leaving the two guitarists to concentrate on developing Sleater-Kinney.

The third member of the band is Janet Weiss. Although Tucker and Brownstein had recorded their first two albums with multi-instrumentalist Laura Macfarlane wielding the sticks, it was when they joined forces with Weiss in 1996, that Sleater-Kinney's identity became fixed. Weiss was, and is, a member of another excellent band: Quasi, a fuzzed up duo formed with her ex-husband Sam Coomes.

At the time of Sleater-Kinney's genesis, guitarists Brownstein and Tucker had been dating, although this had been kept very much a private matter, with neither of the girls' parents being aware of the relationship. However, in the band's first major feature with *SPIN* magazine in 1996, Brownstein and Tucker were outed. Brownstein has said reading the article left her "splintered and smashed", robbed of the opportunity to define her sexuality on her own terms. Much later, she told a *Guardian* interviewer "The part of our relationship that had the most meaning, to both of us, was the creative collaboration. The music: that was the love story."

The CD of *The Hot Rock* drops through my letterbox the following morning. I'm still in my dressing gown and have just sent Misha on his way to school. He's 9 and now lives with Sarah and I full time. His relationship with school is complicated. Last week he apparently shouted at the headmaster "I hope you rot in hell!". Unfortunately, when his form teacher informed me of this, I burst out laughing. I think I might have just about been able to pass off my laughter as a nervous reaction, had I not followed it up by saying "That is *so* cool". I'm not very good at being a parent.

The whole situation is exacerbated by another of my neuroses. As well as claustrophobia, I also suffer from a condition that I can't even pronounce: Didaskaleinophobia. It translates as fear of schools. I only experienced a very minor form of this as a kid. But since I became a parent it's developed quite a grip on me. When I'm within the school environment my heartbeat increases, I become overheated, a sense of dread overtakes me, my thoughts become tangled and I find it hard to articulate myself properly. Although this is probably a good thing, as the overriding thing I want to articulate is that the teachers are all wasting their time and the children should all leave as soon as possible.

If I ever have to go to a parents' evening, or attend any kind of school function, I will knock back two or sometimes three beta-blockers. Although this never quite quells my anxiety, it does ensure that I don't shout "I hope you rot in hell!" at the headmaster.

I make myself some toast and mint tea then slip the Sleater-Kinney CD into the player. Hmm. I was prepared to be blown away by it. But I'm not. A couple of tracks jump out at me, but the album seems all pretty much of one mood. Overall, I'm a little disappointed and wrong-footed. But then I begin to suspect Sleater-Kinney just isn't early morning music. The knocking on the living room wall suggests my neighbour holds the same opinion.

That evening, I play the CD again and it makes much more sense. Once again I feel galvanized and inspired by the band's sound. Aside from the press release, the CD is also accompanied by an additional sheet with a list of tour dates. I'm thrilled to see they're going to be doing a show in Brighton.

* * * * *

Three weeks later, Mike and I are standing in the audience at the Pavilion Theatre. I've spun the album multiple times, both on air and domestically and I'm now completely besotted. There are plenty of people here tonight. It looks like the place is almost full. The band walks on to much applause.

They look relaxed, happy and at ease under the lights, like this is their natural environment. Carrie Brownstein stands stage right. She's 25, lean and pale skinned, with her black hair cut into a short, sharp bob. She wears a black long sleeved shirt, buttoned tight at the neck with a matching black A-line skirt and black leather boots. The only way she could look any cooler would be if she had a big black Rickenbacker 330 guitar hanging around her neck. And it just happens that she does.

Stage left, stands 27 year old Corin Tucker, dressed in a knee length party dress fashioned from bronze taffeta, with white tights and black patent leather shoes. Tucker is even paler skinned, her cherubic face framed by red hair cut into an even shorter bob. She plugs in her white Danelectro guitar, completing another image of near ineffable cool.

Centre stage, where you might expect the lead singer to be positioned, sits drummer Janet Weiss. Aged 34, dressed in black jeans and a black open neck shirt, her black hair cut into a shoulder length bob, Weiss takes out a set of drumsticks. She clicks the sticks and Brownstein begins to play the opening guitar line of 'The End of You'. It twists and folds in on itself with Beefheartian glee. When Weiss and Tucker join in, the energy on stage rockets.

Like the B-52s, Sleater-Kinney have no bass guitar in their line up. Two guitars, two voices and a drummer. The first couple of times I played the album, I didn't even realise. There is no gap, no absence in their sound. On some tracks, one guitarist may play a section in a lower register. But the music is so tightly woven, yet so kinetic, there's no real need or indeed space for a bass. And, partly due to Weiss' fluid use of kick drum and floor toms, there's no lack of bottom end.

The heart of Sleater-Kinney is the dialogue between Tucker and Brownstein, both in terms of how their guitar parts fit together and how their vocals play off each other. On 'The End of You' the two women sing alternate verses. Tucker's voice isn't easy on the ear. It's quavery, yet forceful. And when I've been playing tracks to friends this last couple of weeks, for some, Tucker's voice has been a tall hurdle. My sweet friend Bricknell screwed up her face and said, "She's quite screechy isn't she." But to me, Tucker sounds like she's vibrating with a powerful urgency. Her delivery means every single syllable seems to be loaded with significance. Brownstein's voice on the other hand is more even, more poised. At times she has a sardonic tone akin to Sonic Youth's Kim Gordon.

Weiss plays a continuous roll on the snare. Over this, Brownstein slashes at her guitar strings, windmilling her right arm like Pete Townshend. The song climaxes in a crash of cymbals, but even before the final guitar notes have begun to fade, Weiss clicks her sticks and the band plunge into the next song.

I don't recognise this one. But I love it. Weiss pounds out a thunderous beat on the tom and ride cymbal as Tucker sings *"They want to socialize you! They want to purify you!"*. There is no simple delineation of lead guitarist and rhythm guitarist roles between Brownstein and Tucker. Both play both. And both play neither. Their roles can shift many times within a single song. Each guitarist creates riffs, chords, note clusters, melodic lines and abstracted shapes. Much of the band's magic is in how these sounds weave together, lock tight or contrast and diverge.

Once again, the instant the song finishes and the audience begins to applaud, Brownstein starts straight into the next number. She picks out a sharp figure that wouldn't sound out of place on Wire's *Chairs Missing*. I don't recognise this one either. But I love it. This is the sort of clockwork guitar psychedelia that always catches my ear.

After that, they play 'Start Together'. Here, Weiss' drumming is masterful, making use of the full kit. She has name-checked both The Clash's Topper Headon and Led Zeppelin's John Bonham as influences, and it's possible to see Weiss' work as being a blend of both these distinctive drummers. The bright fills and splashy cymbal work of Headon and the ground shaking bass drum and floor tom attack of Bonham combine to ensure Weiss' contribution is just as crucial as that of the two guitarists.

Next up they play a strident version of 'Banned From the End of the World'. My original Sleater-Kinney epiphany. As a writer, I find the title a pleasing conundrum. Is being banned from the end of the world a positive outcome or a negative one? Live the song is far more staccato with a wilder edge. Yet the band never extend their compositions for live performance. Everything is kept contained and compact. Within two minutes the song is done. And, try as they might, the audience can't find space to applaud, because the band are already playing the next number.

This is a non-stop bombardment of music. There's 5 seconds maximum between each song. It's the classic Ramones performance model; fill your allotted time with as much material and determination as possible and never let the energy drop. Over the next fifty minutes or so, they play many, many great songs I've never heard before, plus a handful of numbers from *The Hot Rock*, including a version of 'Burn, Don't Freeze', which features both vocalists singing contrasting, but complimentary vocal melodies, as a descending guitar line from Tucker reels me in with its barbed hook.

The instant the song ends, Brownstein begins tuning her guitar. Tucker steps up to the mic. "Thank you very much." She says. So, they *are* going to talk to the audience after all. Brownstein turns to Weiss who clicks her drum sticks as the band start straight into 'The Hot Rock'. In the end that was maybe a 9 second gap between the two numbers.

As Mike stands watching the stage, I'm dancing and shaking my head in glee. There are others here tonight who are in more aggressive motion. This is the first gig I've been to for a year or so which has a mosh pit. As usual, it's made up of a small number of would-be alpha males, throwing themselves about in a bid to show how 'into it' they are. Or possibly how 'out of it' they are. Or perhaps how 'it' they are. As someone who likes to end an evening with as few cuts and bruises as possible, I've always avoided mosh pits.

Sociologically, I guess the mosh pit reaffirms music's functionality. It may be facilitated by the music. But it's not *about* the music. For some unfortunate men, directionless aggression would appear to be an inevitable by-product of the state of masculinity. The mosh pit provides a context in which this is seemingly accepted and celebrated. Whilst tonight's would-be alpha males seem content to merely barge into each other, I hear that at some metal gigs, it's apparently perfectly acceptable to throw each other about and land punches. Personally, I suspect I might find it difficult to properly appreciate the music if I was being repeatedly thwacked in the face.

At the close of the band's set, Brownstein unleashes a fat, fast and fuzzy riff that could have been ripped from the heart of the Buzzcocks' debut album. But as always with Sleater-Kinney, the initial suggestion of another artist is erased with the introduction of further elements. *"Damaged goods! Damaged goods!"* sings Tucker in her stinging vibrato. I love what I'm hearing. I want to hear it again. As soon as possible. In the end it will take me a few weeks to track down the song. It turns out to be 'Little Mouth' from their second album *Call the Doctor*. At the climax, Brownstein repeatedly sings *"Oh, you wanna try her, Oh, I think I wanna!"*. Their music connects with me so directly. Its effect is like a battery on the tip of the tongue.

The three women leave the stage to an incredibly positive response. The whole room feels energized. The cheering is not just an attempt to coax the band back on, it's the release of the build up of excess energy generated by the performance. For the hour spent on stage, there's been maybe a minute where the band haven't been playing. And when they play, they play hard. As an audience, we haven't really had a chance to show our appreciation. So here it is, all at once. A barrage of clapping, cheering, yelping, whistling and stamping.

After just a few minutes, Sleater-Kinney return. Even the wait for an encore is kept short and snappy. "Thank you." Says Tucker. That's all. They are one of the least verbally communicative bands I've ever seen. And yet it matters little. There is so much expression in their songs and their performance it feels like they're giving you everything through their music.

Brownstein leans back and carves out a riff that recalls the opening of Siouxsie and the Banshees' 'Jigsaw Feeling'. The same scything tone, the same sensation of building threat. Tucker overlays this with a different, more grinding riff and yawls out the vocal. I can't really catch many of the words. Although one line leaps out at me; *"Do you get nervous watchin' me bleed!?"'* I discover much later, this is the title song from their third album *Dig Me Out*.

In the latter section, Weiss plays a roll on the snare that goes on and on. Over this, Brownstein and Tucker trade slashing chords and vibrating notes. It's the kind of tight yet thrashy workout that recalls The Who in their pop art prime. The effect on the audience is vitalizing. Once again, the song's final note has barely finished ringing out when Weiss clicks her sticks and the trio goes into another number. I don't recognise this song either. But again it feels like something I desperately need in my life. As the song concludes, I realise the gig is almost over. Damn! I feel like a little kid on an outing to the park, who just isn't ready to go home yet.

"We've had a great time." Says Brownstein. "Thank you guys so much for coming along tonight. This is 'I Wanna Be Your Joey Ramone'". This announcement is greeted with bursts of cheering and whistling. I don't know this one either. But the audience's response suggests a lot of people have been waiting for this song. And, when the band kicks it off, I can see why. Tucker's sliding riff is underpinned by Weiss' impulsive drumming, as Brownstein picks out a low melody, which could almost be one of Peter Hook's Joy Division bass lines.

The duo's vocal interplay on the chorus is astonishingly polished, with Brownstein's yelps hooking onto the tail of Tucker's lines, like a couple who know each other so well, they can finish one another's sentences. It's a catchy and vocally manic piece of new wave. And it's the perfect way to end the show.

The band leaves the stage a second time, to an even bigger wave of applause. Mike and I nod appreciatively to each other. "Not bad." Says Mike, his eyes twinkling at the titanic understatement. I chuckle and we wander out of the venue, fizzing with satisfaction.

Sleater-Kinney is a band that exists in a kind of seclusion. True, there are flecks of other groups' influence in their sound: Sonic Youth maybe, or Bikini Kill, plus trace elements of the UK post-punk bands I mentioned. But these manifest themselves as moments within songs rather than as entire compositions. In the end, everything the band play sounds like one thing: Sleater-Kinney. Every song is a perfect balance of force and precision. I may have only recognised five of those songs tonight, nevertheless I've just experienced one of the best gigs of my life.

My first assessment was right too. The stage *is* Sleater-Kinney's natural environment. Over the next year, I'll collect all their albums. They are wonderful documents of some very strong compositions. But the band's live performances are a whole different class of wonderful.

* * * * *

Fifteen months later, on Sunday 30th July 2000, Sleater-Kinney return to the Pavilion Theatre Brighton, whilst touring in support of what remains my most beloved of their albums: *All Hands on the Bad One*. Like that album, their set concludes with the song 'The Swimmer'. Live, they push the piece into uncompromising psychedelic territory, ending the performance in a whirlwind of guitar dissonance. The whole show is intoxicating. I realise Sleater-Kinney are now officially my absolute favourite live band.

* * * * *

Tuesday 12th August 2003. It's two days after my good friend Tim Sagar's birthday. As a treat, I take he and his wife Alice Fox to see Sleater-Kinney, with two strong support bands, at The Old Market Arts Centre in Brighton. First up are a trio called Klang, led by Elastica's Donna Matthews, who deliver a pleasingly terse and spindly take on the Wire sound, with added funky drumming. Second up are Electrelane with a largely instrumental set of moody and filmic post rock. This is the third time I've seen them and they just get better and better.

Tim and Alice are suitably impressed. But once Sleater-Kinney take to the stage, everything else is rendered irrelevant. They proceed to buzzsaw their way through a set that is simultaneously tightly drilled yet filled with moments of sparking abandon. They make most other guitar bands seem dilute in comparison. Every gig I see them play feels urgent and completely authentic. Every gig delivers another clean jolt of direct energy. Every gig feels like the first time.

After the show, I become tongue tied whilst talking to Carrie Brownstein at the merchandise stall. What I want to tell her is "That was one of the best gigs I've ever seen." But what I actually say is "That was the best gig I've seen you play for *ages*." Somehow implying the last few Sleater-Kinney gigs I've attended have been a bit dull. She smiles politely, and says "Thank you." But her eyes say "There are other more intelligent, less rude people I need to speak with."

* * * * *

Sunday 28th May 2006.[2] Pete has come down to Brighton, and is staying with Sarah and I for a few days. On the Sunday evening, I go with Pete, Misha and my friend the talented comedienne Joanna Neary to see Sleater-Kinney play at the Concorde 2. Their latest album *The Woods* is a condensed and weighty affair and it's also one of their very best. Live, the trio hum with energy, attacking the

---

2. The following month, in June 2006, Sleater-Kinney announced an indefinite hiatus. Tucker went on to write and release two albums with her Corin Tucker Band. Weiss continued working with Quasi as well as joining former Pavement vocalist Stephen Malkmus in his band The Jicks. Meanwhile, Brownstein co-wrote and co-starred with Fred Armisen, in the extremely funny counter cultural sketch show *Portlandia* and, along with Weiss, formed the quartet Wild Flag. When, in 2014, Sleater-Kinney announced their return, I was very happy indeed. Their comeback album *No Cities to Love* (2015) was a short, sharp burst of power, which proved the band had lost none of their fire. Their return to the live arena was announced with a series of international dates. Pete and I had initially planned to go and see the band play in Manchester. However, the ticket prices chilled our blood.

new material with vehemence. When they play 'Modern Girl', the passion in Brownstein's voice makes my eyes wet.

Pete had never heard of Sleater-Kinney before today. Didn't know a single song. But, as the four of us walk home along the seafront, Pete says "That was one of the best gigs I've ever been to".

THE STROKES

THE LIFT, BRIGHTON

THURSDAY 1ˢᵀ FEBRUARY 2001

(AGE 37)

I ring the doorbell to Mick's apartment. It's dead on eight o'clock. We should arrive at the venue around quarter past eight.

Mick and I met two years ago in January 1999, when we were both acting in a radio sit-com based around a hapless football team, written and produced by the smart and industrious Paul Hodson. The production team was fun to work with and Mick and I struck up an immediate rapport.

A couple of weeks after recording the first batch of episodes, I bump into Mick at a gig by the neo-Krautrock bands Karamazov and Kreidler, at the Sussex Arts Club. Afterwards, we end up back at his flat, smoking weed, and listening to music. We're the same generation. Galvanized by punk into a life of chasing musical highs. We swap stories about our first gig experiences. I tell him about my Jam related tinnitus. It turns out Mick understands all about the impact of high volume on youthful ears.

"The first punk gig I went to was The Clash." He tells me. "It was the White Riot tour at Wolverhampton Civic Centre. When they went into the first number, the volume was so overpowering I actually pissed my pants. Promise me you'll never tell anybody that.""Course not Mick." I reply. I make a mental note that if, at some future point, I write a book, I'll change his name to Mick.

It turns out that like me, Mick is still something of a serious gig-goer. Also like me, he's got very eclectic tastes. So, over the last two years, we've been out together to see a few more bands: Godspeed You Black Emperor, Bows, Turbocat, Appliance, Birdhouse, Chicks on Speed, Hefner, Things To Do For Boys, Alaska, Laub, Chilly Gonzales, Couch, Bell, Plone, Mogwai, Royal Trux, Holly Golightly, Radar Brothers, Celebricide, Clearlake, Ecologist, Crashland, Candidate, Eeyore, Six By Seven, Mint, The Webb Brothers, Turin Brakes, Oddfellow's Casino, Chimp, Caramel Jack, Land of Nod, Avrocar, Jon Spencer Blues Explosion, Peaches, Ping Pong Bitches, Max Tundra, Willard Grant Conspiracy, Quasi, Aereogramme, Life Without Buildings, Badly Drawn Boy, Domestic4, British Sea Power, Sparklehorse, Placebo, Slipstream, The Kingsbury Manx, Parma Violets, Electrelane, Ladytron and Broadcast. And, unless he's being extremely discreet about it, I don't believe he's pissed his pants at a single one of these gigs.

I've now been standing on Mick's doorstep for a good few minutes. I ring the doorbell again. I wait a little longer. Finally Mick opens the door. I'm expecting him to be wearing a coat and ready to come right out. He's wearing a dressing gown. And he isn't ready to come right out. "All set?" I ask, smiling. Mick is witty, confident and bullish. But right now he looks a little worn out. "Come in mate." He says. "I got a bit delayed. I won't be long." To be honest, it looks like he will be long. But I don't mention this.

I walk up the stairs to his flat. The reason he's behind schedule is he's been on the phone to his wife. I understand. They are in the early stages of divorce proceedings. There are no kids involved and it should be fairly straightforward. They are both reasonable people and they are determined to make the process as civilized and painless as possible. A shame then, that they've apparently spent the best part of an hour bickering on the phone.

Mick goes into the bathroom. "Put some music on. I'll be as quick as I can." I hear him turning on the shower. I flick through his albums and find a copy of Joe Gibbs' *African Dub All-Mighty*. I lower the needle onto the vinyl. There's an initial crackle, then the beautiful smoky sounds tumble from the speakers. I sit on the sofa, take out my notebook and start scribbling down a script idea I had whilst walking over here.

Since the age of twelve – when my grandparents allowed me to stay up and watch Peter Cushing in *Frankenstein Created Woman* – I've been obsessed by British horror films of the 1970s, primarily the output of the Hammer, Amicus and Tigon production companies. I adore their uniquely British sense of the macabre. They are tales that are as much about stately restraint as they are about moments of shock and revulsion. Earlier this year I pitched the idea of a series of comedy homages to these films, to Steve Coogan and Henry Normal at Baby Cow Productions. To my surprise they loved the idea and so took it to the BBC, who promptly commissioned six scripts. So Steve, Henry and I started plotting.

To be able to work with Steve is both an honour and a challenge. He's exceptionally gifted, with an eye for detail and an abhorrence of anything faintly formulaic. *Dr. Terrible's House of Horrible* is an attempt to blend humour with genuine gore and it's a world away from anything else he's previously done.

Whilst Steve is away shooting the story of Factory Records in Michael Winterbottom's *24 Hour Party People,* Henry and I are currently developing storylines and scripts. Henry is a true gentleman and an incredibly gifted comedy creator, and he will become a much-valued friend. I learn more from his mentorship than I ever dreamed possible and over the next decade or so he will end up script editing (i.e. immeasurably improving) nearly 100 of my scripts. But right now, he's busy trying to translate my love of horror films into a workable comedy format. I am a slow learner, but he is a very patient man.

Meanwhile, I'm also still presenting *Totally Wired* on Surf 107, playing a selection of indie, left field dance stuff, dub, local unsigned bands, experimental music, soundtracks – whatever takes my fancy basically. Over the last couple of weeks, I've been giving some heavy rotation to a new US band called The Strokes.

The Strokes' 3 track promo EP *The Modern Age* arrived in a bundle of discs and singles. It's just a CD in a plastic wallet, with a plain white sleeve and virtually no information. But when the music starts, my ears prick up. It's garage rock essentially. Despite its rough and ready surface, the sophistication in the band's songwriting secures my attention.

The Modern Age opens with a tight, blunt riff and a crude, pounding drum pattern. I'm reminded of Jonathan Richman and the Modern Lovers, but they sound seriously polished compared to this. Nikolai Fraiture's bass is mixed low on the verses, but pushes its way forward for the chorus, where Julian Casablancas almost croons the lyrics.

Casablancas' voice has that New York drawl which is perfectly suited to the material. The way the vocal is captured also adds to the charm. There's an intimacy in the recording that matches the conversational tone of the lyrics. In fact, one of the key appeals of the EP is the overall immediacy of the production. You could say the three songs sounded more like rough demos than fully formed productions. But, to my ears, the ragged edges, boxy drums and fuzzy production help create the impression of a band effortlessly throwing down some tracks with a take it or leave it nonchalance.

By the second song 'Barely Legal', I'm completely sold. The opening has the twang and glide of a surf track, summoning up thoughts of both The Ventures and The Jesus And Mary Chain. Fab Moretti's sonorous snare rolls push the band forwards. And the insistent snub-nosed guitar break makes simplicity seem like some kind of threat. The song also contains the best Strokes lyric: *"I don't turn up on weekdays, something you learned yesterday."* There's something so supremely cool and snotty about this. It embodies an outsider arrogance, that stretches from the menacing yelp of Jerry Lee Lewis, through the cocky swagger of The Rolling Stones, the streetwise sneer of The Velvet Underground and the we-don't-care snarl of The Sex Pistols.

And yet, despite their image, skinny outsiders in ripped jeans and leather jackets, The Strokes are a long way away from being rough and ready street urchins. Casablancas' mother is former Miss Denmark Jeanette Christiansen, whilst his father is the multi-millionaire John Casablancas, director of Elite Modelling Management – the man who came up with the concept of the supermodel. Rhythm guitarist Albert Hammond Jr.'s Argentine mother Claudia Fernández was also a model. His father was Albert Hammond, a singer/songwriter who co-wrote a number of songs for other artists, including The Hollies' huge 1974 hit 'The Air That I Breathe'.

These boys grew up in uptown New York, a considerable distance from the wrong side of the tracks. Casablancas, Moretti and lead guitarist Nick Valensi began making music together whilst still at school in Manhattan. Casablancas would go on to meet Fraiture when the two attended the Lycée Français de New York, and the final piece of the jigsaw fell into place when the singer was introduced to Hammond whilst the pair were studying at Le Rosey, an exclusive Swiss boarding school. The Happy Mondays they aren't. Yet, privileged backgrounds notwithstanding, the band have still found a way to plug into the timeless raw energy of garage rock.

Yet The Strokes are not alone in this mission. Right now, there is something tangible happening on both sides of the Atlantic. In the US, bands such as the Yeah Yeah Yeahs, Liars and White Stripes are finding different ways of engaging with the garage form. Whilst British groups such as McLusky, Clinic and Ikara Colt are also creating music shorn of ornamentation and show business flourishes. And yet, this isn't a back to basics slash and burn event, like the punk movement of '76/'77. This isn't a music that necessarily shuns synths, sequencers and drum machines. Indeed, a number of these bands are clearly keen to meld their guitars with the tools of contemporary music technology.

A couple of weeks ago, I went up to London, to visit my friend Colin Newman of the recently reconvened Wire, at his *swim* ~ studios in Southfields. "The next important thing is going to be rock." He says "A return to big guitar sounds – something which gets rid of all the additional debris which accretes to music over time".

Colin proceeds to play me some early works in progress for a projected new Wire EP. It is defiantly rock, crackling with a brutal monochrome power. Although perversely the pieces have been assembled with Pro-Tools, deploying dance floor production techniques. I'm initially a little shocked to hear how the group has abandoned their penchant for psychedelic melodies and textures in favour of an armour-plated sound with the drive of speed metal. And yet, it turns out Wire have judged the moment perfectly. Mutant forms of garage rock will indeed come to dominate the independent music scene for the next few years.

But right now, Mick and I are heading off to a gig that will turn out to have a modicum of cultural significance. Last night The Strokes played their first UK date in Portsmouth, as the support to …And You Will Know Us By The Trail of Dead. But tonight the band will play their first headlining show on British soil. Suffice to say I've been looking forward to this gig for several weeks. Initially I'd spoken with the band's management over the phone and attempted to arrange for them to come in and do an interview for *Totally Wired*. But we couldn't sort out the logistics. 'Logistics' is what we've started saying when we mean arrangements.

Mick's landline rings. For a second, I think of answering it. But I suspect it's his wife calling back, so I decide against it. I return to writing in my notebook. The phone stops ringing.

I hear Mick coming out of the shower and going into his bedroom. I check my mobile: 20:18. The landline rings again. I hear Mick pick up the extension in his bedroom. I can't tell what he's saying, but his tone of voice immediately tells me he's talking to his wife again. He's using the kind of firm, unyielding voice which people only employ with someone they used to love deeply but now find constantly irritating. Mick's muffled voice rumbles on. I check my phone: 20:26.

I realise we're probably going to miss the support band. I feel a bit miffed. I always try to catch the support acts as it frequently pays big dividends. In fact, I'd go as far to say some of the finest performances I've seen have been by support bands I'd never heard of prior to stepping into the venue.

In 1992, at the Brighton Zap Club, Malcolm and I happened upon Consolidated, supporting Meat Beat Manifesto. Consolidated's pummelling union of hip-hop, industrial grit, politically engaged lyrics and video projections was a revelation. Their set was followed by the band carrying out an open soap-box session with audience members which developed into a very heated debate. A long way from your usual gig.[1]

In 1982, John, Owen, Oggy and I caught The Virgin Prunes supporting The Fall at Manchester Polytechnic. Loud off-centre tape loops played through the sound system, then several members of the band wandered on stage looking like a lost tribe, dressed only in loincloths, and proceeded to sit in a huddle, smearing each other with body paint. Guitarist Dik Evans stood in a baggy Oxfam suit, cranking out a massive, slow moving riff, as drummer Mary D'Nellon smashed away at a large crash cymbal that had been cut into a jagged spiral. From then on, it just grew stranger and stranger. Part performance ritual, part art rock catharsis, it was utterly unforgettable.

In 1978, for my fourth rock gig, I went to see Scottish new wave band The Rezillos play at King George's Hall Blackburn. At this point, the band were enjoying their commercial high point, with their single *'Top of The Pops'* – a song which naturally enough saw the band appearing on the very show they were celebrating and lampooning. I went alone as Pete was away on holiday. I wore a yellow T-shirt, on the front of which I'd daubed the word 'Resist' in red paint. I don't know why. I'm not sure what it was I thought I was resisting. I just liked the word. It seemed striking and enigmatic. And yet, I soon came to regret painting it on my T-shirt, as, at various points in the evening, several people came up to me to say "That's not how you spell Rezillos".

The evening's undoubted highlight was support band The Gang of Four. I'd never heard of them. Nobody had. They didn't have any records out and I hadn't seen anything about them in the music press. But I was

---

1. Despite releasing several outstanding albums, Consolidated were never destined to grab the headlines, or achieve major league acceptance. However, they did earn the distinction of having one of their songs covered by Grace Jones. Boasting a chorus of *'Typical male thinks with his dick'*, the track 'Typical Male' is fast moving and funky. Although Consolidated's original is by far the superior cut.

amazed by their set. 'Armalite Rifle' in particular grabbed my attention, with Hugo Burnham's martial drumming and Andy Gill's lacerating monomaniac guitar solo. Although it was 'Love Like Anthrax' that really took my breath away. Literally.

The opening barrage of controlled feedback reverberated my insides, once again making the 14 year old me marvel at the power of sound. I'd seen clips of Jimi Hendrix on TV doing his 'Star Spangled Banner' feedback solo. But there's an enormous difference between hearing guitar feedback coming though the tinny speaker of a small black and white portable TV, and standing at the front of a concert hall with waves of noise rolling from the huge sound system and shaking your innards. It felt unbound by musical form and distinctly dangerous. Had Mick been there, he may well have pissed himself all over again.

After that, The Rezillos struggled to impress. They were high-energy knockabout fun with a Ramones-esque buzz, and they certainly put lots of effort into their performance. But in truth, it was kid's stuff compared to The Gang of Four's astringent punk funk.

Mick emerges from his bedroom fully dressed. He sits next to me on the sofa, pulls on his boots and fastens the buckles. I stand up. Mick remains seated and produces a small bag of white powder from his wallet. "I need a lift." He says. "Do you mind?" I chuckle. "Well yes, I mind if I just have to watch you. But if you're going to include me I definitely don't mind." I sit down again.

Mick takes out a CD case and proceeds to chop a couple of lines. However, as he's doing this, he starts talking about the disagreement with his wife again. As he muses on their situation, he continually chops and re-chops the lines. This goes on for several minutes. "I think those lines are as straight as they're ever going to be." I say. He suddenly realises what he's doing. "Sorry mate. Bit preoccupied." He rolls up a ten-pound note and we do a line each.

Finally, we scamper down the stairs and out into the cold night air. Things accelerate. The coke is buzzing through my system. After a frustrating hour or so, I now feel upbeat and positive. We stride up the street together, chattering confidently, neither of us really listening to the other. We arrive outside the venue: The Lift. It's a room above a pub, just down the road from the train station. We've seen many fine shows here.

We can hear the muffled sound of The Strokes coming from inside. "Shit, they've already started." I mutter. We walk up the staircase to the venue. The music sounds really energetic and noisy. There's a couple of whey faced teenage lads manning the door. "We should be on the guest list." I say. They wave us in without even checking.

We step inside. It's less than half full, but it's buzzing. The Strokes are thrashing out a repetitive two chord instrumental sequence, with waves of controlled feedback sweeping across the room. It sounds more potent and atonal than their EP has led me to expect. It's a noise which prime era Velvet Underground would have been proud to conjure up. It sounds so alive and engaged. I am beaming. This is sonic bliss.

There isn't a stage as such, just an area set back from the room where the amps and drum kit have been set up. There is barely enough room for all five members of the band. Especially when Casablancas and Valensi are leaping about with such abandon. Like all the best garage bands, The Strokes manage to sound simultaneously tight yet loose.

The song concludes in a storm of whistling feedback. But then, to my disappointment, the band strides off to applause and cheers. I glance across at Mick, he gives me an apologetic shrug. "They'll do an encore." He assures me. A young blonde girl next to us snorts. "That *was* the encore." Mick winces. "Maybe they'll do another one." The house lights come up. They won't be doing another one. Fuck.

* * * * *

In April, Henry, Steve and I commence shooting *Dr. Terrible's House of Horrible* at Shepperton Studios – the site where many of the Amicus horror films we're celebrating were filmed in the 1960s and 70s. The series is directed by the extremely talented Matt Lipsey and it attracts some major guest stars. Sadly, when it's broadcast in the autumn, it also attracts a major kicking from reviewers. Although there are some positive reviews and the viewing figures are okay, the general feeling around the show is it is one of Steve's very few missteps. Once again I sit down and start developing some fresh ideas.

In July, The Strokes release their debut album *Is This It*. Producer Gordon Raphael has applied a certain amount of studio gloss and smoothed over the band's rough edges. Although the album will help propel the band to global success, to my ears the polish means The Strokes have inevitably lost some of their renegade appeal. Still, I imagine wealth, fame and film star girlfriends will go some way to easing any similar qualms Casablancas and company might harbour.

Meanwhile, Mick lands a role in a long running soap opera. It's a marvellous break for any actor. Especially as his character turns out to also be long running. I'm pleased for him. But unfortunately this means he moves up north and I lose my most dedicated gig-going companion.

Does this stop me from going to see live music? No. But it does slow me down. Obviously I have other friends who're up for going to gigs, but not everyone is as sonically open-minded as Mick. Not that I resent going to shows on my own, but it isn't quite as enjoyable an experience. Besides which, now I've shaved my head, if I spend too much time standing on my own I will eventually be mistaken for a member of the security staff.

The other factor that slows down my gig attendance is the rolling waves of writing deadlines that inevitably flood into my evenings and weekends. When I was at school I always hated doing homework and yet somehow I have ended up with a career that means I'm doing it almost every night. But writing gives me such pleasure I would never complain.

And yet… over the next few years, due to looming writing deadlines, I will end up missing concerts that I've bought tickets to and have been excitedly looking forward to for months. These include such delights as

Sonic Youth at the Shepherds Bush Empire and worst of all Coil at the Royal Festival Hall. During a lifetime spent going to literally hundreds of gigs it seems churlish to mourn a few missed opportunities. But then even the greatest bands are not around forever.

THE FALL

CONCORDE 2, BRIGHTON

MONDAY 30TH SEPTEMBER 2002

(AGE 38)

Tonight I'm about to watch my 30th Fall gig. This may seem extreme, but having recently consulted Malcolm, he estimates he's seen them play around 125 times. There's no way I'll ever catch up.

But tonight is a special night. Because tonight I am returning to the fold. It's actually six years since I attended my 29th Fall gig. And that was an excruciating experience. Possibly the worst night out in Worthing you could wish on anyone. More of that later.

The Concorde 2 is right down on Brighton beachfront on Madeira Drive. It's a former Victorian tearoom, with windows all down one side, a capacity of around 600 and a solid sound system. The original Concorde Bar used to be about a mile up the road, opposite the Palace Pier. Although it sadly closed down many years ago, to my mind, it was a far better venue. I saw The Fall play there in October 1983. My 14th Fall gig.

I remember arriving feeling grumpy because my girlfriend Louise was supposed to be coming down from London for the gig, but she'd blown me out at the last minute. The start of a swift decline in our relationship. But, by the end of the show, I was in high spirits due to an utterly committed performance that climaxed with a lengthy and fierce iteration of 'Eat Y'self Fitter'.

Apparently, my future wife Sarah had been at the same gig – seven years before we met. She told me she remembers being drunk and dancing in high-heeled boots on broken glass to 'Eat Y'self Fitter'. Oh to have met each other then.

However, my very first live encounter with The Fall was back in October 1978 at the age of 14. And it was glorious. They were playing at a Rock Against Racism benefit gig at a tiny club called Kelly's in Manchester. The thing that immediately struck me was the group's down to earth appearance and low key demeanour. Punk, for all its talk of being a ground zero roots rebellion, still contained strong elements of show business. The majority of punk performances involved the bands projecting themselves into the audience's fantasies via striking poses and jumping around in eye-catching outfits and sometimes make up. For instance, The Clash – often thought of as a group of natural and authentic rebels – had clearly choreographed their stage moves and designed their stage clothes (costumes) to have maximum impact.

With The Fall however, there wasn't even a hint of show business. It seemed like direct communication. As they shambled onto the stage, looking like a bunch of teenagers who'd just been thrown out of some grubby youth club, there was a very noticeable sense of 'Take it or leave it. We know it's good. You either get it or you don't.' I got it.

I'd already bought their debut EP: *Bingo-Master's Break-Out!*. All three tracks shone with an uncanny individuality. But it was the song 'Repetition' which had convinced me I had stumbled into the presence of genius. A hymn to "*The three Rs; Repetition, Repetition, Repetition*", the track is five minutes of slow moving psychosis. It's a sonic statement of intent, which the lyrics describe as having been created for "*All you daughters and sons who are sick of fancy music.*" I played it in my bedroom over and over. There was nothing else even remotely like it on my radar.

Seeing The Fall live for the first time was another kind of revelation. Every song seemed to inhabit its own odd world. Martin Bramah's urgent, choppy guitar, Yvonne Pawlett's tinny, monochromatic keyboards, Karl Burns' energetic drumming, Marc Riley's limber bass lines and Mark E. Smith's smart, off centre lyrics and acidic vocals were a potent force. I was also struck by how many slow songs were in their set. Even as late as 1978, the majority of the music coming out of the new wave was fast paced and hectic. When I heard a band prepared to slow things down, my ears pricked up.

Another fascinating facet of the show was Mark's between song banter. It was like there was no difference between him singing and him talking. Sometimes he made elliptical statements, sometimes he'd be describing what was happening on stage, but everything he said sounded enigmatic and quotable.

After that, I tried to convince several of my school friends of the importance of The Fall. Which was tricky. Even Pete took a while to warm to them. But nobody else really got it. Some of them thought I was joking. Some of them seemed actively hostile towards the group. But the phrase I heard uttered the most often was "It's too weird for me".

The Fall are still a difficult band to defend to those who don't get it. Because well, The Fall are a difficult band. Although they've produced their fair share of songs with hooks and catchy riffs, they are, at root, exponents of a singular brand of art rock. They follow their own path and it's not always easy to tag along. Their music can frequently be abrasive, repetitious, atonal and sometimes deliberately downright ugly.

But for many non-believers, the biggest stumbling block is Mark E. Smith. His voice is neither melodic nor precise. Sometimes, rather than sing, he shouts, chants or rants, sometimes he executes an almost Beefheartian growl, at other times he 'croons' in a cracked and quavery falsetto. But one of the lessons I, and many others, learnt from punk is how virtuosity can sometimes be a handicap to direct expression. The primitives and primitivists also deserve to be heard.

And then there's the matter of Mark's lyrics. They occupy a realm quite separate from most other lyrics. Perhaps this is because he seems to view himself as a writer who works in the field of music, rather than a conventional musical lyricist. Sometimes his words are tightly worked and edited. Sometimes they are off the cuff improvisations. He creates characters and narratives, taking his influences from unexpected sources such as Philip K. Dick, M.R. James, Lenny Bruce, William S. Burroughs, H.P. Lovecraft and, like it or not, Bernard Manning. At their best, Mark's lyrics come across as a form of novelistic kitchen-sink gothic, blending the quotidian with the supernatural and arcane, often locating his songs within his specific home territory of Greater Manchester and the North West.

After that first gig, I became a genuine devotee. And I experienced many more transcendent shows. In July 1980, a couple of months after I left Norden County High School for the last time, I attended the Railway Working Men's Club in Nelson, where the group played a lengthy up-tempo version of 'New Face In Hell' with Mark's vocals drenched in reverb. They also performed a song from the album *Totale's Turns* called 'Cary Grant's Wedding', during which Mark altered the lyrics so the guest list for the wedding included "Three thousand Joy Division fans". By the time the gig was finished, so were the evening's buses. John, Oggy and I trudged the twelve and a half miles home in heavy rain. Yet I never once doubted the gig had been worth it. Besides, we were okay, because we were wearing our long macs.

Another standout was at Manchester Polytechnic in 1982, where The Fall deployed a two drummer line up. They locked into a Krautrock-style motorik and delivered one of the most mesmeric performances I've ever seen, some songs stretching on for nine or ten minutes, with Steve Hanley's sonorous bass lines underpinning the expansive grind.

And of course from their stark and scratchy 1979 debut *Live at the Witch Trials*, through to the dark, dense delights of 1985's *This Nation's Saving Grace* The Fall produced some of the finest albums of the post-punk period. And yet, in the late 80s, I fell out of love with The Fall. They still released some tracks that caught my ear and imagination. But for a couple of years, too many cover versions, multi-formatted singles and a few too many smoothed edges, just didn't seem to be playing to the band's strengths. I caught a couple of uninspired live shows and well, we just drifted apart.

Nevertheless, like many fans that have strayed, I ended up returning to the fold. From 1990's *Extricate* through to 1996's *The Light User Syndrome* The Fall were back in sharp focus, delivering a brace of essential albums which sometimes saw them meshing their experimental garage rock with computer enhanced rhythms. Sadly however, by 1996, their live performances had become notoriously uneven. Which brings us back to Worthing and Fall gig number 29. Which is when I drifted from the fold a second time.

Tuesday, 8ᵗʰ October 1996 was not a day of great merit in The Fall's gigography. The band had suddenly been reduced to a four piece, following the mid tour departure of guitarist and Mark's ex-wife Brix Smith. By the time they hit the stage, they were over an hour late and Mark had been drinking so heavily he was pissed to the point of abstraction. He collapsed twice and spent around half of the forty-five minute gig off stage, leading to several unintentionally instrumental versions of songs. He also berated the generally sympathetic audience for being 'provincial scum' and had to be carried out of the building. I caught the train home, feeling annoyed and saddened.

Unfortunately for The Fall, worse was to come. In 1998, during a drunken and chaotic show in New York, Mark, drummer Karl Burns and guitarist Tommy Crooks came to blows on stage. Mark ended up spending a few days in a police cell and that particular line up came to a very sorry end. However, despite all the signs, Mark would rise again and put together a new version of The Fall.

If The Fall exited the 20ᵗʰ century bruised and battered, they entered the new millennium in sterling form. In 2000, they released a bona fide classic album in *The Unutterable*. If 2001's *Are You Are Missing Winner* is less crucial, it still contains moments, such as the robust and cocksure cover of Lead Belly's 'Bourgeois Town', where Smith and the band tap directly into the primal excitements of rock and roll in a way very few artists can.

* * * * *

And so here I am, in late 2002, thinking the time might be right to venture out to see The Fall in the live arena once more. Malcolm has seen them play a couple times over the last year and a half and has reported them to be on exceptionally fine form. I arrive at the Concorde 2, feeling a combination of excitement and uncertainty.

The venue is already over half full. Each generation of music lovers delivers another congregation of devotees unto The Fall. So their audience is always a mix of ages and types. It's roughly a 75/25 split between male and female. There's a healthy dose of middle-aged balding men, a few of whom seem to have glamorous middle-aged wives in tow. There are students in their late teens and early twenties and a few quite straight looking types. There's a handful of men and women in their mid thirties who still dress like 1981 era punks – studded leather jackets and Discharge armbands – hell, there's even a gaggle of Goths.

I buy a lager at the bar and walk through the double doors into the venue proper. I immediately bump into my good friend Tim Leopard. Dressed as ever, in a sharp pinstriped suit and tie, he's a multi-talented left field artist who operates as a stand up comic, a collagist, vocalist and lyricist. I've seen his band, the wonderfully named Celebricide, a number of times. Like me, Tim is someone whose artistic worldview has been partially shaped by Smith's visions.

Moments later, the support band assemble on stage. They are British Sea Power. I've seen them once before. On that occasion they tried very hard, but they were blown off stage by their support act, the sublime Domestic4. Although they only released one dazzling album and a couple of EPs, the short-lived Domestic4 are, to my ears, one of the best bands of the last 20 years. They share elements in common with both Broadcast and Super Furry Animals. Yet I prefer their songs to both those admittedly fine bands. If that description whets your appetite, I suggest you track down their album *Bungalow Ranch Style*. You will not be disappointed.

British Sea Power try very hard again tonight too. They are a band that put on a proper performance. They have a stage set made up of a collection of stuffed birds and foliage, and they're dressed in outfits that make them resemble extras from *Dad's Army*. At one point, the drummer climbs off the stage and walks around the audience, beating on a large bass drum that looks like it originally belonged to a marching band. Some of the audience are won over by the band's quirkiness and desire to conjure up big rock thrills. They are putting so much effort into their performance I really want to like them. But music either grabs you or it doesn't. And I remain ungrabbed. To me, they sound like a pale awkward imitation of Echo and the Bunnymen, with neither the grandeur nor the grace.

During the interval, whilst ordering a couple of pints at the bar, I bump into the musician Miles Davies, keyboardist with the aforementioned Domestic4. Whilst we're chatting, another young man comes over and joins us. Miles introduces him as the guitarist from British Sea Power. I didn't recognise him without his ARP warden outfit and tin hat. He seems like a really nice guy – witty and articulate. Now I really wish I'd liked his band. However, when he asks me if I saw British Sea Power I opt for an easy lie. "Sorry mate. I've only just got here." I excuse myself and wander back to Tim with our drinks.

The wait for The Fall to take to the stage always seems interminable. But finally the lights begin to dim. A cheer goes up, but the group doesn't appear. Instead, the sound of a muffled home taped voice comes through the sound system, accompanied by bits of background noise. It's Mark muttering and incanting. He refers to Blackpool and the Golden Mile and something about football and "stray electricity". This kind of unkempt experimentation with random elements and chance recordings has always been a part of The Fall's art, and it's something which seems to connect them directly back to the tape recorder experiments of William Burroughs.

When The Fall eventually stride on stage – which they do as ever minus Mark himself – they plunge straight into 'Mansion', a short instrumental piece from *This Nation's Saving Grace*. As a general rule, The Fall tend to eschew their older material. Their forward-looking aesthetic is one of the band's defining characteristics. But tonight's set will take a surprising amount of backward glances at their substantive back catalogue.

'Mansion' sounds a bit thin at first, as the sound engineer struggles to balance everything out. But then, as the band launch into 'Two Librans', everything clicks. Despite guitarist Ben Pritchard's nonchalant body language, clad in jeans and a tracksuit top, he grinds out The

Stooges style riff with real power. The rhythm section of nimble fingered bassist Jim Watts and modish drummer Spencer Birtwistle are fluid yet tightly interlocked.[1]

As a smiling Mark wanders on stage, a roar of affirmation comes from the crowd. He looks relaxed yet focused, a man with a job to do. He's dressed in a pale blue shirt and grey slacks. Along with the suit cut black leather jacket that he often wears, it's a style Mark has maintained for many years. And, whilst it may not really sound like rock star attire, it's a sharp and iconic look which he has made his own. It also means photos of him tend not to be tied down to any particular era.

The guitar and bass punch out a constantly descending riff, Mark holds the mic close to his mouth and barks out the words with utter conviction. *"Tolstoy in Chechnya! Euro reflect on wastage!"*. As always, his lyrics strike the balance between instantly accessible and completely impenetrable.

At the conclusion of 'Two Librans', I lean over to Tim and say "This is already 100% better than the Worthing experience". Tim chuckles. "Yeah. Almost like you're watching a different band." As the applause and cheering continues, keyboardist Elena Poulou walks on stage and assumes her position at her monophonic keyboard. Born in Greece, she's a pale skinned, dark haired woman with a refined elfin beauty that contrasts strongly with the decidedly manly aspect of the rest of the

---

1. One of the things which even non-Fall fans seem to be aware of, is Mark's habit of frequently changing the band's line-up. What is often described as 'hiring and firing'. To me, this has never seemed particularly remarkable. Who knows how many musicians were 'hired and fired' by David Bowie or Prince over their careers? If Mark had spent his career trading under the name Mark E. Smith rather than operating under The Fall banner, it's doubtful anybody would invest a great deal of significance in the line up changes he's instigated. And, unlike Genesis Breyer P. Orridge, the quality of whose recorded output seems to depend entirely on the calibre of his collaborators, Mark's artistic vision is so hefty he's seemingly able to forge a deeply convincing version of The Fall from any assembly of musicians he chooses.

band. She's also Mark's wife. It's no secret that Elena's involvement with both Mark and The Fall has helped guide him from the lowest point of his career to a position of renewed strength and artistic engagement.

Tonight she will only appear on stage to play on a handful of songs. And there are some in the audience who balk at her contributions. Her keyboard lines are frequently atonal and often very abstract. Whilst a good portion of The Fall's core fan base are open to the experimental and chance elements which Mark is always keen to bring into the mix, there are smaller pockets who just want to hear straight ahead rock and see the more exploratory components as unnecessary and irritating.

The set goes on to take in songs from the last two albums, but the live versions easily ace their recorded counterparts. 'Cyber Insekt' is transformed into a hectic rolling beast that Captain Beefheart and his Magic Band wouldn't have sniffed at. The song finishes and there are just a few brief moments before they start into the next song. Unlike The Fall's early performances, when Mark kept up a stream of imaginative and oblique patter between numbers, nowadays he seldom utters a word outside of the songs themselves.

The opening notes of 'Touch Sensitive' are greeted with a cheer. Bizarrely, the tune has recently garnered the band some new fans, having been used in a TV commercial for the Vauxhall Corsa. Tonight Mark even comments ironically about the advert within the lyrics, chanting at one point 'you must buy a car!' This is just one of numerous examples of The Fall's work spilling over into the mainstream. Yet when this happens – for instance, when Mark turns up unexpectedly reading the football results on BBC1's sport service – there always remains a sense of him working behind enemy lines.

As the song ends, Mark walks to the back of the stage and off into the wings. This makes me wonder if things might be about to turn a shade Worthing. With their singer still absent, the band slide into a version of 'Ketamine Son'. It's a slowly building psych grind – the kind of thing that The Fall have always excelled at. A minute or so in and Mark returns, wearing his black jacket and chewing on some gum. He goes on to spit out the lyrics in a performance that turns out to be one of the night's highlights.

During the instrumental sections, Mark wanders around, altering the settings on both Pritchard and Watts' amps. This is something he does several times throughout the evening. He's been doing this on stage for years. There are differing views on his amp fiddling. The main schools of thought being

a)   Mark is dicking about, showing off who is boss.

b)   He's utilizing the amps to create an effect akin to dub, dropping out the guitar, or reshaping its tone, pushing the bass to the fore, or thinning it out. Essentially doing a live mix on stage.

c)   He doesn't have a clue what he's doing.

I believe the truth is in fact a), b) and c). Mark is indeed showing who is boss, by creating a live mix. But he's doing it via random means, with no clear idea of how it will sound. Again he's encouraging chance elements into the performance. But the group is so tightly drilled, they can withstand any amount of experimentation with their sound.

The tumbling opening bars of 'The Classical' cause sections of the audience down the front to immediately start leaping and dancing. In Fall fan circles, the song, from their much lauded 1982 album *Hex Enduction Hour*, is often viewed as one of the group's definitive tracks. Yet, as ever with The Fall, when they dip into their back catalogue, they frequently reshape it. Here, Elena's lopsided off-key keyboard runs stand in sharp contrast with the song's tight beat group dynamic. And, as the song reaches its apex, Mark leans forward and passes the mic to a member of the audience, who proceeds to repeatedly bark out the song's refrain "*I've never felt better in my life*".

This occasional act of handing over vocal duties to random audience members has sometimes been seen as Mark adopting a sloppy approach to his work. But I would disagree. To me it appears to be just another example of him encouraging the inclusion of chance elements into the performance. One thing Mark always seems to be seeking out is the tattered edge, the imperfection, the uneasy collision.

Mark wanders off stage with 'The Classical' still in full flight. Minutes later, the band come to a thunderous climax and, after just a brief wave of thanks from Pritchard, they too depart. Tim and I turn to each other and nod our approval. This was a good one. A very good one indeed.

It takes nearly five minutes of cheering and stamping, but the band eventually return for an encore of 'Dr. Buck's Letter'. With its chugging industrial guitar riff and instantly recognisable bass figure, 'Dr. Buck's Letter' is a perfect calling card for the 21st century Fall. It doesn't sound like anything the band has ever done before and yet it couldn't possibly be anybody else. Tonight Mark extemporises over the music, taking the lyrics in new and unpredictable directions.

This is followed by a high-energy interpretation of 'White Lightning'. The song was written by The Big Bopper and originally recorded in 1959 by George Jones. An intermittent component of The Fall's sets since 1990, it's the story of an impossibly potent alcohol cooked up in an illegal still in the hills of North Carolina. It's an example of how The Fall, despite their ability to continuously push forward and experiment, simultaneously remain connected to the very roots of blues and rockabilly. The band leave the stage to loud applause and calls for more, but the house lights come up and it's time to go home.

Whilst this hasn't been the best Fall gig I've ever attended – after all there's some extremely stiff competition – it was a totally compelling performance, and it felt a privilege to be here. Tonight the band achieved what The Fall at their best always achieve; they made most other bands seem prissy and stale in comparison. It's enough to make that night in Worthing seem like a distant anomaly.

As Tim and I walk back along the seafront, I berate myself for missing so many Fall gigs over recent years. What an idiot.

* * * * *

It's five years after my re-return to the fold. I have now seen The Fall 35 times. I'm busy writing the third series of *Ideal*. There's a storyline about a mentally disturbed Christian builder called Alan. Alan has a vision of Jesus who instructs him to kill Johnny Vegas' character Moz.

But I don't imagine Jesus with a beard and flowing robes. I want him to look like some guy you might meet down the pub. Suddenly it becomes obvious who has to play the role of Jesus.

At the BBC TV building on Oxford Road Manchester, I knock on Mark's dressing room door with trepidation. "Yeah? Come in." I push the door open. Mark is standing at the dressing table in a crisp white shirt and black slacks. He turns and gives me a broad smile. We shake hands. We've actually met several times over the years at Fall gigs and a couple of times when I was working for IKON, but I know he won't remember me.

Graham: "Hi, I'm Graham, I'm the writer. I'm really glad you agreed to do this."

MES: "No problem pal. So, what do you think of this script then?"

Graham: "Well… I wrote it, so obviously I'm reasonably happy with it."

MES: "I've had a few thoughts. I've made some notes for stuff we could do."

Mark picks up his script. It's covered in handwritten notes for additional lines. His handwriting is loose and spidery, frequently alternating between capitals and lower case. It's difficult to make out on first look. You have to concentrate to fully understand both the content and the form. Like The Fall's music.

What he seems to be proposing, is a virtual deconstruction of the scene with references to the fact it's actually a TV show and so on. I love it. It fits in with both Mark's world view, his observation of the process of creating an alternate world in the realm of TV, and it also chimes with the *Ideal* aesthetic, whereby the show frequently peels back different layers of reality. The thing is, we can't jettison the original script altogether. If we do, the episode won't make sense. We need to retain the sense of Mark being a vision of Jesus who instructs Alan to kill Moz.

Graham: "I think that's really interesting. I think the way to go, is to shoot a version of the script as is, then if you're up for it, to try a few runs with you using your ideas."

MES: "Whatever you think cock. It's up to you."

I'm not sure whether it's a good omen or not, but when the clapper board is lifted into shot for the first take of Mark's scene playing Jesus, miraculously it turns out to be slate number 666. This elicits a wave of uncertain laughter from the crew. Mark is clearly out of his comfort zone and initially struggles with running though the material. He's a man who famously doesn't like to do exactly the same thing twice. So repeating the same lines over and over is something of a battle. Peter Slater, the actor playing Alan, has his work cut out to keep the scene moving as Mark's delivery becomes increasingly fragmentary.

At one point, the producer Jane Berthoud sidles over and whispers in my ear "What do you think? Time for a recast?" I shake my head. "It might take a while, but I think we'll get it." We do. In the end, director Ben Gregor manages to tease out a subtle and funny performance. The final on-screen result – Mark bathed in a golden glow, giving foul mouthed godly instructions, soundtracked by the strange celestial music of Coil – is the highlight of the third series. And it's definitely my proudest TV achievement.

After the recording, I ask Mark if he's ever thought about writing narratives for TV. He recalls a few years ago he'd developed some horror ideas for a Welsh TV company. "Nothing came of it in the end. I think they lost them or summat." I say that if he's interested in resurrecting them I'd be keen to help him pitch them to TV companies. "Definitely." He replies. "I'd like to do something that's really weird and properly frightening."

Three weeks later, I'm back home in Brighton and Mark calls up, asking if I'd like to meet up soon and talk about writing some scripts together. I feel like I've just been asked if I'd like to fulfil a lifetime's ambition that I never knew I had.

Over the next year and a half, we meet up every couple of months, either in Manchester bars or London hotels and start mapping out stories for a *Twilight Zone*-esque anthology series for TV entitled *Inexplicable*. As we sit together, he steadily makes his way through a few bottles of pilsner and a couple of glasses of whisky. Yet he never seems to get drunk. Drink has never really been my thing and I usually never drink whilst writing, so I don't even try to keep up. Mark is never short of ideas and frequently refers to historical or literary examples to illustrate what he's talking about. His knowledge of history is impressive and, perhaps surprisingly, his memory is pin sharp.

At first, I'm uncertain as to how the working relationship will operate. But it actually flows pretty well. The meetings tend to consist of free wheeling brain storming sessions, during which I frequently find myself dissolving into fits of giggles at Mark's unexpected flights of humour. I record these sessions on my phone, take notes, write up the ideas later, then send hard copies to Mark. We bat the stories back and forth until they are in good shape.

Sometimes Mark's enthusiasm for the project takes me by surprise. On one occasion my landline rings at 2:30 in the morning. I wake up and answer it, expecting the worst. Expecting to be told that a loved one is ill and that I need to go directly to some hospital or other. However, it's Mark. He's just flown back from doing some gigs in Portugal and whilst on the plane has had "some pretty good ideas for the show". I grab my notebook and pen and wipe the sleep from my eyes.

We manage to put together what we think is a solid pitch. I have meetings with a few TV executives about the idea, but it seems no one wants to pick it up. Some are deterred by what they perceive as Mark's unpredictable personality. But the main thing I hear is "It's too weird for me".

We shelve the project, but stay in touch. Whenever I'm working in Manchester filming *Ideal*, we meet up for drinks and endless talking. Spending evenings in the bar of his local, The Woodthorpe Hotel in Prestwich, or wandering around a range of pubs and bars in the centre of town.

After *Ideal* comes to the end of its seventh season in 2011, I continue to spend big chunks of the next two years in Manchester, co-writing and acting in the BBC2 sit-com *Hebburn*. It's created by Geordie stand-up and all round ball of positivity Jason Cook, and is loosely based on his own family. Gina McKee and Jim Moir (aka Vic Reeves) play versions of his parents and the chemistry between them is palpable. Gina is an actress of superb skill and subtlety. Jim meanwhile has big comedy bones, and can get laughs where you wouldn't expect them. But he also deftly handles the more emotional scenes. A sequence where Gina sits with Jim in hospital as he's recovering from a stroke, makes me well up every time.

Vic Reeves is a huge figure in the comedy world. So much so, that when we're talking on set it's sometimes difficult to remember to call him Jim rather than Vic. He's a fascinating man, though often far more reserved than you might expect. Although that's what they say about me. Apart from the fascinating bit.

Most of our conversations revolve around art and music. He is, unsurprisingly, a Fall fan and he and Mark know each other of old. In fact Jim's singular perspective, his defiantly English persona, his unpredictability and his longevity make him one of the few cultural figures comparable to Mark.

And so, one night I go out on a pub-crawl with Mark E. Smith and Vic Reeves. The problem is, when it comes to alcohol, I am an unseeded amateur, whilst the two of them are operating at an Olympic level.

At the end of a day's filming, Jim and I catch a cab to the 'Kro-Bar', one of a number of large, stylish but anodyne bars that have sprung up in the city centre over recent years. Mark is already here, standing at the bar ordering a drink. As Jim and I approach, he turns and his face cracks into a wide smile. "Alright pal." He says as we hug. He greets Jim with similar enthusiasm. Yet, as we sit at a table, the mood is initially awkward with Jim and Mark seeming somewhat guarded with each other. But as the drink kicks in, the conversation begins to flow and soon I'm creased up with laughter, as Mark goes into a daft routine about how the health service is determined to wipe out the working class male.

After a couple of pints, we wander off in search of somewhere better. We pass a bar that has a beer garden with several large mosaics of Manchester icons on its walls, including one of Mark himself. "You see that place?" Says Mark, pointing at his mosaic. "I'm actually banned from there."

We end up in another bar, where Mark tells a story of a convoluted run in with his neighbours, and Jim explains what a tricky operation it is to purchase Tom Baker's house. By now I've drunk three and a half pints. Which is pretty much my limit for being able to tell a fully functioning anecdote. So I leave it to the professionals.

We move to a pub, the name of which escapes me. We go through into the back garden area so Mark can smoke. Jim pulls out his camera and proceeds to take photos of us. As soon as he sees the camera, Mark begins assuming poses. Yet somehow the poses he assumes are unassuming poses. He pulls out an umbrella and stands nonchalantly against the brick wall. Jim chuckles "Give it to me baby".

Sometime later, we're in another small pub in a side street. Mark buys a round of beers with whisky chasers. I really shouldn't have drunk the whisky chaser. But apparently I did. Because after this, things start to get a bit inchoate. Although I clearly remember the bar maid, who is apparently an acquaintance of Mark's, coming over and inviting us to see their upstairs function room. "It's been completely refurbished." She says. "You'll be amazed Mark."

She leads us up the stairs. It is definitely not amazing. And it doesn't look like it's been refurbished. It looks like a small dusty room with lots of chairs stacked up on the stage. Nevertheless, the bar maid shows us around as if she's unveiling a new Disneyland. Mark nods politely and makes vaguely encouraging sounds. Jim turns to me and whispers "What's going on? Why are we up here?" I haven't a clue.

We return downstairs and Jim orders another round. I opt out as I'm still struggling to make my way through my previous pint. I wander unsteadily to the toilets and on my way back I'm accosted by a plump teenage girl in heavy metal apparel, who appears to have dyed her black hair grey. I can tell this, because her black roots are showing. She tells me she's a big *Ideal* fan and invites me to go home and smoke a bong with her and her mother. She beckons her mother over. Her mother looks about 55, is incredibly skinny, yet dressed almost identically. She however, has naturally grey hair with no need to dye it. I decline their kind offer and totter back to join Mark and Jim.

Jim announces that we are going to move on to another bar. I nod, then pause. On close inspection this is a bad idea. In fact even on distant inspection it's a bad idea. I'm already as topped up on toxins as I will ever need to be. I announce that I have to head back to my apartment. Mark purses his lips and leans his head to one side. "Are you sure about that cock?" They both try to convince me to stick with them on their voyage. But I bow out. Although I don't bow low enough, as I crack my head on the doorframe of the taxi as I climb inside, my coordination shot away. I slur the address to the driver and slump back in the seat.

The next evening Mark phones up and berates me for leaving them. "Why'd you leave so soon?" He asks in a mock angry voice. "Because I can't carry on drinking like you can." I explain. "I had to work today. I had to get up and be responsible on set. Not be so hung over I can't function." As it happened, I could barely function anyway, I'd been hung over all day and at lunchtime, I'd snuck off into the show's pub set and grabbed 20 minutes sleep on one of the padded seats. "You can't hold your drink." Mark says mockingly. "I know! That's what I'm saying!"

A few months later, Mark and I decide to resurrect a couple of the ideas from *Inexplicable* and rework them as a feature film script entitled *The Otherwise*. We develop an idea about a haunted recording studio on Pendle Hill and a gaggle of soldiers from the Jacobite rebellion who are trapped in the present day. The narrative also features Mark and The Fall, who are recording an EP at the aforementioned studio.

I assume that although we're working out the storyline together I'll be the one writing most of the dialogue. However, whilst he's away on tour, Mark starts to send me whole scenes through the post. They are written in his spidery handwriting and often accompanied by his quirky biro drawings. His ear for dialogue is great and in the end it feels like a real 50/50 collaboration. Although it takes a while to complete the script, as we're both fitting it in around other things, we end up with something that feels really exciting and unpredictable. We confidently approach a number of different film production companies with the project. The response is always the same; "It's too weird for me."

DAVID BOWIE

WEMBLEY ARENA, LONDON

WEDNESDAY 26TH NOVEMBER 2003

(AGE 39)

I'm on the phone. I'm being held in a queue. I've been held in this queue for just over an hour. However, my call is very important to them. I can be quite certain of this, because I'm being told it every three minutes.

All I want to do is buy a couple of tickets to see David Bowie playing at Wembley Arena, as part of his A Reality tour. The gig is months away yet, but the tickets will sell out very quickly. I saw the shows advertised in the back of *Mojo* music magazine and immediately decided it would make the perfect birthday present for Sarah. So I noted the day the tickets would be going on sale. And today is that day.

Being held in this queue means I'm forced to listen to an endless piece of bland Vangelis style music – a simple keyboard melody loops over and over... And over and over... And over and over... Suddenly, it abruptly cuts out in the middle of a bar. Finally I'm going to speak with a real human. An upbeat voice informs me that my call is very important to them. This catches me out almost every time. Soon I'm back to the cloying familiarity of the endlessly looping melody...

At the age of 13, after falling under Bowie's spell, courtesy of *The Man Who Fell To Earth* and then having been bewitched by *ChangesOneBowie*, my next move had been to buy his latest single. And his latest single turned out to be 'Beauty And The Beast'. Nothing had quite prepared me for this.

1977/78 was of course a period when various punk bands were releasing singles that aimed to disrupt and disturb. But, more often than not, they were attempting to do so by paring back popular music to its rock and blues roots. Bowie meanwhile, was creating a far more destabilizing soundworld by engaging with technological advances and – spurred on by collaborator Brian Eno – using chance elements in the creation of both song structure and lyrics.

Compared to say the accelerated pub rock of The Damned, or the Doors styled garage rock of The Stranglers, Bowie's 'Beauty And The Beast' came across as some uncategorisable mutant form. With its fat, off kilter squelchy bass line, its seasick synth tones and lyrics which tell of *"slaughter in the air"* and how *"someone could get skinned"* it was an audaciously unsettling choice for a single. Particularly when the album contained the far more radio friendly disco groove of 'The Secret Life of Arabia'.

Suddenly, the tape of the looping piano cuts out and a young woman asks me how she may help. After such a long wait, buying the actual tickets takes just a couple of minutes. They don't arrive in time for Sarah's birthday, so instead I clip out the advert from the magazine and put it inside her card. She's delighted.

Two months later, Sarah drives us up to London. We arrive in plenty of time and find a parking space in a residential area just a short walk from the venue. It's a cool and still night and we wander down towards Wembley Arena, holding hands and chatting in excited voices. We arrive to join the streams of people making their way inside. It takes us quite a while to find the right entrance and once inside progress slows, as we wade through a flood of happily buzzing people.

We make our way up three flights of stairs to the stalls on the right hand side, very close to the front of the venue, second row back, overlooking the stage. The site lines are perfect. And our timing is pretty good too. We barely have time to unbutton our jackets before a portion of the house lights dim and the Dandy Warhols walk out onto the stage. Maybe four or five hundred people applaud, but it doesn't sound like much in this enormous space.

The Dandy Warhols' first three albums succeeded in creating the kind of ersatz garage/glam that means I've always had a soft spot for them. Inexplicably however, for their fourth album *Welcome to the Monkey House*, the band has suddenly decided the best way to operate in 2003, is to start recording songs that sound like they were recorded in 1983.[1] The production is shiny and airless, whilst synths, keyboards and tightly programmed drum patterns are allowed to dominate. Of course they are a band that have always excelled at repurposing secondhand ideas. Even the title of their new album is stolen from a collection of Kurt Vonnegut short stories. But this 80s vision of the band feels too uptight and sterile.

I've seen them play a couple of times before and they always pump a lot of effort into their performances – never more so than tonight. But it's hard to make an impression in such an enormous space, when two thirds of the audience are absent, or finding their way to their seats. Another thing that isn't helping is the volume. They are way too quiet. This is a huge space and the sound of the band just isn't filling it. But then this is all part of stadium gig etiquette. Holding back the impact of full volume for the headliner.

During the interval, Sarah and I sit discussing the composition of the audience. This is without doubt the most mixed crowd I've ever seen at a gig. It's almost like we're being presented with the definitive cross section of the live music audience. There are serious devotees in their 40s and 50s who have probably caught Bowie on most of his tours. At the other end of the spectrum, there are a surprising amount of teenagers. Some may have only recently discovered Bowie and still be encountering the various components of his back catalogue – quite an enviable position to be in really. There are office worker types in glittery outfits and feather boas, looking like they've come out for a 70s

---

1. Musical revivalism is a curious thing. It tends to operate around a 20 year gap. The 1950s were big in the 1970s, the 1960s were big in the 1980s, the 1970s were big in the 1990s, the 1980s were big in the 2000s, whilst the 1990s are big in the 2010s.

night. There are some very straight looking people in their 60s, who probably rarely venture out to see live music. Hell, there's even a gaggle of Goths. And then there's me. The sort of person who thinks he can divide other people into easily definable categories whilst somehow remaining separate from them all. There's a category for us too: Smug.

But the one thing we all have in common is we are very glad to be here tonight. Let's face it, if you're a music fan you will have definitely been touched by Bowie's work. Either you love all his albums and singles, or you love most of them, or you love some of them, or you love just one song. At the very least, you will love a band or artist who has been influenced by him. Like The Beatles and The Velvet Underground, Bowie's fingerprints are all over contemporary culture.

When the house lights dim once more, there is a huge cheer and towering waves of applause. The musicians assemble and play a short instrumental intro. Then, the stage lights slam on, and Bowie is revealed as the band power straight into 'Rebel Rebel'. The eruption of cheers makes me gasp. A collective energy wave of love, respect and admiration surges through the arena, a palpable force. Festivals aside, I very seldom go to gigs of this scale. I generally find them too impersonal. I find it hard to engage with a distant figure and I'm also resistant to the idea of seated gigs. But in this moment, caught in the emotional heat blast of thousands of grateful people, I feel my eyes pricking.

Bowie is dressed in a grey velvet tailcoat, converse trainers, tight fitting black jeans and a bright white T-shirt. His dyed blond hair is cut into a stylish centre-parting, and he looks lean, handsome and still somehow boyish. In fact he looks fitter and sexier at 56 than most men do at 26.

'Rebel Rebel' is a fine choice for an opener. Powered by one of the greatest riffs of the glam era, it's the most covered song in Bowie's catalogue and has a timeless energy that connects immediately with a live audience. And yet, to be truthful, this isn't the best version of 'Rebel Rebel' you could wish for. It feels like the band are holding back, and thereby throwing the song away a little. Whereas one of the biggest appeals of the original cut is the way the riff just keeps driving on and on, here, after the opening four bars, guitarist Earl Slick strips it down to a bare, choppy syncopated rendering of the chords. This works, but it definitely robs the song of some of its innate power. But, when the riff comes back at full force, it lifts the song, and the audience, to a greater height. At the end of the final bar, the music drops away, Bowie purrs out the line *"Hey baby, let's stay out tonight"* and the crowd bursts into cacophonous applause.

"Thank you." Says Bowie. "Welcome." Nothing more than that. But for many it is enough to illicit more cheers of adulation. The band plunges into 'New Killer Star' from Bowie's latest album *Reality*. It's one of his more straight-ahead rock numbers. It's an okay song, but far from a special composition. The band follows it up with the album's title track. This is also played with vim and conviction, but again it isn't Grade A material. In all honesty, although it is a collection with moments of melodic invention and smart lyrical conceits, *Reality* is unlikely to make it into many people's top five Bowie albums.[2]

I take advantage of this early lull to size up the stage. Over the years, Bowie has had some impressive stage sets. The expressionist sky-scrapers of the *Diamond Dogs* tour and the giant neon arachnid of The Glass Spider Tour being particularly notable. Tonight's design isn't quite in the same league as those. Tonight's set is a few upside down tree branches painted white, and some bits of gossamer drapery. As far as set dressing for one of the world's most revered musical geniuses goes, it looks like an austere Christmas display in the Co-op window. But never mind, that's not why we're here.

Next, the band tears into 'Fashion'. And it's only really at this point, when everything comes into focus. The whole song feels jagged and volatile, with second guitarist Gerry Leonard matching the angular bite of Robert Fripp's original guitar parts. Gail Anne Dorsey's bass has real strength and fluidity, whilst Sterling Campbell's drumming injects a

---

2. In case you were wondering, and you probably weren't, but here goes... 1) *Low.* 2) *"Heroes".* 3) *1. Outside.* 4) *Diamond Dogs* . 5) *Blackstar.*

forceful bounce, giving the song far more forward propulsion than the original. Bowie seems to properly come alive at this point too. Despite the size of the venue, he's able to project his persona right out into the furthest reaches of the audience. It's something which I've observed in live performances by other major league stars such as Nick Cave, Grace Jones, John Lydon and yes, if I'm honest, Cliff Richard.

Bowie means different things to different people. Therefore, tonight's highlights come at different points for different people. For some, it's the soul pomp of 'Under Pressure' with Dorsey interpreting Freddie Mercury's part with passion and vigour. For many, it's the glittering treasures of his glam era; a high energy 'Hang on To Yourself', a Beatles-ish take on 'Life on Mars?', a stomping stripped back performance of 'The Jean Genie', where Bowie's harmonica playing has an authentic bluesy swell, or a mass sing-along of 'Starman'. For others, it's his 80s pop moments 'Ashes to Ashes' and 'China Girl'. And it's just possible there are some here tonight for whom the highlights will be 'the new stuff'. They will not leave disappointed either.

Bowie introduces what he describes as "A new very, very quiet track." It's 'The Loneliest Guy', a sad, contemplative song that is very much the highlight of *Reality*. Here, Bowie's voice is supported only by some cool synth pads from dreadlocked keyboardist Catherine Russell and Mike Garson's thoughtful piano work. Garson is a highly skilled and deeply expressive player and it's not hard to see why Bowie has been regularly calling on his services for over 30 years.

Bowie's esteemed producer Tony Visconti once said of him: "Mike Garson listens attentively, then plays whatever the hell he wants". In fact, Garson is reportedly the only member of the touring band who is allowed to improvise. His most famous Bowie collaboration will always be his wild atonal two-chord solo on the title track of *Aladdin Sane*. But Garson has also contributed outstanding work to many subsequent albums and tours. I'm especially fond of his Rachmaninoff style flourishes on 1974's 'Sweet Thing/Candidate' and his endlessly circling lines on 'A Small Plot of Land' from 1995's *1. Outside.*

But 'The Loneliest Guy' doesn't display any of Garson's trademark mania. In fact, it's the gentlest, most low-key thing we'll hear tonight. Yet the audience is largely silent throughout. As the final chords fade, Bowies smiles in appreciation. "Thank you. What a lovely attentive audience you are." He says. "That was really good. Cookies and milk, cookies and milk." The audience applauds the fact they've just been praised by their chosen one. "You get some rock and roll, after a quick nap on the top of your desks." The cookies and milk come in the form of a sprightly version of 'The Man Who Sold the World' followed by a frenetic interpretation of 'Hallo Spaceboy', which powers along on Campbell's double time hi-hat and cymbal smashes, then slams to a halt.

Leonard then starts to pick out clusters of echoing notes on his guitar, Russell adds a sequence of soft synth tones and Bowie begins to sing in his deepest baritone. It's a tender take on 'Sunday' from the *Heathen* album. It's one of Bowie's strongest songs of recent years and, in some ways, it recalls the bruised majesty of mid period Scott Walker. But then, as Bowie steps away from the mic Earl Slick moves into a spotlight and begins an extended and uninspired guitar solo. Showy, yet utilitarian – it sounds like oh so many other guitar solos I've heard. And it's far from the only such moment tonight.

The issue isn't that Bowie's recorded work doesn't contain guitar solos. It's the fact that it contains such strong and idiosyncratic ones. Think of Mick Ronson's emotive solo on 'Moonage Daydream', Robert Fripp's multilayered storm of notes on "Heroes", or best of all, Adrian Belew's contribution to 'Boys Keep Swinging'. Probably the most abstract guitar solo ever to appear on a pop single, it builds and evolves into a manic coruscating barrage. And, at one minute ten seconds, it also takes up just over a third of the song's entire length. Yet it earns every moment of its tortured existence.

In contrast, tonight Slick presents us with standard issue guitar solos. He's an accomplished and seasoned musician and he plays with some brio, but to my ears, his solos wouldn't feel at all out of place in a live performance by say Bruce Springsteen or even Whitesnake. And that is definitely not a good thing.

In recent interviews, Bowie has been continually praising his band. In fact, the *Reality* album seems to have been put together very much with a band aesthetic in mind. With one ear on how it might be performed in public. And Bowie is nothing if not generous, with the performance creating space for the individual musicians to breathe.

Bowie doesn't speak much tonight. But tellingly, when he does, he hardly ever uses the word "I". It's almost always "we" and "us". This is no accident. He wants to give us the impression of a band, not a star with his backing musicians. Or rather he wants to give us the impression of someone who is being *seen* to try and give the impression of a band, not a star with his backing musicians. In reality he knows all the audience are focused on is Bowie.

The set's penultimate song is 'I'm Afraid of Americans'. The band performs it with considerable attack and the song glowers with energy. But unlike the studio version, which has a subtle shifting electronic unease in the verses that contrasts with the chorus' big fat power chords, here the whole thing is levelled out to a form of brutal, polished but ultimately anonymous rock.

"Thank you for a real good time." Says Bowie at the song's conclusion. Like the phrase "cookies and milk", it's another Americanism that speaks of a man who has spent his most recent years living in New York. Then, the band pitch into a song which will most likely be near the top of most people's wish lists tonight: "Heroes". Although, like the opening 'Rebel Rebel', it is performed in a stripped down fashion, throwing away the original's emotional dynamics. Most of the ambiguity and anxiety that are manifest in the original are ditched in favour of the song's more celebratory aspects. But it seems churlish to complain. After all, this is one of the greatest stars of our age, playing one of the greatest songs of our age.

"Thank you so much." Says Bowie. "From *all of us*, thank you so much." He waves, bows and is gone. His set has lasted for an hour and forty minutes, but it's felt like 25 minutes tops. In contrast, the cheering and clapping and calls for more seem to go on forever.

Finally, Bowie and his band return to the stage. The wait has been just long enough for us to start thinking maybe they wont return after all. We couldn't *be* more grateful to see them again. Bowie has changed into a short jacket and has a white Supro Dual Tone guitar over his shoulder. "I feel like I know each and every one of you." He says. Pure show biz corn of course. But what he *does* know is that this is what each and every one of us wants to believe.

Suddenly we're plunged into a pumping version of 'White Light/White Heat'. And Lou Reed's breakneck hymn to the agonies and ecstasies of methamphetamine has never sounded more vital. Way, way better than The Velvets at Glastonbury, this is a tour de force. It's exhilarating to hear three rhythm guitars hammering away at the same simple chord progression. And that's one of the strengths of what's happening here. The band is keeping it simple. No elaborate solos, no fussy arrangements. Garson's piano work is sublime, colouring the song with his splashy unhinged playing, whilst Russell and Dorsey's soulful, full throated backing vocals add considerable depth to the sound.

As the song ends and applause fills the arena, Bowie passes his electric guitar to a roadie and straps on an acoustic guitar. The next song is 'Five Years'. So attuned are the audience, that there are cheers of recognition at simply the first three drumbeats. Bowie's performance on the recorded version is one of his best of the era. And tonight he serves the material well, his voice alive with shifting emotion, whilst the chorus provides another opportunity for a mass audience sing-along.

"Thank you." Says Bowie. "We'll keep going to that place shall we huh?" The venue fills with cheering. This encore will be pure vintage 1972 Bowie. He grabs the mic stand as the band drive into the instantly recognisable opening of 'Suffragette City'. The story goes that Bowie had originally offered this song to Mott The Hoople. They rather surprisingly declined it, leading to Bowie himself recording the song as a late addition to the *Ziggy Stardust* album.

With its high-energy riff and rolling Little Richard-esque piano line, 'Suffragette City' is made for live performance. As Slick slides into a brief guitar break, Bowie peels off his jacket and tosses it aside. Then, as

Russell's keyboards effortlessly mimic a full horn section, the band build to the song's most famous moment. The sound of over a thousand people shouting *'Wham-bam thank you mam!'* is simultaneously ludicrous and totally life affirming. Then the band plunges into the extended outro. Once again, Garson's keyboard work has space to shine. His playing is so bright and euphoric I feel myself getting choked up by his sheer abandon.

The song reaches a climax and Bowie waves at the audience. "Thank you. Goodnight folks. We'll see you again. Miss you. Oh yeah." Another collective energy wave moves through the building. This one radiates a sensation which says "Oh no! He's going!". But Bowie is the consummate showman. It's been reported that in press interviews he employs an unusual technique. When the allocated time for the interview is up, his assistant will come in to inform Bowie and the interviewer of this. But then Bowie invariably says something along the lines of "Oh? But we're having such a nice time, let's just have ten more minutes." After that, how could a journalist write anything negative about such a generous soul?

Here tonight, he pulls a variation on the same trick. Bowie really knows how to make an audience feel grateful. He's already said "goodnight". We think he's going for good. But he's *not* going. He's *staying*. In fact he's about to do another song. And it's *that* song. Another collective energy wave moves through the venue. This is gratitude on an epic scale.

The opening notes of 'Ziggy Stardust' are met with near euphoria. For many, this will always be Bowie's definitive statement. A rock icon playing the role of a fictional rock icon. A feedback loop establishing him as one of the brightest stars in the cultural firmament. That twisting riff is possibly the most potent of all Bowie's compositions. And again the band keeps it simple, avoiding elaboration. But it is Bowie's voice and words that carry us along to that final line. He draws out the word "played", then draws out the word "guitar" even further, still able to hold a pitch perfect note. And the arena explodes into rapturous applause and cheers. And Sarah and I are right there with them. This may not have been the best gig I've ever been to, but that was without question, the best encore I've ever seen.

Bowie takes a step forward, towards the lip of the stage. Scores of people are down there, reaching up towards him, a coral reef of arms swaying at his feet. Bowie reaches down and briefly touches one guy's hand. A simple but powerful gesture. To make contact with two or three audience members would be sweet but meaningless to the rest of the crowd. But to touch just the one has a symbolic resonance. Bowie is connecting not just with that person, but with the entire arena. The audience instinctively sense this and the gesture is met with a roar of approval. Bowie knows his stagecraft inside out. He then bows, making sure he does so to each area of the arena in turn. The applause and cheering eclipse any response I've ever heard at a live music event.

He beckons his band forward. They assemble in a line, sweaty and beaming. Bowie beckons them closer. They collectively shuffle forwards. He holds up his hands to halt them, then indicates they should shuffle back a little. They do so. Smiling, Bowie indicates they should stop. They do so. This seems calculated to display what a tight knit and playful crew they are, whilst subliminally showing us that Bowie is unquestionably the one in the driving set. He skips over to the line up of musicians and slips in between Campbell and Russell. Arms around each other's shoulders, Bowie and his band bow. Again they are careful to bow to each and every area of the auditorium. The applause goes on and on and on. We would be happy to watch Bowie bow all night.[3]

* * * * *

On the morning of Monday 10th January 2016, I walk into the kitchen to make myself some breakfast. I didn't sleep well and I'm feeling a little

---

3. Stretching from 19th August 2003 through to 25th June 2004, in terms of individual dates, the A Reality tour was the longest Bowie would ever undertake. And, although he would make sporadic live appearances at one off events, this would turn out to be his last ever tour.

vague. I fill the kettle. As the water splashes, I catch the radio news announcer saying something about Bowie confirming that his father has passed away. "Wow." I think. "Bowie's dad must have been a ripe old age!"

I sit down at the breakfast table and I'm about to start flicking through Facebook on my mobile phone when I tune in properly to what's being said on the radio. *David Bowie* is dead. What I'd first heard was a report of Duncan Jones confirming that *his* father had died. It never occurred to me that David Bowie *himself* could have died. I mean, how could he have died? He's *David Bowie*. Tears are spilling out of my eyes.

Suddenly I have a vision of myself back in another kitchen. Back at my parents' house in 1980, hearing of the death of Ian Curtis and staring blankly at a bowl of Rice Krispies. Whereas that news numbed me, this has bitten me deeply.

The only other time I've been so swept away by the death of a public figure was on the 25th October 2004, when I suddenly received a text from my good friend Steve North, which simply read 'Fuck! Peel's dead!' With Bowie's passing, like John Peel's, there's the realisation of how much blander the world would have been without their presence. All the innovations, all the advances, all the differences, all the chain reactions, all the ripples. Throughout his career, Bowie was unconsciously writing permission slips for wave after wave of contemporaries and younger artists.

I text Sarah and Pete and a few other friends for whom I know Bowie is of totemic importance. Across the country, thousands of people are doing the same thing. Texting or calling friends about their sense of loss and disbelief. I spend the rest of the day lying on the sofa, vaguely trying to work on a script. But I can't concentrate. Yet, despite the fact many radio stations are now playing non-stop Bowie, I can't listen to any of his music today. It would just swamp me with sadness.

All day yesterday I was listening to what I suddenly realise is Bowie's final album: *Blackstar*. It's by far his strongest set since 1995's *1. Outside*. Like that album, it's dark and detailed, with elements of both art rock and jazz in an amalgam which privileges mood, atmosphere and stark dramatics. The highlight may be 'Girl Loves Me', a slab of morphine-paced sidereal funk, partly articulated via homosexual polari and the nadsat of *A Clockwork Orange*. Over the coming weeks it proves impossible to listen to *Blackstar* without becoming entangled in both the shock and emotions summoned by Bowie's passing and the deeply personal nature of the lyrics.

2016 turns out to be the year of celebrity death overload. Swathes of broadcasters, actors, writers and sports personalities are cut down. But the world of music perhaps suffers the most, with the death of not just Bowie, but Leonard Cohen, Prince, George Michael, Rick Parfitt, Lemmy and George Martin. It's the year Britain votes to leave the EU. It's the year Donald Trump, a gnawing ache in human form, wins the US elections. It is a negative, destructive and spiteful year.

A joke begins to circulate that David Bowie made his exit at the very start of January because he knew what a garbage fire of a year 2016 was going to be. Another thought is advanced, which suggests that Bowie had been the glue that had been holding everything together. As the awful year grinds on, this begins to feel less and less fanciful.

* * * * *

I never met David Bowie. Let's face it, if I had have done, I would have mentioned it by now. Although, I do know a few friends who were fortunate enough to meet the man. And I must confess I'm pretty damn envious. The closest I ever came (and to be honest, it's not very close at all, in fact it's a looooooong way off) was meeting *Angie* Bowie.

In 1994, Malcolm and I were developing a sit-com script with the transgender comedienne and singer Lana Pillay. Lana was working as a compere at a stand up night that took place at The Broadwalk, 19 Greek Street in Soho – previously the site of Peter Cook's fabled 1960s comedy club The Establishment. Angie, who is a good friend of Lana's, turned up at the launch night, accompanied by Leee Black Childers – a man steeped in counter cultural history. Childers was a photographer at Warhol's Factory, and besides having managed some of Bowie's tours, he had also had the unenviable task of working as day to day manager of both Iggy and the Stooges and Johnny Thunders and the Heartbreakers.

Childers was 48 but looked older, his face creased with laughter lines. Ever the rocker, he was clad in brothel creepers, skinny black jeans, leopard skin shirt and tightly fitted satin jacket. He was chatty and friendly, especially since I was asking the kind of fan boy questions he must have been asked innumerable times before.

But it was the 45 year old Angie who dominated proceedings. Dressed in a short black dress and grey tights, her peroxide blond hair cropped stylishly short, with her broad smile and high, clear voice, she was a big presence. She was already a little drunk when she arrived and was acting daft, but her enthusiasm for life was infectious and she made me laugh a lot. Weirdly, although I felt quite comfortable probing Childers and asking what it was like trying to keep early 70s Iggy Pop under control ("The guy was damn near unmanageable." being the perhaps unsurprising answer) I somehow didn't feel I had the right to ask Angie about her past. If there is such a thing as awe by proxy, I felt it that night.

THROBBING GRISTLE

HEAVEN, LONDON

SUNDAY 21ST JUNE 2009

(AGE 45)

Today is Father's Day. I've always struggled with my own role as a father. I still feel too much of a kid myself to be a dad.

Also, like just about every other man, I simply don't feel qualified. However, as I do have three sons, maybe I should have mastered it by now. Either that, or at least stopped worrying about the fact I'm so utterly useless at it.

Sarah and I have two young boys: Lucian is 8, lean as a whippet, thoughtful and soulful with large blue eyes, like a Lucian Freud portrait – hence his name. Marius is just 2 years old, impossibly cute and full of burbling enthusiasm for life. Misha turned 19 this year. It's fair to say he's always been sonically open-minded. For his 17th birthday, we went to a Nurse With Wound concert. That's the level of parenting we're talking about here.

It's been a real pleasure introducing him to all kinds of music. But it's been an even greater pleasure having him introduce me to bands I was unaware of. I can remember the joy I felt the first time he played me the *Cryptograms* album by Deerhunter. They are a band that has gone on to become a household favourite. I'm talking about my *own* household here obviously. I don't imagine the entire nation enjoys sitting down to eat dinner accompanied by 'Tape Hiss Orchid'.

It's been a good weekend. My old friend John Blackett has come down to stay with us. These days he lives just outside Preston with two young sons and a lovely wife called Helen. Although we talk on the phone from time to time, John and I don't get to see each other much – maybe once every couple of years. But whenever we do meet, we click straight back in. No awkwardness, no small talk. And hardly a mention of our shared past as Long Macs.

Last night, John and I went out for a drink and sat outside the Tin Drum wine bar. He said it felt a bit odd being in Brighton, as he knew an old ex-girlfriend lived here now. Many years ago, they'd been very much in love, but things had gone sour and they'd parted on very bad terms with lots of unresolved issues. They'd since lost contact and he didn't know how to get in touch.

A couple of minutes later, we're talking about music, when John gives a little gasp. "God!" He whispers. "That's her!" I see a slender woman with long dark hair walking on the opposite side of the road. She glances over, seems to notice John, but then walks on.

Brighton is a decent sized city. The odds on her walking past us – and at this exact moment – seem slight. "That was definitely her." Says John. He agonizes over whether or not to go after her, but in the end decides that as she definitely saw him, if she'd have wanted to talk, she would have come over. The conversation moves on, but John's mind is clearly a little blown by the close encounter.

This morning, after I receive sweet hand drawn Father's Day cards from Lucian, Marius and Misha, John and I visit a nearby boot market. I've got into the habit of coming here every week and I've found some excellent boot market bounty – a beautiful glass paperweight the size of a football, an old fashioned metronome and a small and slightly battered lithograph by the surrealist Yves Tanguy. This week however, does not look like a vintage week. John and I wander past trestle tables of bric-a-brac and boxes of old vinyl albums, blankets laid on the ground covered with kids toys, displays of once adored ornaments and car boots full of unwanted books.

Suddenly, John grips my arm. "Graham, I can't believe it!" He whispers. "That's her again!" I glance back, a couple of stalls away from us, the same dark haired woman is standing behind a table full of books and household items. The odds on this happening seem slighter still. John takes a moment then goes over to talk to her. In the absence of finding any boot market bounty, I wander off to buy some free-range eggs.

Later, back at the house, John tells me how glad he is he made the effort to go and talk. The two of them were able to open up, clear the air and part on good terms. *That* was today's boot market bounty.

John leaves mid afternoon for the long drive back up to Preston. I wave him off, go back inside and phone my Dad to wish him a happy Father's Day. My relationship with my Dad is loving but distant. It's like we're always slightly shy of each other. I tell him I'm going up to London later to see a band. I don't mention that it's Throbbing Gristle. It won't mean anything to him. And let's face it, even if it did, it's hardly likely to suggest anything positive. "It'll be a lot busier in London these days than when I first used to go." This is what he's started saying whenever I mention going to London.

Afterwards I manage to squeeze in an hour's worth of writing. There remains nothing outside of sex that gives me as much pleasure as writing. I have occasionally pondered on the possibility of finding a way to combine the two activities. Sadly I think it would lead to an awful lot of typos. Having said that, I do usually combine writing with another of life's great pleasures; listening to music.

Recently, my writing has been soundtracked by Fever Ray's eerie self titled debut, Telepathe's warm and witchy album *Dance Mother* and Dälek's *Gutter Tactics* – a marriage of strident hip-hop and post rock textures. However, the album that has probably been annoying the neighbours the most is the latest offering from the reformed Throbbing Gristle: *The Third Mind Movements*.

Formed in 1975, Throbbing Gristle, grew out of the confrontational performance art group Coum Transmissions. They consisted of Genesis P. Orridge on bass, violin and vocals, Cosey Fanni Tutti on cornet and guitar which was manipulated rather than played, and Chris Carter and Peter 'Sleazy' Christopherson on a variety of prepared tapes, synths and electronic devices, many of them home made. Throbbing Gristle's early sound was abrasive and pugnacious. There was no drummer in their line up, yet their music frequently deployed strong rhythmic pulses, whilst P. Orridge's vocals were often spoken, intoned, shouted or chanted.

Throbbing Gristle referred to their music as Industrial and set up their own label: Industrial Records. Initially, they chose as their subject matter the most base and abject elements of humanity – murder, totalitarianism, sex crimes and so on. Yet, once these became perceived as Industrial music's normative topics, Throbbing Gristle began to integrate other interests such as arcane magick, personal empowerment and musical exotica.

Yet, I missed all this. Unlikely though it seems now – when I consider what a huge impact they have had on my creative work – during their original lifetime, Throbbing Gristle passed me by. Although perhaps that's not entirely surprising, as despite regular record releases and live appearances, most of the time, the British music press of the late 70s and early 80s treated the group with contempt, viewing them at best as arty poseurs, at worst as degenerate con artists. That's if they bothered to write about them at all.

Consequently, I'd heard the name but remained unaware of their music. It was only through my inspirational introduction to Psychic TV in 1983, that I got acquainted with Throbbing Gristle's back catalogue.

Their 1977 debut *Second Annual Report* is a deeply unsettling collection, largely culled from early live appearances. It's a brutal, ugly and very, very bleak album. In direct contrast, this was followed by the single 'United', a sweet and melodic synth-pop love song (albeit one which quotes Aleister Crowley). Their second album: *D.o.A. The Third & Final Report* (1978) retains their predilection for confrontational sounds, but also takes in more minimal pieces, found recordings and Tangerine Dream style electronics. This was followed by *20 Jazz Funk Greats* (1979), which, despite its title, is actually a blend of all the styles they had mastered thus far, with the addition of some subtle spectral instrumentals. And, whilst none of the album's recordings come anywhere near being jazz funk, they do also briefly experiment with a form of mutant disco.

However, their masterpiece is *Heathen Earth* (1980). A live album, but one recorded in their own studio, in front of an invited audience.

A richly pulsing compound of electronics, adorned with P. Orridge's manifesto like lyrics, heavily treated washes of guitar and bursts of wailing cornet, it perfectly encapsulates the group's appeal. I am in thrall to much of their work, but *Heathen Earth* is the album I return to again and again.

People tend to have a lot of preconceptions about Throbbing Gristle. Often, they have decided they hate them, without having heard a single note of their music. I'm happy to say I've played *Heathen Earth* to several of these people and ended up converting them. It's a recording where the group sound like nobody but themselves and the music is presented as a seamless flow of expression and invention. In fact, if you're in the mood for a piece of crass reductionism, *Heathen Earth* is Industrial music's *Dark Side of the Moon*. There, I've said it. And instantly regretted it.

In spite of the censorious and ignorant nature of the contemporary music press, since their termination in 1981, Throbbing Gristle have cast a pitch-black shadow over nearly 30 years of music. Their influence has been evident in a diverse range of musicians, artists and DJs. From Soft Cell to Carl Craig. From Antony Hegarty to Nine Inch Nails. From Andrew Weatherall to Jake and Dinos Chapman. In fact, many of the group's experiments have prefigured entire musical movements. The looping pulses of trance, the brittle melodies of 80s synth pop, the spacious caverns of techno, the rigid uber-on kick drum of gabba, the bestial assault of grindcore, the claustrophobic bass pressure of early dub step, the sparking walls of noise in power electronics, all of these and more were elements of Throbbing Gristle's soundworld during their original period of operations.

And yet, despite the pervasive nature of their influence, Throbbing Gristle remain steadfast outsiders. Unlike many other musica*l bêtes noires*, they seem impervious to absorption into the world of advertising. Over recent years, aside from seeing The Fall help to sell Vauxhalls, I've seen The Velvet Underground's 'Venus in Furs' used to flog tires and Iggy Pop's 'Lust For Life' soundtracking commercials for Saga holidays. However, Throbbing Gristle have a diamond hard carapace that cannot easily be digested by the caustic juices of the mainstream.

As I walk into Brighton train station, the murky breath-steps of Throbbing Gristle's 'Perception Is The Only Reality' are playing through my ipod headphones. I buy a return ticket to London and board the largely empty train. I see Simon Fanshawe sitting at a table. I go and join him. He's a smart, witty and friendly man. He started out as a stand-up comedian and we did a few gigs together, at The Zap back in the early 80s, when I was performing with Obelisk. But Simon was always in a different league and he went on to win The Perrier Award, at the 1989 Edinburgh Fringe. These days, he works as a consultant with public and private companies helping to promote equality and diversity.

Simon asks where I'm bound. I tell him I'm meeting my friend Malcolm and we're going to see Throbbing Gristle in Heaven. "Oh?" He says, slightly amused. "You don't look how I imagine Throbbing Gristle fans look." I'm six foot two, with a shaven head and a goatee. I think he might be surprised just how many Throbbing Gristle fans look like me. Although perhaps he's referring to the fact I'm wearing a brown linen suit. That said, the group have a far broader fan base than popular myth would lead you to expect. Whilst they have a reputation for being an incredibly niche concern, appealing only to seekers of the extreme, I am frequently surprised by the people I meet for whom Throbbing Gristle are a major touchstone.

I say goodbye to Simon at Victoria Station and catch the tube to Embankment. I meet Malcolm in The Princess Of Wales pub on Villiers Street, just across the road from Heaven. He's in good spirits and as ever makes me laugh way too loud. We stand on the pavement outside, sipping lagers, the heat from the day still rising from the paving stones. We discuss reformed bands we've seen, and who has and who hasn't lived up to our expectations. Misha and I went to see My Bloody Valentine's return at The Roundhouse last year and it was everything I'd hoped it would be – tight, psychedelic and nerve janglingly loud. On the other hand I saw the reconvened Echo and the Bunnymen and couldn't figure out who was the most disinterested; me or them.

Despite a handful of positive experiences, as a rule I'm not a huge fan of going to see reformed bands. The majority of such performances seldom deliver more than a burst of nostalgia. And nostalgia, for all its comforting qualities, is not an essential part of a healthy culture.

On the other hand, I would never criticise bands for reforming in order to make money. It is and always has been near impossible to make a living as a musician producing original work. For certain bands it must be infuriating to write and record strong and individual music that is critically acclaimed, yet garners you no remuneration. Then, to watch later generations of artists picking up on your stylistic nuances and enjoying commercial success must be galling in the extreme. It's easy to see how the temptation to reform, reclaim the limelight and finally see some financial reward for your endeavours must become overpowering.

Naturally of course, for many fans, the opportunity to see a group whom they first enjoyed during the flush of youth can be very appealing. And there's also an obvious pull for those who missed the group first time around because they were too unhip, or too young, or too unborn. But the margin of disappointment is a fairly wide one. The Velvet Underground's almost wilfully underwhelming Glastonbury performance being a case in point.[1]

In fact, in terms of impact and reputation, Throbbing Gristle are one of the very few groups who are in some way comparable to the Velvets. Indeed, they were described by the esteemed US critic Richard Meltzer as "the Velvets of a new age". Like The Velvets, their groundbreaking work was frequently ignored or vilified in its own time. Yet both bands have come to be seen as providing a variety of templates for how a modern music group can operate. And there's another matter in which Throbbing Gristle mirror The Velvets. I had assumed I could count on them to stay dead.

Since Throbbing Gristle's termination in 1981, each of the four ex-members have created huge bodies of work which dwarf the output of their parent group in both volume and scope.

---

1. Since the Velvets reunited, all manner of bands with irreconcilable differences have reconciled. The Sex Pistols, The Stooges and Led Zeppelin all succumbed to the lure of reformation funds.

Since my encounter with Psychic TV at the Haçienda in 1984, Genesis P. Orridge has continued to record and perform under the PTV banner, with a frequently changing and evolving line up. After their Velvet Underground inspired drone rock of the mid 80s, they briefly flirted with a plastic art pop with chart pretensions. Which is where I lost interest. Then inspiration struck P. Orridge in the form of acid house. Which is where I became interested again. This was followed by a return to psych-pop. Which is where I lost interest again. This was followed by experiments with ambient soundscapes and spoken word pieces. But, eventually, P. Orridge himself seemed to lose interest, as from 1998 onwards he mainly concentrated on writing and visual art. Then in 2003, he relaunched Psychic TV. This time, despite continuing to craft interesting lyrics, he assembled a group of musicians who serve up a brand of psychedelic rock so standard issue, it makes the Dandy Warhols sound like Stravinsky. Lumpy cover versions of 'Foggy Notion' or 'Jumpin' Jack Flash' anyone?

More interestingly, since 1993, P. Orridge and his second wife Lady Jaye Breyer have been involved in a project known as Pandrogeny. In order to try and closely resemble each other, the duo have spent $200,000 on body modification, including hormone therapy, lip plumping, eye and nose jobs, cheek and chin implants and breast implants. He has also changed his name to Genesis Breyer P-Orridge. Although whether this makes him sound more normal or more abnormal is open to debate. The duo has also adopted gender-neutral pronouns. Therefore from now on Genesis Breyer P. Orridge will be referred to as s/he.

Following their joint departure from Psychic TV back in 1983, Sleazy and his partner Geoff Rushton (aka John Balance) operated as Coil, experimenting with multiple genres and producing a massive catalogue of recordings. Their work encompasses everything from synth pop to ultra-minimal drones, from acid house club cuts to expansive kraut-prog workouts, from subtle string arrangements to industrial grind – all encrypted with a defiantly queer sensibility. Since Balance's tragic accidental death in 2004, Sleazy has been developing music composed almost entirely of vocal samples under the name Threshold House Boys Choir.

Meanwhile, Chris and Cosey have been consistently producing subtle and sensual electronica. Early albums such as *Trance* (1982) and *Techno Primitiv* (1985), with their looping rhythms and warm pulsing electronics graced by Cosey's spectral and sexual vocals, prefigured much of what would happen in the late 80s house and trance scenes. Yet Cosey's use of the cornet as well as Chris' predilection for heavily processed granular noise mean their recordings always have a sound which is far more distinctive than many dancefloor interlopers.

Chris has also released a number of instrumental solo works, whilst Cosey continues to create visual art, films and performance pieces alongside her own solo recordings. At the dawn of the twenty first century, as the pair rebranded themselves as CarterTutti, their music began to display an increasing engagement with a wider musical palette. Their most recent album, 2007's *Feral Vapours of the Silver Ether*, contains work of delicacy and mystery and it may just be their finest achievement.

In short, it appeared that each ex-member not only had plenty to keep them busy, but they had also worked hard to carve out their own creative space, well away from the group which made their names.

But, in 2004, against all expectations, Throbbing Gristle rose from the dead. They delivered an excellent EP called *TG Now*, followed by a handful of international live shows. In 2007, they produced an album of substantive new material: *Part Two – The Endless Not.* The same year, they undertook several recording sessions at the ICA London, where, in front of an audience, they worked on a cover version of the entirety of Nico's 1970 *Desert Shore* album. A typically paradoxical gesture, in that it both demystifies and mythologizes. Then, just a few months ago, they released another new album – the aforementioned *The Third Mind Movements*. Throbbing Gristle are, as we briefly used to say in the late 80s, back in full effect.

Malcolm and I enter the venue. Heaven usually operates as a gay nightclub. But, due to its location and superb sound system, from time to time it's also used as a rock venue. Today, bizarrely, Throbbing Gristle have already done a matinee show here. This helps me keep my expectations of tonight's show in check. Is it possible the group could channel the amount of energy and passion required for the creation of their music twice in one day? Unlikely I think.

We buy drinks from the bar and survey the capacity crowd. I spot my friend Andrew Lahman and The Pop Group's Mark Stewart. As I mentioned earlier, Throbbing Gristle attract a far more eclectic audience than one might expect. There are men in leathers, both biker style and fetish style. There are women in their 30s with crimson lipstick and long, straight 60s hairstyles. There are Japanese boys and girls in their early 20s who are probably art students. There are people in their 40s who look like they've just returned from raving in Ibiza. There are numerous morbidly overweight men in their 50s, wearing combat fatigues adorned with TG and PTV patches (it's entirely possible some of them are the same men I saw at the PTV gig at the Haçienda in 1984, grown older and wider). Hell, there's even a substantial gaggle of Goths.

There are also quite a few straight looking people here tonight. And I guess, I'm probably now in that camp too. Long gone are the days where I might daub the word 'Resistance' on a T-shirt and wear that. Gone too are the days where I'd wear a long mac, even indoors. Now, I wear the clothes that I feel confident and comfortable in. In my brown linen suit and black cotton shirt, I suppose I look like a father on Father's Day.

Suddenly, Throbbing Gristle begin to assemble on stage. No lighting change, nothing. All around us people are clapping, whistling and whooping. The sound of awe and respect. It's only now, as the group are taking a few moments to sort out their equipment, I realise I have no idea what to expect from tonight's performance. Will they play new material? Greatest 'hits'? Cover versions? All of these are a possibility.

On the left hand side of the stage, stands Cosey Fanni Tutti – impossibly glam in her black diaphanous top, black glittery leggings and shiny candy apple red knee high latex boots, her snub nosed Hohner guitar around her neck. Centre stage is Genesis Breyer P. Orridge. Hair cut into a sharp blonde bob, s/he's dressed in a set of very feminine pale pink clothes that are so tastefully styled, s/he could have almost stepped out of the pages of a Toast catalogue.

At the rear of the stage, occupying the space where you might expect a drum kit to be placed, there's a table covered with a black cloth. Sleazy sits on the left hand side, laptop open in front of him. He wears a white and black gown with a fur trim, which looks part oriental priest and part Cruella de Vil. Opposite him, leaning over a battery of electronic devices, is Chris Carter, dressed in a white lab coat, looking like a concerned technician in a science fiction film. Their combination of outfits could be seen to symbolise the unlikely coalition at the heart of the group – the meeting of the beautiful, the grotesque, the camp, the mystical and the scientific.

"Oh it's so *wonderful* to be back in London." Sneers Breyer P. Orridge, their tone dripping with insincerity. And yet this still elicits applause and cheers from certain sections of the audience. "Home of political corruption and asshole politicians. Don't you just love this country? Where no one tells the truth." It seems a surprisingly straightforward statement. Trite even. But then, just to put a bit of a spin on things, s/he adds "Gordon Brown, I want to suck your cock." Hmmm. As I stand in the densely populated environs of Heaven, I wonder if Throbbing Gristle will still be able to disturb, confound and exhilarate.

Suddenly, all qualms are blown aside, as a deep primeval thud reverberates through the venue. I can feel it in my guts. Another enormous thud. And another. And another. This isn't a rhythm. It's a series of timed depth charges. It's the kind of sound that seems designed to trigger my fight or flight instinct. Malcolm looks across at me beaming, yet somehow also looking concerned. Each thud is coated in a thick, sickly synthetic tone that increases the sense of deep dread. This is a surprising reinvention of the ironically titled 'Very Friendly', one of the group's earliest compositions.

As the evenly spaced thuds continue to pound into the very foundations of the building, Cosey's distorted guitar creates darts of noise that pierce the song's corpus. Then Breyer P. Orridge begins to intone *"It was just an ordinary day in Manchester, Ian Brady and Myra Hindley drinking German wine."* The narrative goes on to describe the hacking up of a corpse in the couple's living room, as Eamonn Andrews blithely presents *This Is Your Life* on the television set. Blood splashes on the screen and runs down Andrews' chin. This is music with a very strong, very sour flavour.

People sometimes ask why anyone would actively choose to listen to music that makes them feel unsettled or even scared. Although the question is a valid one, interestingly it's a question that is rarely asked of cinema, or literature, or fine art. The paintings of Francis Bacon are unremittingly bleak and unsettling, yet there is no question over his genius or the validity of the work. Similarly the books of Stephen King, and the films of David Lynch contain huge swathes of material specifically designed to frighten and deeply disturb. Again we accept that they are masters of their craft. But it would seem that music, the most abstract of the arts, should expect to be judged by different criteria.

Despite the popular image of the group as purveyors of unleavened doom, they have so much more in their armoury than provocation and matter of fact terror. Unlike many of the Industrial bands that followed in their wake, Throbbing Gristle always engaged with a genuine range of emotions and ideas. 'United' is a sincere love song, 'Exotica' is a piece of subtle drifting ambience, 'Hot on The Heels of Love' smoulders with dance floor sensuality and 'AB/7A' exudes electro exhilaration and positivity.

However, in live performances, Throbbing Gristle do tend to lean more heavily towards the darker side of their work. And songs don't come much darker than 'Very Friendly'. After eight punishing minutes, the song closes in a tsunami of echoing vocals. There's enthusiastic clapping, cheers and whistles from the packed audience. I feel relieved the song has finished, but exhilarated by the primal assault. "Well thank you. That was the first song we ever wrote, in 1975." Says Breyer P. Orridge, before adding "It was a love song."

The arpeggios of 'Convincing People' start to roll from the speaker cabinets. The 4/4 beat is set in motion. Kick drum stamping like a bull. Synthetic snare cracking like a dominatrix's whip. Cosey generates a squall of subtle dissonance and I find myself smiling. This is one of the pieces I'd hoped they'd play. Taken from *20 Jazz Funk Greats*, and centring on notions of control and manipulation, 'Convincing People' is a signature composition which both musically and lyrically uses cycling repetition to hypnotic effect. The 1979 studio version is bright and crisp. But what we're hearing right now is far more dense and murky. And all the better for that.

Breyer P. Orridge's voice, fat with reverb and distended with delay, delivers an altered version of the lyrics. *"You can take their money, you can lie about your expenses"*. Another reference to the current MPs' expenses claim scandal, something which is clearly bugging the singer. But at its heart, it remains the same song. *"You are the people!"* S/he sings. And it's true. Here tonight, we *are* the people. We are the people who are convinced. We are the people who are convinced of Throbbing Gristle's worth. We are the people who believe that Throbbing Gristle themselves are very convincing people.

Next they plough into the lengthy instrumental 'Live Ray'. As Carter and Sleazy generate a barrage of synth noise, Breyer P. Orridge saws away on a white violin and Cosey creates detuned glissandos on her guitar. The sound is savage and thunderous. Malcolm leans over and shouts in my ear "I didn't expect it to be anywhere near *this* good!" I nod and shout back. "I know! Amazing!" I had wondered if there'd still be a space for Throbbing Gristle. I don't mean in my heart. They are there forever – like a benign growth. But I'd wondered if there was a place for Throbbing Gristle in contemporary culture. Although, during their long absence I've never stopped playing their albums, I'd thought that possibly live, they might feel somehow anachronistic. But this sounds and feels dynamic and still defiantly modern. How could I have doubted them?

"It's so nice to know how lethargic you are in London." Drawls Breyer P. Orridge, still in full sarcasm mode. "Oh yes, it was so exciting I can almost make my hands clap". Seemingly the audience isn't offering up enough appreciation for the group's liking. "Well, you've really encouraged us. We're so excited to be here with all of you apathetic people." This spurs certain sections of the audience to cheer and clap with greater enthusiasm. "Oh it *is* London! Wow!" Shouts Breyer P. Orridge. "That's better. You bitches!"

The fan boy in me finds this a little ironic, as on Throbbing Gristle's album *Funeral In Berlin*, the final track 'Trade Deficit' consists solely of all the audience applause from two Berlin gigs spliced together. In an interview with Chris Bohn in the *NME*, Breyer P. Orridge explained "We would put in so much, and people thought all they had to do was clap! That applause was their part of the bargain." But these are different times. After a life during which their work has been dismissed and ridiculed – perhaps it's natural to hunger for the sweet blessing of veneration.

And, whilst there are many first generation fans in the audience, there are a lot of younger, more recent converts here too. "Half of you were virgins, when I was making love to three people at a time." Observes Breyer P. Orridge, ever the flamboyant decadent.

The sound of a life support machine begins to beep regularly through the speakers, as synth tones shimmer like a sickly heat haze. Breyer P. Orridge uses a tiny horn to create a little three note motif which cries out like an ancient Egyptian call to arms. Cosey is making the barest of movements on the guitar strings, yet causing huge, granular wedges of noise to echo across the venue. *"No eyes, no ears, no tongue"* intones Breyer P. Orridge *"She was burnt from the waist up"*. It's an almost unrecognisable interpretation of 'Hamburger Lady', taken from 1978's *Dead on Arrival*. This is one of Throbbing Gristle's most notorious tracks – a shivering dirge with a deeply unsettling 'lyric', which is in fact a partial transcription of a letter to Breyer P. Orridge from William Hogg Greathouse (aka mail artist Al Ackerman). Its subject is a woman who has been hospitalized due to horrendous burns from the waist up. Someone for whom every living moment is agony.

To many observers, this kind of material might seem to be an exercise in wallowing in negativity. But Throbbing Gristle have always prided themselves on covering aspects of life which are ignored by others. The world over, there are people suffering in burns units and having to cope with the daily horror of existence. As are those who care for them.

The first time I heard 'Hamburger Lady', I was at my friend Carl's house. It immediately made me feel spaced out and queasy. I'd never experienced such a negative physical effect from a piece of music before. And yet, due to the disorienting vibrato effect on Breyer P. Orridge's voice, I wasn't able to make out the lyrics on my initial listen. So the song's sickening impact was purely due to its musical elements. The next day I went out and bought the album so that I could hear and experience the severe disorientation of it again. Why? Well, I can only liken it to the thrill to be had from riding on wild fairground rides. You get off, so relieved and thrilled you survived you have the immediate urge to repeat the experience.

After the oppressive confines of 'Hamburger Lady', 'Almost A Kiss', comes as decidedly light relief. It's one of *The Endless Not*'s undoubted highlights. It has a deftly shuffling rhythm, sustained synth strings and backing from what sounds like a celestial choir. There's a tenderness and sadness to the music that is quite unlike anything else in their catalogue. To my ears, 'Almost a Kiss' sounds less like Throbbing Gristle and closer to Coil – like a piece which could have come from one of their *Musick To Play in the Dark* albums. Lyrically an exploration of a half way state, it's by far the gentlest and most reflective piece they will play tonight. And it's an intriguing side step, as there are certain sectors of their audience who just want to hear extreme noise and see anything else as a bit of a distraction. But here again, Throbbing Gristle revel in avoiding what their audience might want.

They start into a new piece called 'Springbankistan'. As a grainy thumping comes from the speakers, Sleazy triggers some deep booming bass tones that press right against my chest. Cosey picks up her cornet and begins to play long, mournful notes through a delay. The effect is like chem trails in the song's atmosphere. It's difficult to tell exactly what Breyer P. Orridge is singing about, but the lyrics clearly mention Afghanistan, Pakistan and Iran.

At the song's climax, s/he lets out a cry of *"I want to be a man!"* and the main body of the song drops away to near silence. The audience applauds, but the piece is still in motion. As the clapping peters out, I become aware of a recording coming through the sound system. It's someone playing the piano. It could be one of Erik Satie's more abstract 'Gymnopédies'. Whereas everything else we hear tonight has been treated and manipulated, the piano has a clean, natural tone. Perversely, in this context, it makes for an oddly alien sound.

Moments after the piano cuts out, a sudden deep electronic roiling starts up. It's the unmistakable sound of 'What A Day', another song that originally appeared on the *20 Jazz Funk Greats* album. It's designed to bludgeon and chafe. And it does. Consequently, over the years, it has often prompted me to skip it and move on to the album's closing track.

As I say, one of the group's specialties has always been the investigation of topics and states of mind that would normally fall outside rock's remit.[2] On 'What A Day', the topic is disappointment and the misery of frustration. Breyer P. Orridge's vocal line is deliberately blunt and oafish, moaning near incoherently about what a dreadful day s/he's had. *"What an awful day! What a terrible day!"* Musically, the song is founded on a locked half rhythm, with the minimum of adornments. Just a few curlicues of synth and some brief and muted washes of guitar. It's pure sonic irritant.

Yet, tonight, Throbbing Gristle are retooling the piece. Without question, the song's moronic architecture is still in place. But it's being used to create something far more subtle and multi-layered. Carbon copies of a band's well-known recordings are often what is expected and requested at reunions. But this is something very different. This is

---

2. Punk had initially opened up the possibilities for songs that encompassed subjects other than love, lust, loss and rebellion. There were songs about boredom and stasis (The Buzzcocks' 'Boredom', The Fall's 'Repetition', The Mediators' 'Monotony'), songs that addressed fallibility (Subway Sect's 'Ambition', Alternative TV's 'Splitting In Two', The Prefects' 'Faults'), songs about impotence (Alternative TV's 'Love Lies Limp', The Snivelling Shits' 'I Can't Come') and so on. But Throbbing Gristle pushed the envelope far more than most, with pieces about severe physical trauma ('Hamburger Lady', 'Hit by A Rock'), masturbation ('Something Came Over Me'), death threats ('Death Threats') exhilaration ('Adrenaline') and so on.

an almost complete reimagining. As the churning continues, Sleazy is overlaying what sound like heavily filtered samples of a Japanese koto. This lightens the piece and goes some way to exoticising something which was previously crude and lumpen.

Cosey is playing slide guitar. Or rather she's using a steel finger slide to generate glistening sweeps of electricity. Also, somewhere in there, there's a noise which sounds almost like a balloon deflating. It's impossible to tell if this sound is being generated by Carter's battery of electronic devices or Sleazy's laptop. The song even seems to have acquired a seductive swing. Here again, Throbbing Gristle undercut expectations. A song that I would have assumed would be one of the night's low points is actually one of its high points. Finally, the piece slows to a halt, to be greeted by much cheering, clapping and whistling.

They conclude with 'Discipline'. It's a song that, although a fairly late entry to the group's original body of work, has become something of a signature piece. *"Discipline, discipline!"* Chants Breyer P. Orridge. *"We need some discipline in here! Are you ready boys!? Are you ready girls!?"* To me, the song seems primarily to concern the assertion of self-discipline in order to maximize your potential. Although other interpretations are available. Could it be about Breyer P. Orridge expecting loyalty from their fans? Or is it about the notion of discipline as a form of sexual control? Or perhaps it's about totalitarianism. It's probable that all these interpretations are equally applicable.

The clangourous electronic rhythm is tight, stunted and brutal, with walls of synth and guitar noise building over the top of it. But what's grabbing me most of all is the throbbing sub-bass deep in the mix. Sub-bass is a wonderful thing to experience at a gig or club. It's importance and proliferation in both house and drum and bass has come about because sound that is at such a low register (anything below 60 Hz) isn't so much heard as *felt*. Within modern dance music, sub-bass is a potent tool because it connects directly with the body rather than the mind.

Right now however, Throbbing Gristle are applying sub-bass to facilitate a different kind of 'body-music'. Although it is possible to dance to Throbbing Gristle – and many people are doing so – the sub-bass is being used less to move the feet and more to shift the internal organs. To create an awareness of our own physicality. I can feel it moving inside my chest. It's a feeling with the potential to both soothe and unnerve. And currently it's somehow doing both.

The beat stutters to a standstill leaving only feedback hanging in the air. A sense of release and relief. Suddenly the electronic rhythm returns at double speed. We are travelling forwards at full tilt. The mood is frenetic. Like a machine operating beyond its limits. Sleazy is kneeling down by a monitor, using some kind of palm pilot device to send bursts of distortion ringing through the venue. Cosey stands stroking huge squalls of fizzing noise from her guitar. Carter remains at the table, looking thoughtful in his lab coat, as he gently tweaks the controls before him.

The pace increases again. It's the sound of technology going haywire. The noise is smothering and oppressive. Breyer P. Orridge stands at the very edge of the stage, as if caught in a wind tunnel created by the music. S/he opens her mouth wide and wedges the whole of the head of the mic into their mouth as s/he groans like a wounded beast, then takes out the mic, pulls their blouse to one side to reveal their bare breast and proceeds to repeatedly rub the mic around their nipple. It's a spectacle that is simultaneously carnal, grotesque and plain daft.

By the last couple of minutes, everything is at maximum speed and maximum volume. The sub-bass tones reverberate through my insides. The treble of the guitar and electronics feel like they're piercing my skull. The rhythm is now like the most insane infinitely accelerated breakbeat. It's impossible to dance to it. I just have to let it pebble-dash me. The sound is so enveloping, it prevents me from thinking about anything else. The desire to surrender to this exhilarating sonic assault is irresistible. I close my eyes and beam in the bombardment. This is music as psychic massage.

Suddenly, it's over. The four of them exit the stage. They have played just eight songs, yet the performance has lasted an hour and twenty minutes. Everything has been given the space to breathe. Their songs haven't been reiterated, they have been explored. Malcolm and I are smiling at each other, dizzy from enjoyment. The show has completely exceeded our expectations. "It's always so much more than just music isn't it." Says Malcolm. He's right. I don't just feel entertained and thrilled by the sound of Throbbing Gristle. I feel truly purged.

I still know plenty of close friends who dismiss Throbbing Gristle's music, saying they are mere sensationalists, or that it's self-indulgent experimental nonsense, or that it's not real music. There's also a strong resistance to seeing past Breyer P. Orridge's unpleasant on-stage persona.

"His music is deplorable. A rancid smelling aphrodisiac. It fosters almost totally negative and destructive reactions in young people." A tabloid reaction to the sound of Throbbing Gristle? No. A reflection on the early rock 'n' roll of Elvis Presley by none other than Frank Sinatra. To my ears Throbbing Gristle's music seems to embody the very qualities that horrified adults back in the 1950s. It's raw, it's godless, it's primal, it's brutal, it's lewd, it's anti-establishment, it's depraved, it's deafening, it's not music, it's just screaming. Maybe Throbbing Gristle is rock 'n' roll distilled to its purest form.

As the crowd starts to thin out, Malcolm and I chat with a few other people. We're just about to slip away, when a skinny Irish guy in a Throbbing Gristle T-shirt and denim dungarees comes up to us. He introduces himself as Terry. He's running the merchandise stall. "You're not going are you? Cosey would love to see you." Could tonight get any better? Apparently it could. And is doing. Terry guides us up onto the stage and out through the side, to the green room area. The mood here is ebullient and a shade more show biz than I'd expected. The space is packed with a combination of friends of the band, musicians, artists and performers of one kind or another.

Terry takes us over to Cosey. She greets me as if we're old friends. I introduce Malcolm, whom she recognises from playing the role of the overly-intellectual art gallery owner Warren Keys in *Ideal*. The pair of us gush about the impact of the gig. Cosey says how liberating it is to be able to be more freeform during these gigs as opposed to the more controlled pieces she and Chris perform as CarterTutti.

Chris joins us. We shake hands. "I'm so glad you could come." He says. I can't stop myself from gushing further. I find myself telling him *"Heathen Earth* is one of the major achievements of the 20th century".

Malcolm tells him he was taken by surprise by how intense the gig had been. "Yes." Says Chris. "Tonight was one of the better ones." I mention the effect of the sub-bass. Chris nods. "Charlie really knows what he's doing." He says, modestly deflecting the praise to their live engineer. Chris asks if I'd mind having my photo taken with him. I can barely formulate an answer. Chris hands Malcolm his phone and he takes a snap. When I see the image a couple of days later on Chris' Instagram page, it makes me chuckle, as we both look happy yet somehow bemused.

Chris introduces us to Sleazy, who seems relaxed and quite amused by the fuss surrounding the group's appearance tonight. He also says he may have just completely deafened himself in his left ear.

Although Sleazy's name might not be one to drop outside the confines of 'Industrial society', his cultural legacy is a substantial one. Aside from his pioneering work with Throbbing Gristle, along with Storm Thorgerson and Aubrey Powell, Sleazy was also one of the partners in the Hipgnosis design team. Hipgnosis were responsible for creating some of the most iconic album sleeve images of the 1970s and 80s, with Sleazy's photography and design work featuring on album artwork including Pink Floyd's *Animals*, 10cc's *Deceptive Bends* and Peter Gabriel's first three solo albums.

Sleazy was also a major musical force on the first two (and best two) Psychic TV albums. Then of course there's his work with John Balance in Coil. They produced an astounding run of albums which display a truly open ended creativity, including 1986's hugely ambitious *Horse Rotorvator* with its global field recordings and orchestral flourishes, 1991's acid house tinged *Love's Secret Domain* and the nu-kosmische of 1999's *Musick to Play in the Dark Volume 1*. For my money, Coil are one of the truly great British groups, who deserve to be accorded the kind of reverence reserved for the likes of Leonard Cohen and Nick Cave. In truth, I am even more obsessed by Coil than I am by Throbbing Gristle.

On occasion, I pause to wonder how there is enough space in my head to accommodate all my obsessions. How there's room for all the information I seem to have stored on various groups and movements and labels and films and directors and artists and artworks and books and authors and television shows and actors. And then I think about all the friends and family birthdays I forget and all the grown-up stuff I never quite get around to doing. Then I know how I've found the storage space.

As Sleazy and Malcolm chat further, I turn to look at Breyer P. Orridge, sitting on a sofa talking with a couple of friends. I ponder whether or not it would be a good idea to go over and say 'hello' and congratulate them on the gig. And should I mention our unfortunate 'interview' at the Haçienda on bonfire night in 1984? And should I acknowledge that I'd been such a tripping dick? No, of course I shouldn't. Or should I? Would s/he remember the encounter? I seriously doubt it. But then maybe s/he would. Or, even if s/he didn't remember, would s/he pretend that s/he did? Clearly I'm overthinking it. I finally decide that I will go and say 'hello'. But that I wont mention our previous meeting. I'm about to head across the room when Malcolm taps me on the shoulder. "Aren't you going to miss your train?" I check the time. Shit! I say a hurried goodbye and rush off to Embankment tube station.

* * * * *

Sixteen months later, on the 23rd October 2010, Malcolm and I go along to Village Underground in Farringdon London. Throbbing Gristle are giving the first 'disconcert' of a brief five date international tour. Once again, the gig is completely sold out. Whilst the show in Heaven was an intoxicating fusion of the confrontational and the celebratory, the Village Underground event is far more sonically varied, moving from the unsettlingly dissonant to the ethereal.

They play a few pieces from their archive, including psychotropic interpretations of 'World Is A War Film' and 'The Old Man Smiled', plus a clamorous version of 'Discipline'. Here, Breyer P. Orridge shines, part showman/woman, part shaman/woman, s/he channels maximum energy into the vocal. During the song, a man in his early 30s climbs out of the audience onto the stage and strips naked. Breyer P. Orridge, smiles and whacks the man in the genitals with a bunch of roses s/he's been handed. The naked man then dives back into the audience and Breyer P. Orridge tosses the flowers after him. At any other show, this would be a moment of extreme aberrance, but the rest of the group barely seem to register it, so caught up are they in creating the claustrophobic cacophony.

But for me, the most important aspect of the show is the fact there's plenty of new material. Much of it is instrumental, slow moving and abstracted. You might be tempted to call it ambient, except for the fact it's frequently imbued with a sense of deep, brooding dread. At one point, an incredibly strong sub-bass vibrates not only my innards but also the very air around us. Simultaneously, sharp trebly 'pings' are piercing through the atmosphere. If these noises were any higher pitched, only canines would feel the benefit.

This is one of Throbbing Gristle's signature techniques, eschewing the mid range and focusing on sounds that occupy the extreme ends of the spectrum of audibility. Then broadcasting these sounds at near deafening levels. This is without doubt mind-altering music. It impacts on my sense of space and balance and afterwards my head is swimming for about a quarter of an hour. And yet, during many of these new pieces, Breyer P. Orridge seems disengaged from proceedings, wandering around and contributing little. But it doesn't seem to matter, as the music is so thick with detail created by the other three members.

Four days after the gig, to everyone's surprise – and especially to the rest of Throbbing Gristle – Breyer P. Orridge announces that s/he's leaving the group. Well, s/he actually announces s/he's leaving the tour. The distinction is an odd one. This leaves the group's plans in disarray, but with very little ado, Cosey, Chris and Sleazy announce they will be fulfilling their concert obligations as a trio, operating under the name X-TG. It's a smart plan, which in the light of the Village Underground performance makes perfect sense. In the end however, X-TG only play one gig together. A month later, Sleazy dies from a heart attack in his adopted home of Thailand. What should have been a new beginning turns into a full stop.

* * * * *

Father's Day 2012. I phone Dad to wish him well. He asks if I'm busy. "Yes. I've got to go up to London a couple of times this week, for pre-production meetings." "It'll be a lot busier in London these days than when I first used to go." He observes. I ask if he can remember the first time he ever visited London. "When I was in the army." He says. "When I was delivering cipher codes to the war office." I chuckle at the gag. Then I realise he isn't joking. "Seriously? *Did* you?"

"Yes. It was 1949, 1950, when I was stationed at Wilton House. We were using one of the Enigma machines. And there was a British version called the Typex machine. I used to travel down to London regularly with the cipher codes". I'm flabbergasted. My whole life he's never mentioned this to me.

"It took about 80 minutes on the steam train to get down to London. To be honest, I think the best part was walking across Waterloo Bridge and seeing them building the Festival of Britain. I used to walk to the War Office in Whitehall. Then after they'd destroyed the codes, you'd get chauffeur driven back. Happy days."

MASSIVE ATTACK VS. ADAM CURTIS

MAYFIELD DEPOT, MANCHESTER

THURSDAY 4TH JULY 2013

(AGE 49)

My Dad died four weeks ago. Cancer. He was 82.

He'd been feeling increasingly weak and tired for over a month. But from diagnosis to death it was just six days. He was a private and shy man, but proud and strong. Over those six days, although to some degree I reconciled myself to the fact he was dying, the thing I found hardest to deal with was seeing him so diminished.

On the morning he finally passed away, we were all there; my Mum Christine, my sisters Carolyn, Gillian and Susan and my half sister Pauline. All of us gathered around the hospital bed, reaching out and touching his hands and his arms, as if to receive the dwindling warmth of a fire that has been reduced to embers.

There were a couple of times during that last hour when we thought he'd died. He seemed to have stopped breathing. I checked for a pulse in his neck. It was still there. Faint and irregular, but he was still with us. His breathing shallow and uneven, his throat rattling, his eyes closed. Another few minutes passed. And then he really did stop breathing.

As soon as Dad was dead, everybody seemed to leave almost immediately. Mum kissed his forehead and said "goodbye." But I couldn't go. I didn't want to. So I remained by his beside for another 40 minutes or so. I wanted to take some control of the moment. I wanted to say my farewell in silence and calm.

I even took a couple of photos of him with my mobile. Dad always hated having his photograph taken. Consequently I don't have many pictures of him. It's a shame, as he was a handsome and distinguished looking man. Yet, when his hair started to thin, he became self-conscious about his looks. Not only was he extremely resistant to having his photograph taken, but, as far as I know, he hadn't deliberately looked in a mirror for well over 30 years.

At home, when he wanted to comb his hair, he would draw the curtains in one of the lounge windows, then go outside and comb his hair as he looked at his darkened reflection in the glass. He felt comfortable doing this, because he couldn't see his hair, or himself in any real detail.

It seems as odd to me now as it did at the time. Because he still had plenty of hair. He never went properly bald and was clearly still a good looking man. But his vanity meant he fell short of how he believed he should look and he didn't want to face the reality.

I recall, visiting my parents in the summer of 1991. It was the day before Pete's wedding. He was getting married to Caroline, a woman I had first introduced him to in 1980, when we had all been at college in Blackburn.

I arrived at my parents' house, having bought an ornately framed mirror as a wedding gift. "Did you find a present?" Asked Dad. "Yeah, look." I pulled the mirror from a large carrier bag. Dad literally recoiled, quickly turned his head away then walked off into the kitchen without a word. Mum looked at me and gave a subtle shake of the head. It was the kind of subtle shake of the head that implicitly says "You should know better than to show your father his own reflection." Almost like we were characters in some ancient Greek myth.

Today I came back up North again. I have a couple of meetings tomorrow, but tonight is the opening of the Manchester International Festival. It's a biennial event and what makes it particularly exciting is the majority of the shows are new commissions and/or debut performances. The festival's managing director is Christine Cort, whom I've known since we were 17. She sent me the festival programme a while ago. As soon as I opened it, one thing immediately seized my attention: *Everything is Going According to Plan* – Massive Attack vs. Adam Curtis. "What?" Was my initial response. Followed by "How's *that* going to work?" Then another "What?".

Adam Curtis is the UK's most prominent left field TV documentary maker. Massive Attack meanwhile, are a rare example of a group who have successfully found accommodation within the mainstream for a unique and uncompromising musical vision. And, as their work has become increasingly experimental, their worldview seems to have become increasingly politicized.

I'm staying at Manchester's Townhouse Hotel. I checked in about three hours ago. Since then I've been sitting and writing, with music playing on random from my iTunes library. Pete is coming over for the show and should be here any time. I save the script document, step away from the laptop and go to the window. Whenever I stop working, my mind begins to focus on Dad. His absence from my life. His absence from the world. His death has hit Sarah and I hard, as we're still finding our feet following her Mother's sudden death from pneumonia just over a year ago.

My room is on the 6th floor. There's a great view of Manchester, with its blend of Victorian, 1960s and contemporary architecture and of course the ever present cranes in the process of building yet more new blocks. I take this in, but my mind is elsewhere. Massive Attack's 'Babel' starts to throb from the laptop. Even with its bottom end severely diminished, the track comes over as deep and slippery.

Bottom end is one of Massive Attack's big passions. From the very beginning they've engaged with the power of bass to move both the hips and the emotions. The group has its roots in a sound system collective that operated in Bristol from 1983. Known as The Wild Bunch, its core members were DJs Grantley Marshall (aka Daddy G), Milo Johnson, Andrew Vowles (aka Mushroom) and Nellee Hooper and rappers Robert Del Naja (aka 3D) and Adrian Thaws (aka Tricky). They mixed their own vocals with combinations of hip hop, post-punk, soul, R&B, reggae and ambient electronics, with the emphasis on slower rhythms.

Del Naja, Mushroom and Daddy G formed Massive Attack in 1988, with their initial recordings drawing on cohorts from The Wild Bunch, including Tricky and singer Shara Nelson. From the start, Massive Attack deployed a range of guest vocalists. Something that can make their albums feel like mix-tapes. Their 1991 debut *Blue Lines* was hailed as a masterpiece. I heard it and thought it was okay. I listen to it now and it sounds astonishingly good. But in 1991, my biggest crushes were LFO's *Frequencies*, Coil's *Love's Secret Domain*, WIR's *The First Letter* and My Bloody Valentine's *Loveless*. In comparison to those envelope pushers, I found *Blue Lines* fairly traditionalist, its soulful, jazzy laid back sound only intermittently laced with evidence of the wonderful hybrid abstractions to come.

I didn't really get on board until 1994's *Protection*. This is Massive Attack's coming of age album. The moment where, emboldened by success, they leave the more obvious traces of their influences behind, striking out for new territory. Every track is a miniature realm of crafted sonics. But the high point is the gorgeous, slow moving title song, featuring vocals from Tracy Thorn. It sounds like love in suspended animation.

The Mad Professor remix album *No Protection* pushes the songs into even more spacious dubwise shapes. I played that album into the ground. And yet 1998's *Mezzanine* is even better. The last set to be constructed by the original trio of Del Naja, Daddy G and Mushroom, the vocals are largely provided by ex-Cocteau Twins singer Elizabeth Fraser and roots reggae master Horace Andy. Perhaps surprisingly, the majority of the samples deployed are decidedly 'rock' choices. Led Zeppelin's 'When the Levee Breaks', The Cure's '10:15 Saturday Night', The Velvet Underground's 'I Found a Reason', Pink Floyd's 'Up the Khyber', Manfred Mann's Earth Band's 'Tribute' and Iron Butterfly's 'Get Out of My Life, Woman', all serve as strong elements in *Mezzanine*'s soundworld. If the Fraser voiced 'Teardrop' is the album's defining moment, the deep and dense cover of John Holt's 'Man Next Door' featuring Horace Andy is no less engaging.

By the time of 2003's *100ᵗʰ Window*, Mushroom had been ousted. And, due to various disagreements, Daddy G largely absented himself from the recording process. Also absent were samples. It was the first Massive Attack album to be constructed from all original sounds. The mood is more introspective, reflecting a sound palette that features an increasing amount of guitar work and draws as much from the world of post-punk as it does from funk or dub.

Daddy G returned for live touring with Massive Attack later that year, and he and Del Naja have continued collaborating ever since. Their most recent album, 2010's *Heligoland*, showcases another eclectic collection of guest vocalists, including Blur's Damon Albarn, Mazzy Star's Hope Sandoval and TV on the Radio's Tunde Adebimpe. Although, as an album, it doesn't excite me quite as much as some of their previous releases, there are moments, such as the purposeful groove of 'Atlas Air', or the shimmering horn pierced thrum of 'Girl I Love You', where they sound like artists at the top of a game they are still in the process of inventing.

A knock on the door. It's Pete. The last time we saw each other was three weeks ago, at my Dad's wake. We hug. "You okay?" I ask. "Yeah." He smiles. "We're still here." This is what we've started saying to indicate we're basically okay and we still have each other. We stand, staring out at the view, talking over the events of the past couple of weeks. He and Caroline have recently separated. We're both feeling emotionally dislocated, he freshly divorced, me freshly bereaved.

Pete produces a four pack of lagers, sits at my laptop and clicks onto YouTube. He wants to play me a track that's currently obsessing him. He thinks I'll like it. It's 'Pursuit' by Gesaffelstein. I *do* like it. It's a sleek and strict piece of Teutonic techno. Even coming through the laptop it's got real power. We listen to it three times in a row, its dark shine and restless energy helping generate our escape velocity.

We set off walking to the venue: Mayfield Depot – a disused train depot. I have no idea where I'm going. As usual, when I'm with another adult, I let them lead the way. My sense of direction is so bad, that during our school days, Pete gave me the nickname of Pathfinder Duff. The pavements are full of people, many of who seem to be heading to the show. We turn onto Fairfield Street and join the crowds making their way towards the building.

Mayfield Depot is a huge imposing red brick edifice. Built in 1910, it originally operated as a railway station. But it has lain disused and deserted since 1986. And it sounds like the space hasn't been overly spruced up for the festival, as there are warnings in the publicity about how attendees are advised to wear sensible footwear.

We queue at the box office for a little while, before I give my name to a red haired girl with a clipboard. "Hi, I should be on the guest list. It's Graham Duff plus one." As ever, I don't actually expect my name to be on the guest list. I always feel that, in some way, I've been put on there under false pretences and I'll get found out and refused entry. Nevertheless, we're crossed off the list and given passes. A steward offers us small packs of bright yellow earplugs. Pete declines but I take a pair. I probably won't use them. Maybe I will. But I probably won't.

We enter the main space. It's enormous. There are 14 screens, each approximately 25 feet high, fitted flush to each other, side by side, all the way around three walls of the vast hall. There are also numerous metal support pillars in the room, to which speaker stacks have been attached. In a normal venue, these pillars would restrict the audience's view, but here, there are so many huge screens, there's no danger of that. However, the one thing that is noticeably absent is a music stage. I begin to wonder if what we are about to experience is simply the screening of an Adam Curtis documentary that has been soundtracked by Massive Attack. Interesting enough in its own right, but not the thrilling cross-cultural event I'd been hoping for.

Curtis describes himself as 'neo-conservative' and yet his work is frequently treated as if it's operating from a left wing standpoint. His idiosyncratic documentaries are assembled from existing footage and have a mosaic-like aesthetic. Curtis finds unexpected links and themes in political power structures and social movements. For over 25 years, he has continually refined his aesthetic, and one thing that he excels at, is creating creeping disquiet through his gradual unveiling of interconnected theories of power, control and manipulation. His most recent series for the BBC was *All Watched Over By Machines of Loving Grace* (2011) which investigated the limiting and oversimplifying influence of computer systems.

As I say, tonight's collaboration with Massive Attack initially seemed a surprising one. Although, in view of Curtis' frequent foregrounding of cross genre, cross era musical recordings within his work, perhaps it's actually quite fitting. After all, Curtis and Massive Attack can both be said to be working in the medium of collage.

Music is obviously one of the documentary maker's abiding passions. As a youth, he attended Sevenoaks School in Kent, where he was friends with Andy Gill and John King of Gang of Four, and Tom Greenhalgh and Mark White of The Mekons. Both bands would go on to set early examples of post-punk artistic expression away from conventional models. Initially, The Mekons operated more like a collective, where their line up wasn't fixed and theoretically anyone could join in. Nor were roles within the band fixed, as instruments were swapped between musicians.

Meanwhile, Gang of Four's heavily politicized lyrics, artwork and sleeve notes side stepped easy left wing sloganeering and obvious polemic in favour of a more wide-angled approach which incorporated elements of direct reportage and Situationism. This could easily be viewed as a pre-echo of the approach Curtis takes to his material.

The Mayfield Depot's capacity is 2,200 and tonight's opening show is completely sold out. People are standing around chatting, but in amongst the buzz of excitement, there's also a feeling of reverence. Massive Attack have that effect on some people. I've decided to avoid too much pre-publicity about tonight's show, so I have no real idea of what to expect. Although to be fair, Pete has been reading up about it and still says he hasn't the faintest idea what's going to happen.

Suddenly, traditional Afghani music begins to pour from the various speakers. The enormous screens light up all around us, filling the hall with a sombre glow. News footage plays on the screens. Curtis narrates.

His smooth, authoritative yet ever so slightly bemused middle class tones lending his words an instant aura of credibility.

Sometimes all 14 screens show the same image, sometimes there can be two, three, or four different pieces of footage playing out on separate screens. And, in typical Curtis fashion, within a couple of minutes, the sound cues have switched from The Shirelles to This Mortal Coil to Chubby Checker to Burial. There is so much visual information being presented and the volume of the music is so high, it's disorientating. It suddenly occurs to me that the show may possibly be a little overwhelming in my current vulnerable state.

And then, lights fade up behind the screens at the far end of the hall. Although much of the space behind the gauze of the screen remains in shadow, we can see it's set up as a music stage. Former Cocteau Twins vocalist Elizabeth Fraser stands alone, picked out in a cone of bright ivory light. Also on the screen we see the shadows of other musicians – two guitarists, a seated keyboardist and a man standing at a set of vibraphones. There's an enormous cheer from the crowd. Fraser begins to sing the Burt Bacharach and Hal David song 'The Look of Love'. It's the most stripped back interpretation imaginable. Apart from a handful of very sparse vibraphone notes, Fraser carries the tune completely unaccompanied. She is close in on the mic. Her vocal is intimate and unforced. The enormous crowd is completely hushed. We want to catch every nuance.

She would seem a small, distant figure were it not for the fact a camera has been trained on her and is now projecting a twenty foot high image of her face onto the screen. The face is so huge that the real on stage figure of Fraser behind the screen barely reaches up to her bottom lip. Her hair is cropped close and she sings the whole lyric with eyes closed. Fraser's voice has always been an instrument of true beauty. But seldom has it been heard in such splendid isolation. The lyrics have a direct simplicity and Fraser's performance of them is so tender, so pure, tears are soon running down my cheeks. To be fair, in my current frame of mind, I'm easily moved to tears. But there is something in her delivery that lifts the song into another emotional realm entirely.

'The Look of Love' was originally written as an instrumental in 1966, but Hal David added lyrics for the version included in the 1967 James Bond comedy spoof *Casino Royale*. Frankly, that silky smooth cocktail lounge version, sung with effortless grace by Dusty Springfield, is wasted on the soundtrack of a film that is a sprawling indulgent cavalcade of half formed ideas, misfiring jokes and ill-used talent.

This is part of what's making me cry. I remember so clearly sitting with my Dad, at the age of 11, at the height of my Bond obsession, watching *Casino Royale* on television – him tutting at some of the lame gags and me feeling an odd sense of distance from the film. I hadn't expected it to be a comedy. But once I realised it *was* a comedy, I did at least expect it to be funny. There had been a version of 'The Look of Love' on the first music cassette I ever owned: *Roland Shaw's World of James Bond Adventure*. I'd played it to death before I'd ever seen the film. The sense of disappointment was quite something.

However, 'The Look of Love' went on to transcend its ropey cinematic origins and become widely recognised as a standard. It's been covered by, amongst others, Dionne Warwick, The Delfonics, Isaac Hayes, The Four Tops and Andy Williams. Massive Attack have also tackled the song before. Twenty-five years ago. When they were still in their larval form, and operating under the name of The Wild Bunch, they released a version of 'The Look of Love' as the B-side of the 1988 single 'Friends and Countrymen'. That iteration, with Shara Nelson handling the vocals, is an extremely minimal electro hip-hop workout. And yet, it is fussy and cluttered in comparison to the delicate interpretation we are presented with tonight.

Pete glances over, and sees my wet face, puts his arm around me and rests his head on my shoulder. "It's alright brother." I nod. It isn't all right. We both know this. But him telling me it is, at least confirms the idea that one day it might be. Fraser sings the last line *"I love you so"*, and I feel goose pimples running up my arms. As the audience applaud and cheer, I wipe my eyes. Christ. If it's all going to be as good as this I'll be in shreds by the end of the night.

The spotlight on Fraser snaps off and suddenly the entire band bursts into life, drums pounding, guitar crashing. It's the most rock thing I've ever heard Massive Attack play. But they clearly have the power. In contrast with the delicacy of Fraser's performance, this is like a lump hammer to the chest. I look around to see several audience members inserting their free bright yellow earplugs. It sounds like it could be something by Alternative TV. But what the group are in fact playing is a song entitled 'Everything is Going According To Plan' by Yegor Letov's Russian punk band GROB. Grob is short for Grazhdanskaya Oborona, which translates as Civil Defence.

All around us, the huge screens are infused with red light. Robert Del Naja is at his keyboards, side on to the audience, wearing a black suit, white shirt and black tie, with a white armband, he stands erect, hands by his sides as he sings into the mic. About fifteen feet away, bassist Sean Cook stands facing him, wearing a matching outfit and singing the same vocal line – both sing the original Russian lyric. To their right, behind another screen, we can see suited guitarist Angelo Bruschini and behind a screen to the left, drummer and percussionist Damon Reece wearing a white shirt and black tie.

Images of forests at night come up on the screen. The words 'Everything is Going According To Plan' flash over and over. Cook and Del Naja sing the chorus over and over. The sound of a cold, cruel wind fades up. Suddenly the music cuts. A gasp of breath from Del Naja is left hanging in the air.

As the sound of the cold wind swells, images of a 1980s Soviet mental asylum appear on the screens all around us. Due to intervention by the KGB, the song's author Yegor Letov was interned in a mental asylum in 1985 where he was 'treated' with anti-psychotic drugs. He was released after three months, although the drugs had done little to diminish his anti-authoritarian stance.

As the images roll on, the disparate sound cues segue into one another... Benjamin Britten, Suicide and Gavin Bryars all pump from the speakers, with the group adding their own textures. This isn't an elaborate cinematic backing for a music gig. This is a fully integrated multimedia event. The assemblage of documentary footage, Curtis' narration, the group's songs, the sound cues and the text, all are of equal importance. In short, this *is* the thrilling cross-cultural event I'd been hoping for.

As the ominous sound of Nine Inch Nails' rich droning instrumental 'Corona Radiata' swells through the hall, images flash up on the screens of Russian scientists in radiation suits going into the Chernobyl reactor.

Cut to footage from a black and white gangster film. Gunfire. Explosions. The drone increases in volume. Bright red and purple lights fire off all around the hall. Bruschini creates a hail of spiked noise that hovers over the pounding drums. It's an overpowering assault, full of precipitous menace. Pete turns to me and nods his head in approval. Suddenly the tune peaks. Huge text comes up on the central screen…

'THE NEW WORLD ORDER'

Images of Nicolae Ceaușescu, the Communist leader of the Socialist Republic of Romania, and his wife Elena… Elena wanders around a garden… Elena stands next to Queen Elizabeth on a state visit to the UK in 1978…

Bruschini sends the opening chords of The Jesus And Mary Chain's 'Just Like Honey' flowing from the speaker system in thick, gritty waves. Reece measures out the beat on the kick drum. Cook takes the lead vocal, with Del Naja providing backing vocals. I love this song. In fact I love most of The Jesus And Mary Chain's songs. But I especially love their 1985 debut album *Psychocandy*, from which 'Just Like Honey' is taken. It's a song that welds huge distorted chords and a deep minimal drum pattern, with a sweet and bleary vocal line. A sound that is bizarrely both grounding and uplifting.

On the screens, Jane Fonda is leading a workout class. Fonda's hair is heavily styled for lots of volume, her body clasped in a bright blue leotard. As she exercises, she is continually smiling at the camera. Either side of her, twenty feet high images of Del Naja and Cook's faces singing *"I'll be your plastic toy"*… I realise that, as if to mirror the way in which Curtis works only with found footage, Massive Attack's contribution consists of found songs; cover versions. And the selection of songs is decidedly eclectic.

The screens are showing images of Siberian woodland. Guitarist Bruschini begins to pick out a sequence of slow, gentle arpeggios. On screen the text tells us

'Yegor Letov fell in love with another Siberian punk'.

Shot of an attractive working class Soviet women in her 20s.

'She was called Yanka Dyagileva.'

Bruschini's guitar continues unaccompanied. Then, Fraser appears again in a centre stage spotlight. She sings the line *"These are the eyes that watched him walk away"*. It's a tender interpretation of the American classic 'My Coloring Book'. But Fraser has discarded the first two verses and begun with the third. Here again, she's backed by just one instrument – another chance to hear her voice unadorned. The song itself was written by John Kander and Fred Ebb[1], and it's been interpreted by a host of vocal talents, including Aretha Franklin, Julie London, Dusty Springfield and my old mate Cliff Richard. However, it was first recorded by Barbra Streisand and released as her second single in 1962.

Five years later, Streisand would fall prey to one of show business' most legendary cases of stage fright. During a concert in New York's Central Park in 1967, she forgot the lyrics to the song 'When the Sun Comes Out'. Streisand was traumatised by the experience. She began to fear she would continue to forget the lyrics to songs during performance. And so, she remained absent from the live arena for over 20 years.

Whilst Fraser herself hasn't actually experienced stage fright, she has been largely absent from the worlds of recorded and live performance since the demise of The Cocteau Twins in 1997. A guest appearance with Craig Armstrong on 'This Love' (1997), one promo 12" for an unreleased track called 'Underwater' (2000), one proper solo single,

---

1. Kander and Ebb were enormously prolific and successful. They wrote numerous hit musicals, amongst them *Cabaret* (1966), *Zorba* (1968), *Chicago* (1975) and *Kiss of the Spider Woman* (1992), whilst their scores and songs for film include *Funny Lady* (1975) and *New York, New York* (1977).

the charming 'Moses' (2009), and a smattering of contributions to film soundtracks. In fact, the handful of recordings and appearances she's made with Massive Attack constitute her most high profile work of the last 16 years. However Fraser and her partner, drummer Damon Reece, are known to have been working on a solo album for a number of years. Last August she made a one-off live appearance at London's Royal Festival Hall. So maybe, just maybe, she's about to properly re-emerge and we'll finally get a chance to hear her long awaited album. I hope so. As listening to her voice tonight is pure pleasure.

Except for the fact it keeps making me cry. As she sings the last note of the song, I find tears escaping my eyes once more. Pete turns to me and squeezes my arm. "You okay? Do you want to go?" I shake my head. "God no. It's amazing. I'm just a bit easily overwhelmed." It's not that I can't cope, it's just that I feel so suggestible, so emotionally porous.

On all fourteen massive screens, BBC chat show king Terry Wogan is interviewing Donald Trump and his wife Ivana in 1990. Trump, middle aged and tanned, his hair still brown, talks of how he originally ran his various businesses "for the money". But he now claims "I really enjoy doing what I'm doing". "Do you count your money?" Asks Wogan. Guest Barry Humphries, in his Dame Edna Everage disguise, chips in. He seems to be praising Trump, saying the multi-millionaire businessman does what he does out of love; "The love of the gift which Dame Nature has given you".

The sequence is underscored by a lush orchestral arrangement of gently ascending strings. It's the 6th Movement from Olivier Messiaen's *Turangalila Symphony* (1949). The sound is romantic, conjuring a sensation of celestial harmony. Curtis' narration tells us "Donald Trump was one of the heroes of this new era. In the 1980s, he had reshaped the battered ruins of New York, building hotels and skyscrapers covered in gold and marble."

A couple of guys in their mid twenties and dressed in sports gear, are standing next to Pete and I. They don't look happy. One of them, a lean handsome lad with a neatly styled beard leans over and talks in my ear in a broad Bolton accent. "Whose this bloke doing all't talkin'?" "It's Adam Curtis." I tell him. "He made this documentary." He shakes his head. "Fuck!" He nods to his mate. "We thought Adam Curtis were a rapper." I shake my head. "Do you think it's all gonna be like this?" I nod. He pulls a face. A few minutes later the pair of them wander off. I ponder for a moment on how many people here are also wondering if it's all going to be like this.

On the huge screens, O.J. Simpson stands in a courtroom holding up both hands to show off the gloves he's wearing…

The opening drum sound of 'Karmacoma' rings out around the vast space. This is one of only three Massive Attack originals the group will play tonight. Cook nudges the huge bass sound to the forefront of the mix. Pockets of the audience cheer. For some, this is what they've been waiting for. Hits they recognise. A spotlight flashes on, picking out Daddy G centre stage, sitting on a bar stool like a nightclub crooner. More cheers. His participation was in no way guaranteed. *"Are you sure you want to be with me?"* He sings. *"I've got nothing to give."*

He looks so cool and stylish, dressed in a smart black suit, with a white armband, his head crowned with short spiky dreads. The man seems ageless, looking no different now to when Massive Attack first sprang to prominence 25 years ago. He sings the first verse in his distinctive deep, smoky voice. But then, as he sings the line *"Now take a rest"*, the music completely drops away to be replaced by a gentle orchestral loop.

On the screens, news footage of civil unrest, US police clash with protestors… A man throws a refuse bin through a large office window, huge shards of glass hit the pavement…

Suddenly 'Karmacoma' starts up again, the rhythm moody and sensitized. Lights up on Del Naja, sitting at his keyboards. He sings the second verse. But, as he utters the lines *"I drink on a daily basis though it seldom cools my temper, It never cools my temper"* the music cuts dead once again. The reverb from Del Naja's voice fades.

On the screens, a woman with short blonde hair is being interviewed in the street. Her hairstyle and clothes suggest the late 80s. "Where were you in the building? And where was the explosion?" The woman is about to answer when a loud blast rings out. She squeals in terror and ducks down. Thick smoke billows out over the street.

The music kicks back in. Lights up on Daddy G again. He sings the third verse. *'Duplicate, then you wait for the next Kuwait'*. Live footage of him singing appears on one of the screens. A close up on Daddy G's face, projected twenty feet high next to images of violence in Kabul and O.J. Simpson on trial.

"Karmacoma, Jamaica an' Roma, Karmacoma, Jamaica an' Roma."

Although meaning and intent is often unclear in Massive Attack songs, I've always believed the line *"Jamaica an' Roma"* was a reference to the group's mixed ancestry. The recorded version was originally sung as a duet by Del Naja – whose father was from Napoli in Italy – and Tricky, whose father was Jamaican. The line seems to be saying 'this is us, this is our mix'. In contrast, footage of an impossibly white Michael Jackson appears on screen talking to camera, looking like some bleached out pixie. Again the drums and bass drop away and Bruschini's guitar picks up the tune, filling the space with his expansive wah-wah chords. Then this too cuts out.

Suddenly, the loud and startling sound of machinegun fire rings out of the speakers. Dazzling white lights flash in time with the gunfire. The effect is disorienting, unnerving. It goes on for nearly half a minute. For a moment, I consider putting in those earplugs.

'Karmacoma' starts up again. Reece slots straight back into the rhythm as Cook's bass sends plangent notes deep into the ground. Despite the interruptions, the groove is sure and solid. It's typical of Massive Attack's contrarian nature, that even in the middle of an evening of otherwise unrecorded material, when they play one of their hits, they interrupt it, deconstruct it and reorganise it, punctuate its hazy narcotic atmosphere with disturbing news reports and rapid machinegun fire. *"Don't wanna be top of your list"* croons Daddy G.

As the final notes of the song fade, a blurry image appears on the screens of a man having make-up applied. Del Naja plays a shimmering synth tone. Images of Tony Blair speaking in parliament… A huge open plan office… Men stare at banks of computers… The illuminated windows of New York office blocks in the night sky…

"A Strange feedback loop came into existence." Says Curtis. "We imagined what we feared. And we feared what we imagined."

The sound collage underscoring the images moves from the synthetic tones of This Mortal Coil's 'Dreams Are Like Water' into the drum loop from Massive Attack's 'Unfinished Sympathy', but it's been slowed right down and distorted. The vocal is slurred, quavering and grotesque. For some, 'Unfinished Sympathy' will always be Massive Attack's high watermark. Soulful and elegant with a string-laden down tempo groove, it's a song a large portion of the audience will be hoping they're going to play tonight. Yet, once again striking a contrarian stance, the group chooses instead to smuggle a portion of the song into the soundtrack in a virtually unrecognisable form.

On the screens, a smiling chubby pre-teen girl tells of her positive experiences with Prozac. Bruschini begins to strum a slow autumnal figure on the guitar. It repeats over and over. It's a version of 'Where Did You Sleep Last Night?', a tale of suspected infidelity and bloody revenge. Cook begins to sing *"My girl, my girl, don't lie to me, tell me where did you sleep last night?"*.

A traditional Appalachian folk song, dating from somewhere around the 1860s, 'Where Did you Sleep Last Night?', is also known by the titles 'Black Girl' and 'In the Pines'. The earliest recorded version is believed to be by Lead Belly – one of a number of musicians who are credited with creating the blues. But his life was scarred by violence, attempted homicide and murder, for which he served seven years in jail.[2]

---

2. Lead Belly (aka Huddie William Ledbetter), was born in 1888, on a Louisiana plantation, the only son of a sharecropper. He was a virtuoso 12 string guitarist, multi-instrumentalist and individual vocalist and, by the age of 16, he was earning a living as a performing folk musician. Lead Belly is a fascinating figure in the history of songwriting, in that his own lyrics often contained elements of reportage, with songs concerning news events and celebrities. His

In the 1990s, 'Where Did You Sleep Last Night?' became closely associated with Nirvana, who performed the song as part of their MTV unplugged performance in 1993. And effective though that version is, it's nothing compared to what Massive Attack are creating on stage tonight. As it progresses, they add more and more layers of guitar and keyboard texture, slowly building up to a howling salvo of noise. Reece pounds at the toms with timpani mallets. The sound builds and builds, the chugging power of its simple repetition, recalling Cook and Reece's bluesy psych work with Spiritualized.

The screens show footage of a parade of support for Stalin, his face on banners flapping in the breeze... Young couples dancing...

The instrumental section reaches a climax. Only the keyboard drone remains. Then, as that too fades, Lead Belly's original crackling recording of the song begins to play through the sound system, his voice is old and bruised. On the screens, ancient footage of a US prison. All the convicts are black.

"In the 1930s Lead Belly was imprisoned on Angola Farm Prison in Louisiana."

"It was the most brutal prison in American history."

"Its aim was simply to punish and exact retribution."

Massive Attack begin to play along with Lead Belly's recording. Once again the music is subsumed by the howling of a wintery wind. On screen images of the doomed British 1960s pop artist Pauline Boty...

Suddenly the lights go up behind the screen revealing vocalist Horace Andy at the mic stand. At 62 years old, the Kingston born Rastafarian appears cheerful and relaxed. Dressed in jeans, a grey cotton shirt, with his sleeves rolled up and metal-rimmed glasses, he looks like a benign granddad. Since his debut album, 1972's *Skylarking*, Andy has released over 30 albums of reggae and dub. He's been collaborating with Massive Attack since *their* debut album, and his warm rootsy vocals are one of the finest weapons in

---

compositions include 'Mr. Hitler', 'The Roosevelt Song', 'The Titanic' and 'Howard Hughes'.

their armoury. His arrival tonight is unexpected and welcome. Just when I thought I'd got a handle on the mood of impending doom which seems to have been woven through the entire performance, Andy and the group wrong foot me with a version of The Archies' 'Sugar Sugar'.[3]

This is perhaps the most incongruous moment in an evening of incongruous moments. Massive Attack, whose arsenal of musicians are more often marshalled to summon up a sense of dread, are here re-creating one of pop music's most lightweight confections. And, rather than rework the song into some bass heavy dub experiment, the band remain true to 'Sugar Sugar's all conquering bubblegum spirit. Reece's snare pushes the song forward as Bruschini mimics the original song's irresistible hook. Meanwhile, Andy's voice is so seasoned he's able to inject a soulful vibe into this piece of giddy pop. As if to enhance the glow of pure entertainment, there's also two longhaired dancing girls, gyrating on stage in contour hugging costumes.

Massive Attack have always possessed the skills and song craft to, with a few minor tweaks, push their sound out to a bigger audience and thereby earn bigger bucks. To, as the saying goes, sell out. And yet instead, with Del Naja at the helm, they have moved in the opposite direction. They have evolved into something far harder and darker. But here, with their take on 'Sugar Sugar', they toss out something that, if

---

3. 'Sugar Sugar' was originally created for the US cartoon series *The Archie Show* about a pop group formed by a bunch of clean-cut teenagers. In 1969, the song was inescapable, becoming a number one chart hit in the US, Canada, the UK, Ireland, Germany, Austria, Norway, Belgium and Spain. The song is often dismissed as being the epitome of bubblegum, yet its co-writers, Andy Kim and Jeff Barry, are not without merit. Kim also wrote and recorded 'Rock Me Gently', whilst Barry's credits are staggering. He co-wrote 'Do Wah Diddy Diddy', 'Da Doo Ron Ron', 'Leader of the Pack', 'Then He Kissed Me', 'Be My Baby', 'Chapel of Love', 'Baby I Love You' and 'River Deep – Mountain High'.

released as a single, could easily be a huge hit all over again. Something tells me they would never dream of doing such a thing.

On the screen behind Andy, there's monochrome footage of a dance routine from the BBC TV entertainment series *The Black and White Minstrel Show*. The figures of three male black face dancers tower above him, maybe eighteen feet high. They look grotesque as they execute some kind of soft shoe shuffle. The music may be light and bouncy, but these gigantic spectres lend proceedings a feeling of discomfort. A black artist of undeniable stature, dwarfed by giant white men masquerading as black men. Dwarfed by a history of disrespect and appropriation.

I look around to see pockets of the audience dancing. But the song is over in just a couple of minutes. The dancers come to a halt and the depot rings with the sound of applause. Appreciation for a feel good moment in an evening dominated by foreboding.

On the screens, images of laughing faces… A clip of Bambi looking for his dead mother… This dissolves into more footage from *The Black and White Minstrel Show*. This clip has been slowed down, rendering it even more ugly… A disenchanted Kurt Cobain shakes hands with members of the MTV audience then wanders off. The camera lurches away from him… The screens are saturated in bright red light…

The sound of Bruschini's gently strummed guitar… The two dancing girls appear in silhouette once more, framed against the tall red centre screen. Andy steps to the mic for a version of the Burt Bacharach song 'Baby It's You'.

This is a total bull's-eye as far as I'm concerned. I think it may well be Bacharach's best song and over the years it has been recorded by some supremely talented artists.[4] Tonight the group is so tightly drilled, the

---

4. The Shirelles cut a light and sweet version of 'Baby It's You' which skips along with an easy charm. The Beatles also tackled the song on their 1963 debut album *Please Please Me*. Their interpretation, with John Lennon handling the lead vocal, is harder edged, but maybe a shade workmanlike. However, the ultimate version will always be the 1969 single by US one-hit-wonders, a band named Smith, with

arrangement so nimble and Andy's voice so sweet, it would be a hard heart indeed that didn't feel touched by the performance.

On the surrounding screens, images of Nicolae and Elena Ceaușescu dancing at some function… Jane Fonda leading her exercise class… Hamid Karzai… A neutron bomb test in the desert – the ground collapses away, leaving an enormous void… Bambi in the woods crying out for his mother…

As Andy sings the line *"It doesn't matter what they say"*, the screens go black. The music cuts with a surge of electrical static, like the plug has been pulled. Big white text comes up on the black screens…

"AND ALL YOUR OWN WORSE FEARS"

On a personal level, the sequences that touch me the most involve fast cutting between different eras of television. From the 60s up until the end of the 90s, television provided one of modern society's few collective experiences. My very earliest memory may well be of being five years old and watching the *Doctor Who* story 'The War Games' with my Dad. In fact, looking back at my childhood, I have as many memories of the television programmes I watched as I do personal memories.

A simple drum machine pattern pounds from the sound system. Over this, Reece adds the high and gentle chiming top notes of vibes. It's a version of Suicide's 'Dream Baby Dream'. Like The Velvet Underground and Throbbing Gristle, Suicide were frequently vilified during their original lifetime. And again, like those other forward thinking outfits, the passing of time has conferred upon this New York electro duo the status of unrecognised prophets.[5]

---

vocalist Gayle McCormick's uplifting performance wringing every last drop of passion and longing from the text. It's three minutes 25 seconds of perfection and if you haven't had the pleasure, I suggest you have it as soon as you can.

5. I saw Suicide supporting The Clash, in Blackburn, on their 'On Parole' tour in July 1978. My second ever rock gig. As a 14 year old recent convert, I was far too in thrall to the new punk orthodoxy to be able to fully understand Suicide's sound. Yet, in reality, Suicide were so extreme and so modern, they made The Clash seem like Gerry and the Pacemakers. The

Although much of Suicide's work has a confrontational and sometimes ugly aesthetic, 'Dream Baby Dream' is a gentle balm of a song, with a clear and positive message. In recent years, against the odds, it has been covered by several artists. The most unlikely of these being Bruce Springsteen, who, in 2008, turned the song into a banal and mawkish splurge of saccharine. That isn't going to happen tonight. Massive Attack have a firm grasp of 'Dream Baby Dream's spirit, staying true to the nervousness at the heart of the song's optimism.

The surrounding screens are filled with images of a youthful and recently inaugurated Vladimir Putin standing at a podium… Eastern teens eat French fries. "Delicious!" says one… Bin Laden sitting at the head of a board room table…

Del Naja's keyboards begin to play the song's high, sustained chords. Heroic shots of bin Laden on horseback in the desert…

Cook sings the song's main refrain, his voice is warm, with a slight vibrato *"Dream baby dream, dream baby dream…"*

Shots from *Independence Day* and *The Day After Tomorrow*. Citizens stand in busy city streets, lines of traffic at a standstill.

"Dream baby dream, forever, forever, forever…"

The citizens stare awestruck at the sky. One by one, they begin to turn and run… Panic in the streets of New York and Washington DC…

"Gotta keep that dream burning, forever…"

Hollywood movie images of immense office blocks. A low angled shot looking up at a skyscraper. It towers above us, thousands of feet high. Suddenly it explodes, glass flying out of every window, it's an enormous blazing inferno…

---

audience largely hated them, showering Alan Vega and Martin Rev with gob, bottles and glasses. Vega ended up with a cut on his forehead and The Clash's Joe Strummer had to intervene and remonstrate with the audience. To add insult to injury, on the day following the gig, Suicide were arrested for possession of cannabis by a Blackburn police officer named Mr. Ray. This event was later immortalised in the song 'Mr. Ray (To Howard T.)' which appeared on their second studio album *Suicide: Alan Vega • Martin Rev* (1980).

Simultaneously Bruschini's fuzztone guitar starts grinding out the song's chords, turning the song into a huge power surge of longing. The sound of the exploding buildings blasts through the sound system at such volume, it's competing with the music. More and more skyscrapers burst into flames and collapse… Re-edited blockbuster footage of a tsunami sweeping between the twin towers of the World Trade Centre and through the streets, flipping over buses and cars… The top of the Empire State Building plummets to the ground below… It falls over and over and over again… A flying saucer topples the Washington Monument… Fire entirely engulfs the city… A UFO shoots at the White House. It erupts into flames… More explosions… More collapsing buildings…

"Dream baby dream, forever, forever, forever…"

The group stops dead, leaving just a guitar note hanging in the silence. The screens go black. The sound of a nuclear winter.

"AND THEN THE DOORS TO THE PANIC ROOM CLOSED"

Reece starts up a hard, thumping beat on the kick drum. The enormous screens are alive with a blazing green light. Sean Cook begins to play a series of deep, widely spaced notes. Reece adds echoing rim shots. The penny drops. Massive Attack are actually playing a version of Bauhaus' debut single 'Bela Lugosi's Dead'. They've upped the pace slightly, but it's unmistakable. Pete turns to me with a raised eyebrow. "I wasn't expecting *this*." Me neither. This is perhaps the evening's most unlikely detour. Yet Massive Attack's interpretation is surprisingly faithful, with the group sticking close to the source material.

I remember hearing the song as a teenager, on John Peel's show. For the first couple of minutes, I was hooked. But when Pete Murphy's vocal came in, it blew it for me. His voice takes the song swerving off into the world of pantomime. Murphy's industrial strength moodiness just didn't ring true. With Massive Attack's version, there is no such clash of taste. Whereas Murphy's vocal is portentous and arch, Del Naja's voice is even and matter of fact. The lyrics – in truth just a handful of words which would look perfectly at home on a sixth form poetry website – take on an air of reportage.

With its rattling percussion, and deep, descending bass line, 'Bela

Lugosi's Dead' has always owed a serious debt to the dynamics of dub. And Massive Attack are just the group to exploit such possibilities. Cook's deep bass notes make it impossible not to move your body in some way, even if, for some, it's just a continuous slow nodding of the head. Bruschini's guitar begins to generate caustic tendrils of noise that blossom in the cavernous spaces between the bass and drum.

More text comes up on the blazing green screens. This time it's in big white capitals twenty feet high.

"IF YOU LIKE THAT YOU'LL LOVE THIS"

The same words flash up, again and again, the huge text filling the screens. As the other instruments drop away, the song ends in a burst of echoing rim shots, firing off into space. This is one of the most unpredictable live shows I've ever attended, and consequently one of the most satisfying. The constantly changing roster of vocalists and the wide-ranging genre of songs performed help make the show feel like the ultimate live mix-tape.

Right now, the group is playing the unmistakable tight shuffling bass line of Massive Attack's 'Safe From Harm' – the opening cut from *Blue Lines*. This is only the third self-penned piece they've played tonight. Yet, here again, the group chooses to reshape the song. Its original mood of sensual urgency supplanted by a sense of accumulating panic. A dizzying spiral of synth noise pierces the atmosphere like an air raid siren, its pitch climbing ever higher.

The on screen images cut back to Russia. To Yegor Letov's punk friends staging a protest at the Finance Ministry in Moscow, burning documents and unfurling Soviet flags…

The music cuts suddenly. As if severed by an editor's blade. Replaced by the sound of a bitter Siberian wind. The on screen text informs us that Letov died in Omsk, of heart failure, at the age of 43…

At which point, the group reprise their version of Grob's 'Everything is Going According to Plan'. Reece's snare cracks and Bruschini rolls out the riff with Stooges style intensity.

"The MANAGED WORLD promised to make us safe."

"But no one feels safe any more."

The screens are blazing red. A rapid fire cut up of what looks like all the images we've seen tonight, over and over. Suddenly, we hear the loud screeching sound of music rewinding at very high volume. Eventually the music stops, but the rewinding noise continues. All the lights black out, plunging us into darkness. The noise squeals around the huge industrial space. Bursts of applause break out in different areas of the audience. Whistling and cheering. The rewind spins on. It runs through so many different blocks of fluctuating tones and at such length, it feels probable we're listening to the entire audio content of the event being rewound. For me, no matter what speed it's played at, there remains something magical about hearing sound in reverse. The sound of the rewind is the sound of one of the building blocks of reality being tampered with.[6]

---

6. I remember, as a child, the thrill of discovering the uncanny thing that happens to recorded sound when you turn the record turntable counter-clockwise. I recall my Dad bringing home a reel to reel tape recorder in 1974, and my sisters and I collapsing in giggles at the sound of our voices sped up and reversed. Later, I became gripped by The Beatles and their reversal of both George Harrison's guitar and John Lennon's voice on 'Tomorrow Never Knows'. Later still, I became engaged with reggae and dub, where the sound of tape rewinding is often used to great effect. Another inspirational interpretation of the magical powers of magnetic tape and its reversal appears in the science fiction writer John Wyndham's short story 'A Long Spoon' (1960). A man is editing a tape on a reel to reel machine, when he plays a recording of his own voice backwards. In so doing, he accidentally summons up a demon called Batruel, who manifests in the centre of a vague pentacle formed from discarded lengths of metal oxide tape on the floor. The tale provides a prescient foretaste of the moral panic surrounding so called 'backmasking'. The Beatles experiments with tape reversal would fuel the 'Paul is Dead' craze in 1969. Much later, in 1990, heavy metal band Judas Priest would find themselves in a Nevada courtroom, after two teenage boys decided to take their own lives, having claimed to have heard subliminal backmasked messages in songs featured on Judas Priest's 1978 album *Stained Class*. Of course, the key question here, is why would a band want to kill off their fans? Wouldn't that tend to cut into their profit margins?

Suddenly, the rewinding stabs to a halt. The applause swells. But then, stage lights come up, illuminating all the screens, bathing everything in a rich purple light. Spotlights come on behind the central screen. Visible behind the gauze are three people. Bruschini stands, picking out a sparse cyclical melody on his red Stratocaster. Reece is at his kit, simply hitting the bell of a cymbal. And, centre stage, stands Fraser. She sings in a clear, bright tone, lyrical and tender. But it's not English. These lyrics are Russian. The song is called 'My Sadness Is Luminous' and it was originally written and performed by Yanka Dyagileva. Although both the tune and the melody sound sweet and lilting, in reality, the lyrics speak of depression and disillusion. In contrast, a set of positive statements begins to appear on the central screen.

"The future is also full of POSSIBILITY"

"IT IS NOT PREDICTABLE"

"YOU CAN MAKE ANYTHING HAPPEN"

"YOU CAN CHANGE THE WORLD"

This last minute swerve into positivity is surprising to say the least. Up until this point, it would have been pretty easy to read the subtext of the evening as 'We're all completely fucked.' As the song concludes, Fraser steps back from the mic into the shadows. The screens are once more drenched in purple light. A message is spelt out in huge white block capitals. On every screen, the same message:

"NOW FIND YOUR OWN WAY HOME"

No solutions, just the possibility of solutions. Now the depot fills with the sound of 2,200 people applauding and cheering. That was easily one of the best live shows I've ever seen – musical or otherwise. I hadn't known what to expect. I had no idea how, and indeed if, the two forms could work together. But they did. It was satisfying and provocative. If you came along to dance you may just have left disappointed. If you came along thinking Adam Curtis was a rapper, you would have definitely left disappointed. But if you came along with an open mind, you will have almost certainly left feeling educated, entertained and informed.

The audience is encouraged to exit through a portion of the warehouse that is littered with huge piles of broken bricks and breeze-blocks. As we pass through, we are monitored by a couple of tough looking security personnel. They have guard dogs on leads, and rake the area with dazzling torches. It's the perfect coda to the event. Like the show itself, it's a compulsive but unsettling spectacle.

Pete and I wander back through the city to Albert Square. Manchester's huge Victorian gothic Town Hall towers over an area that, for the duration of the festival, is positively bustling. There are pop up restaurants, bars, displays, places to sit and chat and a small stage. We watch an Asian women's choir in brightly coloured saris sing a selection of pieces before heading into a marquee where drinks are being served. In the entrance, we bump into the Festival's managing director Christine Cort. She's a powerhouse of energy and enthusiasm, with a pin sharp intelligence and a striking beauty. The opening night of the festival must be very stressful, yet she appears cool and relaxed, seeming to have time for everybody.

Accompanying Christine is her husband, the illustrator Paul Shorrock. Paul and I were on the Arts Foundation Course together in Blackburn in 1981. Even then, he was gifted and driven. "Sorry to hear about your Dad." He says. I thank him. I'm still in the state of mind where every time someone mentions it, I have to assess how I'm feeling about it. Am I feeling centred enough to talk about it in any depth? Or do I just want to acknowledge it and move on? Or, am I feeling so wobbly that I can only nod and hope that I can hold myself together? I've already notched up a few quiet sobs tonight, so with Paul I'm able to talk briefly about the situation. He lost his Dad a few years ago and we compare scars.

Pete wanders off, drink in hand, keen to mingle with the Asian women's choir. Christine introduces me to Massive Attack's drummer Damon Reece. A handsome, friendly and youthful looking 46, his fair hair is fashioned into a short side parting. Aside from his work with the Bristol ensemble, he's performed on scores of other recordings, including a couple of albums I rate very highly, namely Spiritualized's

Ladies And Gentlemen We Are Floating In Space and Goldfrapp's *Seventh Tree*. I mention this. He seems surprised I've even heard of him. He's clearly underestimated how much of a music-nerd I am. He informs me he's a big fan of *Ideal* and I blush. We stand for a moment, smiling at each other, unsure what to do. It's like a first date that's started off too well and now neither of us knows what to say next.

Fortunately, at this point we are joined by his partner Liz Fraser. I congratulate her on her performance, telling her 'The Look of Love' moved me to tears. "Thank you." She says, nodding politely. I get the impression such complements make her feel uncomfortable. Fair enough. Damon tells her I wrote *Ideal*. She seems pleased the subject has moved away from her. "Oh Damon loves that." She says. "I sometimes have to stop watching it though. I find it too frightening."

We talk for a while, about music and the logistics of tonight's show. "Listen." Says Damon. "Let me know if you ever want to collaborate on something." This sounds like a grand idea. Although I have no idea what it might be, or how it might work. As we are swapping mobile numbers and email addresses, Pete rejoins us, having failed to pull a member of the choir. He's drunk. And he's starting to lean like a daffodil in a stiff breeze. It might be time to take a cab back to the hotel. "You okay?" I ask. He smiles. "We're still here".

Just before we leave, Damon introduces me to Robert Del Naja. I tell him how blown away I was by the show. He gives a little nod. He seems less impressed by the evening. "Thanks. There's a lot we want to change." He seems a bit down. I can't tell if it's the inevitable anti-climax after the build up to the first night. Or, if he really feels this isn't the show he wants it to be. He says they've been rehearsing the material for nearly a month, but Curtis has been reediting the visual components right up until the last minute.

"Will you release the songs as an album?" I ask. He doesn't even pause. "No." No explanation, no elaboration. But the music fan in me hates to think this would be the last time I'd ever hear Massive Attack's versions of these songs. "It'd work really well though." I protest. "Like a Bowie *Pin Ups* kind of thing." He shrugs. For want of something smarter to offer, I say "It would definitely sell." Del Naja smiles and shakes his head. "Yeah well, never mind."

* * * * *

In the year following Dad's death, there were several negative milestones. The first Father's Day without him. The first Christmas without him. My first birthday without him. *His* first birthday without him. Also, during that year, I repeatedly found myself seeing or hearing things that made me think "I must tell Dad about that". Followed by the immediate re-realisation.

The actual anniversary of his death hurtled up with obscene haste, the swift passing of time over that first year seeming in itself disrespectful. The phrase "Life goes on" is often invoked to suggest solace, but it's just as likely to summon sadness.

A year after his death, I'm on holiday in France. Holidays are really the only chance I get to read novels these days. So I've brought a stack of new books with me. And, for comfort reading, I've brought my tattered copy of the complete short stories of H.G. Wells. I first encountered these tales in my late teens and I've lost track of the number of times I've read them since. Yet they never lose their power to bewitch and startle. One afternoon, I'm reading the story 'The Purple Pileus'. It concerns a shopkeeper who attempts to kill himself by eating poisonous toadstools, which in fact, turn out to be magic mushrooms. Like many of Wells' stories, it's smart and witty with opulent visual imagery. "Funny." I think. "How few of these have been adapted for the screen." Suddenly, I know what my next TV series could be.

The Nightmare Worlds of H.G. Wells' journey, from inception to pitch, to commission to shoot, turns out to be the fastest I've ever experienced. From the outset, I decide the series should have a very different feel to the usual costume dramas. One of the first ideas I have, is to avoid the traditional approach to scoring period dramas – pianos, cellos, decorous woodwind arrangements and so on. But I also want to avoid the vogue for using contemporary rock songs in period dramas. Many of Wells' ideas are about the shock of the new, so I figure a more electronic score could help foster the feeling of unease. I email Damon and Liz, asking if they'd be interested in scoring the series. I think it's unlikely they'll go for it. But they say 'yes'. And I grin a lot.

Two months later, I catch a train from Brighton to Bristol Temple Meads station. Damon greets me with a hug and drives us to their home. Damon, Liz and I spend a couple of hours in the kitchen, sipping tea, chatting about the project, about Wells' stories and their ideas for the score.

Damon and I go downstairs to their basement studio space. It's airy and bright and kitted out with a huge battery of different analogue synths and keyboards. We spend a few minutes playing with a vintage ARP synth, its warm, wiggly tones swarming around us. Then Damon plays me recordings of some initial sketches he and Liz have been working on for the score. It's so inspiring to hear these works in progress. The music sounds mysterious and modern with hints of John Carpenter.

"Is this where you've been recording Liz's album?" I ask. Damon nods. "Would you like to hear some of it?" I was secretly hoping he'd say this, but didn't want to come right out and ask. The album has been in development for eight years.[7] Amongst fans, it has started to acquire a mythic quality, something which is always just out of reach. Surely it must be inching towards a release sometime soon? I can't believe I'm actually going to hear some of it, in the space where it was created.

Damon plays me a couple of pieces, including one lengthy composition that's maybe eight minutes long. Its prog credentials are furthered by the fact the song is composed of several quite different sections. And there's some intricate 12 string guitar work which turns out to have been contributed by Steve Hackett of Genesis. The post-punk purist inside me doesn't know what to think! But of course the centre of attention is Liz's vocals. And they do not disappoint. Unlike her work with the Cocteau Twins – which was frequently gilded with reverb and effects – her voice here is close mic'd and quite dry of studio treatment, creating an unmediated intimacy.

---

7. As of the time of writing (Winter 2018), Elizabeth Fraser's solo album has yet to see the light of a release schedule.

In truth, I want to be able to listen to the whole album right now. But I haven't quite got the cheek to make that request. What I've just heard sounds so singular, so artfully arranged and so honed, it's impossible to imagine how it could be improved upon. A few minutes later, Liz enters the studio. I tell her how much I love what I've heard. "Yes." She replies cautiously. "It's starting to sound quite good isn't it".

WIRE

THE HAUNT, BRIGHTON

SUNDAY 13TH APRIL 2014

(AGE 50)

It's the sunny yet cool afternoon of Saturday 6th September 1980. Pete and I are 16.

We left Norden County High School back in the spring. On Monday, I'm due to start a fine arts foundation course at Blackburn Technical College. But, for the past nine weeks I've been working in the loading bay of Debenhams department store. In a daylight free environment, I've shifted fridges, I've stacked heavy boxes and I've chucked a never-ending stream of refuse into a compressor.

One day I trip and fall into the compressor whilst it's in operation. As a metal wall moves inexorably toward me, I scramble up a slippery pile of refuse, sliding back and flailing. Finally I manage to extract myself. But only just. I pull my left foot from my trainer just in time to see my footwear crushed to a singularity.

Pete meanwhile has started an apprenticeship at his Dad's engineering factory, learning how to operate a machine that puts the foam backing on carpets. Apparently, it's even less fun than it sounds. On the plus side, we've both suddenly been earning just over eighty pounds a week. This means we can afford to plug the gaps in our record collections and probe back beyond punk's arbitrary year zero.

On several Saturdays over the summer, we've returned from Manchester with heavy, arm lengthening bags of vinyl. I've got acquainted with Captain Beefheart, Can, Brian Eno, King Tubby and

Lee Perry. My appetite for music which side steps the mainstream is insatiable. Yet somehow, inexplicably, Wire have passed me by.

Today, Pete and I have travelled to Preston. It's good to see these places whilst you're still young. We are skulking around a branch of Tandy's electrical store, in the mistaken belief we can simply buy a few electronic components and by mid evening we'll have built, and be composing songs on, our own synthesizer. Whilst the shop assistant patiently explains that we are idiots, I happen to notice a modest rack of albums.

I pick up a 12 inch square of pure white, into which a few hard-edged coloured shapes have encroached. It's like looking at a small area of a much larger abstract image. The more I gaze at it, the cooler it seems. It gives absolutely nothing away. I turn the cover over; the same shapes in a different arrangement. Finally, I think to check the spine: *Wire – 154*. Even the title has no obvious meaning or connotations.

When I get the album back home and lower the needle onto the vinyl, it becomes apparent the artwork is in fact a fair representation of the contents; mysterious yet immediate, muscular without being macho, sleek yet spiky, motorik but concise. The music has an experimental edge. It isn't always constrained by the verse/chorus format, and there's nothing so obvious as a solo. Importantly however, these are still clearly recognisable as songs – with hooks, melodies and a keenly crafted dynamism. An inventive and subtle use of synths and keyboards melds perfectly with Colin Newman and Bruce Gilbert's effects heavy rhythm guitar textures, whilst Robert Gotobed's drumming is direct and uncluttered.

I spend the whole of the next day, listening to the album, reading and rereading the lyrics that are printed on the immaculately designed inner sleeve. If the cover sparked my interest, and the music seized my imagination, then the lyrics push my mind into inspiration overdrive.

Bassist Graham Lewis appears to be their most prolific lyricist, his texts crammed with turns of phrase which are simultaneously sharp yet ambiguous. Sentences that fold in on themselves, words whose usual meaning are sometimes reversed. These are lyrics that demand to be examined and deciphered. And, in Newman and Gilbert, Wire also boast two further articulate and adventurous lyricists.

In Wire's hands, lyrics can be about several subjects at once, they can be stories, they can be snapshots, they can be psychological profiles, they can be fragments of a larger narrative, they can be wide ranging lists, they can be descriptions of mental states, they can be incidents where atmosphere is privileged over exact meaning.

When, on the opening 'I Should Have Known Better', Lewis sings *"I haven't found a measure yet, to calibrate my displeasure"*, does he mean he is royally pissed off? And what about Newman's *"When yellow has turned green to brown, divide by four"* on the song 'On Returning'? I experience a thrill as I decide this must be a description of the changing seasons' effect on plant life. The album's closing lines – Gilbert's *"In between are where only edges can be seen of the spaces in between"* – chime with my understanding of the cover artwork and also seem to imply that, despite my determination, Wire's songs cannot simply be decoded into single interpretations.

The actual language used by the group is a revelation in itself. I lose count of the number of words and turns of phrase I first encounter through the lyrics of Wire (*prehensile, servile, noblesse oblige, IDL, cartologist, denuded…*). Prior to this, most new and unusual words and phrases have come to me via *Doctor Who* (*polymer chains, liberty hall, serendipity, transcendental, entropy…*).

It is of course perfect I discover Wire just as I arrive at art school. After all, they are probably the most overtly art school derived band to emerge since Roxy Music. Their approach to songs as sculpted rhythm and noise and Gilbert's description of the band as "Artists who have chosen sound as a form of expression" both strike a deep chord with me.

But this isn't the sound of earnest chin stroking. Again, like early Roxy, Wire exhibit a perverse sense of humour. Take for example the way *154*'s potential hit single is bestowed with the wilfully anti-catchy title of 'Map Ref. 41°N 93°W'. Or the way Newman sings the word *"chorus"* just before the band glide into the track's gloriously uplifting chorus. Is the song deconstructing itself? Or are Wire larking about? I quickly decide both are true. One part Marcel Duchamp to one part Spike Milligan.

I spend the first week on the foundation arts course feeling increasingly out of my depth. I soon discover I'm not nearly as artistically talented as I'd previously believed. From the age of 6 or 7, I'd got used to people telling me "You're a good drawer". At school, there'd been nobody else in the art class with much of an idea. I'd been impressed by books I'd found in the library on Surrealism and Francis Bacon and, via a news item in the *NME*, I'd become fascinated by Gilbert & George. But I'd never met anybody else even vaguely interested in fine art, least of all Norden County High School's art teacher Mr. Duckworth.

In Mr. Duckworth's lessons, he had sat with his feet up on his desk, dressed in a blue blazer, smoking Woodbines and reading the *Daily Mail*. In front of him, two hand written-lists. One was entitled *Everyday Subjects*. This included At the Library, At the Green Grocers, In the Park and The School. The other list was entitled *Imaginative Subjects*. This included The Stagecoach, In the Castle, On the Mountain and the especially imaginative The Airport.

You chose a subject, took a sheet of A3 grey sugar paper and a piece of charcoal, then returned to your desk. What was crucial was that your picture should include, as Mr. Duckworth repeatedly reminded us, "Five big figures at least half the size of the page". Once you'd sketched the scene out in charcoal, and he'd given you his approval, you then filled in the image using poster paint. We did that for every single art lesson for five years.

I tell a lie. There were two lessons in 1978 when we used pastel crayons to draw a red geranium in a plant pot. And another two lessons in 1979 when the class had tackled life drawing. This entailed one of the children sitting on a chair in full uniform at the front of the room, whilst the rest of the class drew them in pencil. But I missed out on that. Because I was selected to be the model.

I should also mention that Mr. Duckworth's art lessons were carried out in complete silence, with absolutely no talking. If you were caught talking, even whispering, you were given a severe dressing down, had the back of both your hands whacked with a ruler, then had to spend the remainder of the lesson sitting alone in an alcove, copying out an essay from a school history book.

When other people tell me about their school art classes, they frequently describe them as havens from the rest of school life. Somewhere where the atmosphere was more carefree, with a lively exchange of ideas, and a sense of creative experimentation. Where maybe the art teacher would play albums by King Crimson or Free. In contrast, our art lessons had a bleaker, more Kafka-esque tone. A room full of people ordered to churn out the same images, week after week, year after year, in an oppressively silent environment, under strict threat of punishment and isolation. But, I knew what I was doing. Again and again I had been able to prove that I was indeed a good drawer. And a vaguely passable painter.

Now however, at college, I'm in a class with students who have far greater technical skill than me. Presumably because they'd had teachers who'd actually *taught* them rather than merely sat in the same room as them. Here are students who've worked in a range of media, including pottery, photography and woodcarving. People with portfolios! And here am I, with a few pencil drawings of rock musicians I've copied from photographs in the *NME*, and several A3 paintings of libraries and green grocers, containing five big figures, at least half the size of the page.

Each day I return home and spend the evening in my bedroom trying to improve my drawing skills. To soundtrack this, I play *154* relentlessly, exploring its dynamics, its subtleties and its hidden textures. I haven't been so completely absorbed and obsessed with an album since the release of *Unknown Pleasures* last year.

The following Saturday, I go to Reidy's Records in Blackburn, where I acquire Wire's previous album, 1978's luminous *Chairs Missing*. The album contains some of post-punk's defining moments, including the breathy shivering pulse of 'Heartbeat', the near Byrds-like delicacy of 'Outdoor Miner' and the dizzying mania of 'Another The Letter'. So many ideas, so many approaches.

About a month later, I finally track down Wire's thrillingly fragmentary 1977 debut *Pink Flag*. Here, spread across a single album, are a staggering 21 tracks. Some, such as the frenetically detailed 'Brazil', 'Field Day for The Sundays' and 'Straight Line', last less than a minute. Others like 'Strange' or 'Reuters' are built on a Velvet Underground style slow grind.

Unlike my discovery of The Fall two years earlier, I'm fortunate enough to find others who either already love the band, or fall head over heels when they do hear them. I meet two lads at college who are fans. Paul Shorrock is in the year above me, studying graphic design. He's a smart and skilled draughtsman, and he knows a good thing when he hears it. "No list of writing credits will ever scan better than Newman, Lewis, Gilbert and Gotobed." He says. And I have to agree.

Another lad on my course is Douglas Jones. Bright eyed and witty, he lives in nearby Clitheroe and produces thoughtful artworks that balance the conceptual and the emotional. Doug is not only a Wire fan he's also into Gilbert and Lewis' more eccentric *Dome* album. Whilst Pete remains fairly unruffled by Wire, when I play *154* to John he is appropriately impressed. "I think they might be one of the most important bands I've ever heard." He says. Again, I have to agree.

With my discovery of Wire, I feel like I've stumbled upon the gold standard for modern musical excellence. Unfortunately however, I make this discovery at the exact point Wire decide to embark on a 5-year hiatus.

* * * * *

Sunday 18ᵗʰ July 1985, age 21.

Having graduated from Brighton Polytechnic last month, I'm working for four weeks, with my girlfriend Natalia and our friend Trevor, decorating a townhouse near Ladbroke Grove. Way too much of the money I'm earning is being exchanged for albums at the nearby Rough Trade shop. We spend the days painting and painting, whilst listening to my recent acquisitions. The fumes of white gloss mingling with the haunting opiated grandeur of Current 93's *Live At Bar Maldoror* and the labyrinthine delights of Mad Professor's *Dub Me Crazy Vol. 5*.

One evening, Natalia is looking through a copy of *Time Out* magazine when she spots Wire are playing at the Bloomsbury Theatre in three days time. What!? Wire!? Together Again!? Playing live!? Wire!? I phone the venue, but the show sold out several days ago.

Undeterred, on the bright sunny Sunday evening of 21ˢᵗ July, we head along to the venue in a bid to acquire some returns. As we arrive, I realise we are far from the only folk who've had this thought. We join the queue. Surprisingly there seem to be quite a few returns. Then, just as we reach the front of the queue, we're told the show is now officially sold out.

We walk away, my mood somewhere in between heartbroken and sulking. Later that night, we end up at a basement reggae blues party in Notting Hill. A seven foot tall Rasta sells me five pounds worth of weed which he refers to as Lamb's Breath. The dance floor is packed and smoky. Natalia and I share a joint and dance to the deep throb of the sound system. As Johnny Clarke's divine 'Come Back To Me' begins to radiate from the bass bins, tears prick my eyes.

Over the next two years, Wire play another four London gigs; annoyingly I'm unable to attend any of them. I'm either otherwise engaged, or I find out about them too late.

One day, at Camden Market, I happen upon a bootleg cassette stall. Row upon row of tapes of different bands. Photocopied sleeves of red, yellow, green or blue. Live gigs and John Peel sessions. The cassette is still king. I spot a red spine with the word WIRE written in capitals. It's a tape of the band playing live at Chalk Farm. New songs by Wire! The recordings are distinctly lo-fi, but the band still sounds so special. Still so individual and unpredictable. I play the tape until the oxide begins to flake off it.

* * * * *

Saturday 23ʳᵈ August 1986, age 22.

I'm in the tiny Virgin Records shop on Queens Road in Brighton, flicking through the racks. Suddenly, I happen upon Wire's new 12" EP *Snakedrill*. What!? I had no idea this had been released! I can't understand how the music press isn't alive with this news! My eyes widen. The black and white cover is stark, stylish and mysterious. Just the way I like it. I can't take the sleeve to the counter quick enough. And I've never ever carried home a record with a greater sense of anticipation and excitement.

I am not disappointed. The sound is different to the band who pressed pause six years earlier, but it couldn't be anyone else. This is Wire in the digital age. The sequenced and sampled components are more pronounced and the surfaces of the compositions are smoother. But it works wonderfully. All four tracks have clear identities, smart arrangements, and as ever, the words manage to be both vivid and enigmatic. Lead track 'A 'Serious' of Snakes' immediately takes its rightful place as one of my top Wire songs. It sounds completely contemporary, whilst in some indefinable way, reminding me of *Magical Mystery Tour* era Beatles.

For nearly two weeks I play the *Snakedrill* 12" to the exclusion of almost all other music. One day I return home and I can't find it. It turns out my flat mate Tony has hidden the EP, in a bid to encourage me to play something else.

* * * * *

Saturday 25th July 1987, age 23.

Today I'm happy. Today I am very happy. Today, after seven years of listening to their music on a weekly basis, I am finally going to see Wire play live.

I've travelled up to Finsbury Park in London, with Natalia, Malcolm and his girlfriend Alex for the day long Capital Radio Festival. Aside from the hollow testosterone of openers Gaye Bikers on Acid, Wire are part of an impressive line up of post-punk luminaries, comprising Psychic TV, The Fall and headliners Siouxsie and the Banshees.

When, in later years, I hear people bitching about bands reforming, saying how they only do it for the money, I always remember myself standing here, in this packed crowd, inside this enormous tent in Finsbury Park. Beaming with anticipation, unable to believe my luck.

Yet, for band and fans alike, this is no exercise in nostalgia, no rolling out of the tunes of yesteryear. Since Wire resumed operations in 1985, one of the things which has marked them is their abject refusal to play anything from their 1970s catalogue. Instead, they choose to focus exclusively on new compositions. I love them for this.

So today, the main thing I'm hoping is that they play some songs I don't recognise.

Wire's 'comeback' album *The Ideal Copy* came out three months ago. After the glittering promises of the *Snakedrill* EP and the full-bloodied attack of the live bootleg cassettes I've amassed, *The Ideal Copy* is something of an anti-climax. The songs are great. The problem lies in the production. It feels unsympathetic and brittle, too bound up in studio technology to exploit the band's unique dynamic. So I still tend to play the live bootlegs more than I spin the album itself.

Natalia has managed to charm her way into the photographers' area, where she's been shooting Super 8 footage of Psychic TV. Malcolm and the lovely Alex have gone off to get drinks. So, when Wire come on stage, I'm standing on my own. Well, I'm standing on my own, in the midst of a few thousand people.

They start straight into a song I haven't heard before: 'Silk Skin Paws'. Newman's plosive opening chords kick the song into life, even as Gotobed's sharp snare slices through the heart of the piece. Lewis' bass line is carrying the melody, but this is one of those Wire songs that exploits the luxury of having two rhythm guitarists. Together Newman and Gilbert weave a rich, thick web. The skin on my arms prickles. *"You have nothing to fear"* sings Newman. *"I'm just making enquiries."* Whilst Gotobed wears a black sleeveless T-shirt, the rest of the band is dressed in dark suits and shirts. Wire's appearance is defiantly anti-show business. Looking less like a band, more like the enigmatic organisation *behind* a band.

They play tracks from *Snakedrill* and *The Ideal Copy*. Live, these songs have a grit and intensity that elevates them way above their recorded counterparts. They also play 'Kidney Bingos'. Yet to be released on disc, this song has appeared on the live bootlegs I've been listening to. Newman's guitar chords ring out with a chiming optimism, but when they're joined by the compressed chug of Gilbert's riffing, the song develops a more earthbound feel. Like much of Wire's best 1980s output, 'Kidney Bingos' has a bright sparkle masking a sinister centre.

I'm bootlegging this gig myself, with a Walkman I borrowed from my friend Olly. There are so few contemporary Wire recordings available

I'm not going to miss this opportunity. At the conclusion of 'Kidney Bingos', I estimate the band's set must be about half way through, so I press eject and take out the TDK D60 cassette. Running out of tape mid song is not an option. The cassette's smoky grey plastic reflects the red and green of the stage lights. I hurriedly turn it over and slide it back into the Walkman. I snap down the lid as quickly as I can, and immediately depress play and record. Missing the beginning of a song is not an option.

Seconds after the Walkman's recording head hits the tape, Wire start into a version of 'Over Theirs'. As Gilbert's guitar creates a deep drone, Gotobed's drum track thuds and shakes like a huge industrial machine. Wire never really struck me as a festival band, yet they seem well able to generate the required energy to connect with the huge audience.

Lewis introduces a new song called 'For Girls Only'. Ah, good news. More new Wire. Newman and Gilbert create cycles of fizzing guitar, whilst Lewis' bass line has a lean bounce, powering the song forward like a speedboat cutting across a choppy sea. By the time it's released on next year's album *A Bell Is A Cup... Until It Is Struck*, the song's title will have been changed to 'It's A Boy' and it will have had its sharper edges sanded down.

Throughout the remainder of the 1980s, Wire is a schizophrenic group, leading a dual life. On stage, they present their songs via a stripped down beat group format – two guitars, bass and drums – Gotobed's cymbal-free kit consisting of just snare, hi-hat and kick drum. Yet, on disc, they take the same songs and reconstruct them as digitally driven studio assemblages, where the drums are programmed and guitars are often sampled rather than played. Wire have always experimented. And at this point, one of their experiments is a simulation of what a pop band might sound like in a parallel world.

* * * * *

Friday 28th August 1998, age 34.

I'm due to present another instalment of *Totally Wired* on Surf 107 at 11pm tonight. I'm in the living room, sorting out a bunch of CDs and vinyl to take down to the radio station.

There are always so many great new releases to play and never enough time on the shows to cover everything. I seldom look back. Today however, I pull Wire's *A Bell Is A Cup...Until It Is Struck* off the shelf and slip it into my shoulder bag. There'll always be space for Wire. Somewhere in tonight's show I'm going to play 'It's A Boy' or maybe 'Free Falling Divisions'.

For the past six years, Wire have been silent. Their last album was 1991's *The First Letter*. Released under the name Wir, following the departure of Gotobed, it contains moments of sublime left field pop such as 'So and Slow It Grows', but on the whole, it's one of their more experimental outings, and for me, it's one of their very best.

But as I say, that was six years ago. Since then, Wire have been on another hiatus. Except, right now, I don't know it's a hiatus. It feels like it's actually over. It feels like I'm living in a post-Wire world. The needy fan in me has been only partially sated, by intermittent solo releases. Lewis' album *Immanent* (1994) released under his H.A.L.O. alias, and Gilbert's intimate, surreal and creepy spoken word album *The Haring* (1997) being two unacknowledged career highlights.[1]

Throughout the 90s, Newman has been particularly industrious. In collaboration with his wife Malka Spigel – formerly of Minimal Compact – he's released several albums of near devotional instrumental electro-kosmiche under the name Immersion, as well as a curious solo album entitled *Bastard*. Together, the couple run their own label *swim* ~ which has delivered a killer run of electronica albums by Ronnie And Clyde, Lobe, G-Man and Spigel herself.

---

1. Wire's solo releases would seem to illustrate the perceived creative division at the heart of the group – that Gilbert and Lewis are responsible for their more experimental aspects, whilst Newman is the standard bearer for their pop potential. Yet, in reality, things are far from being so black and white. In his guise as He Said, Lewis has been responsible for such glossy and glamorous pop compositions as 'Could You' or 'Pale Feet'. Meanwhile, on pieces such as 'But No' and 'How Long Is A Piece of String' Newman has delivered a sound as brutal and untethered as anything produced by his band mates.

Mid evening, I walk down to the radio station. I get there about 50 minutes before the show is due to start. Surf has a fax machine I can use to send back reaction sheets to the various pluggers and promoters about forthcoming releases. I finish faxing, then sit at one of the computers and send a few emails to small labels whose mailing lists I'm keen to insinuate myself onto. I've been meaning to email Newman at *swim ~* for some while, but I've kept putting it off. Tonight I do it. It's just a short message, commenting on the label's releases, especially the debut album by Lobe, which I adore. I also explain a little about the radio show. I don't mention Wire.

Two days later, I'm at home writing, when the landline rings. "Hello, can I speak to Graham please." It's Colin Newman. I recognise his voice immediately. I become tongue-tied. He thanks me for the positive things I said in the email. I struggle to keep up my side of a chat about what the *swim ~* label is doing. In the end we arrange for he and Spigel to come down to the radio studio in Brighton the following Sunday afternoon, to do a prerecorded interview for *Totally Wired*. I don't mention Wire.

On the day, Mike Bradshaw and I do the interview together. I'm glad Mike is there with his unflappable demeanour and relaxed interview manner. I think any professionalism I might possess could easily dissolve were I to undertake this on my own. We discuss Spigel's forthcoming album *My Pet Fish*, we discuss the *swim ~* label and its roster, we discuss current artists whom they find inspiring such as Pole, Aphex Twin and Scala. I don't mention Wire. Partly because six years after their dissolution, there's nothing new to say. But mainly because I don't want to start gushing like an unattended fire hose.

Nevertheless, after the interview, I sheepishly produce the copy of *154* I bought in Preston 18 years earlier. "Would you mind signing this?" Newman laughs. I tell him it's the album that I've played more than any other. He nods appreciatively. "Thank you. That's really nice of you to say so."

We stay in touch. Over the next few years to my scantily concealed glee, we become good friends. Colin and Malka are two of the most hard working, creative and prolific people I know. Colin and I talk on the phone every month or so. We talk about what music we're listening to, we talk about our various projects, we talk about our kids. But I don't mention Wire. I think if Colin really knew how much Wire there is in my diet he'd be worried for me. No matter how much other music I absorb – and I absorb a hell of a lot – the gold standard remains the same.

We're talking on the phone one day when Colin says "By the way, do you know about the thing that's happening with Wire?" My skin prickles. I'm immediately on high alert. As casually as I can, I say "There's a *thing* happening? With *Wire*?"

* * * * *

Saturday 26th February 2000, age 36.

That thing is happening with Wire. It's a cold crisp winter evening. Sarah and I step out of the Embankment tube station in London, climb the steps to the Golden Jubilee Footbridge and walk across the Thames toward the South Bank. After 9 long years, against all expectations, Wire have reformed for a performance at the Royal Festival Hall.

We enter the venue. It's a late 1940s built modernist palace of culture, with impossibly high ceilings and expansive marble floors. No matter whether a show is sold out or not, the building's entrances, seating and bar areas are all huge wide-open spaces. And tonight is definitely a sell out, with a fully charged buzz of expectation.

As Sarah and I queue at the bar, I glance around at the enormous crowd. I remember something Mike said to me after surveying the audience at a 1994 gig, by the newly reformed Faust; 'These are my people'. I laugh to myself. But it's true. They are. There are men of around my age and a little older, whom are dressed in cool, dark clothes, yet whose faces are filled with boyish delight. There are stylishly clad women and girls, some in glamorous evening dresses, others in functional but chic leisure wear. There are art students both old and new. And there are plenty of misfits. People who were never quite punks, people who side step trends, people who hear in Wire something they cannot locate elsewhere. Yes, these are my people. And there's also one or two Goths.

We take our seats, uncertain what to expect. To my surprise, Wire turn in a set which cherry picks from the band's 70s and 80s oeuvre. This is pretty much the first time during their career Wire have looked back. Up until this point, during any performance by the band, the most mature material on display would have always been around a year old. But – like Throbbing Gristle, The Fall and Massive Attack – Wire excel at confounding expectations. Just as I think I have their MO pinned down, they change tack.

The noise they make tonight is glorious. 'A 'Serious' of Snakes' sounds better than it ever has before – drum and bass thunderous, guitars creating hard melodic knots. As the applause dies down, Bruce uncoils a repeating series of bent notes and Robert Grey[2] starts a strict and coppiced rhythm as the group hurtles into 'Another The Letter' from *Chairs Missing*.

When I first heard this song, age 16, during the second week of my nascent Wire obsession, it smacked me right between the ears. It's a startling piece that could only be the work of Wire. Grey's hi-hat and snare drive the song relentlessly forward, as Graham's one note bass line throbs like a motorbike engine. From its obscure title, to its frenetic pace, and lyrics which partially read like a description of a Francis Bacon painting, this is one of Wire's signature songs. It thrills, it bewilders, it tells a story, it engages emotionally. And it achieves all this in less than a minute. It's a perfect example of Wire's ability to construct an oblique yet dramatic work that uses minimal components and operates within an abbreviated time frame.

---

2. Wire's drummer was born in 1951 and christened Robert Grey. However, he later learned his original family name had been Gotobed. His Grandfather, tired of jokes and jibes, had changed it, in favour of the far less extravagant Grey. In his youth, in search of his artistic identity, Robert decided to readopt this original surname. Ironically of course, at the time of the band's emergence in 1977, the name Robert Gotobed sounded just as made up as Johnny Rotten or Captain Sensible. However, with the dawn of the 21st century, feeling more secure in his own identity, Robert Gotobed once again became Robert Grey.

During 'Heartbeat' the band are joined on stage by Michael Clark's Dance Company. As the music scratches and pulses, a cluster of lithe, body-stocking clad figures execute strange minimal moves. The band closes their set with a version of '12XU'. It sounds tense and savage. No half measures.

As I step out of the auditorium, into the cold London air, I feel a kind of elation. Now Wire are back, I plan to see them as often as is humanly possible. Because I'm like that.

* * * * *

Monday 7th October 2002, age 38.

Tonight Wire are playing in Brighton at the Concorde 2. I'm standing in the audience with my friends Daniel Nathan and Lance Dann. The gig is a sell out. Wire's new releases have proved to be successful both critically and in terms of sales. I feel happy for the band. And I feel happy for me. All those years of saying "My favourite band is Wire", only to be met with uncomprehending stares.

I stopped DJing on the radio just over a year ago. The station was taken over. The programming completely changed. I wasn't required. Yet my desire to proselytize hasn't left me. I find myself making endless mix CDs for friends. Over the last few months my biggest crushes have been on Interpol's *Turn on The Bright Lights*, Boards of Canada's gorgeous *Geogaddi* and Kid606's exquisitely titled *The Action Packed Mentalist Brings You The Fucking Jams*. But more than anything else, it's Wire's latest EPs *Read And Burn* and *Read And Burn 2* which have been hammering at my head.

The venue lights dip right down, plunging us into near darkness. An electronic bass line begins to throb from the sound system. The sound is ripe with menace. Out of the blackness, four dazzling beams of light come shining into our eyes. The music increases in volume. As the bass continues to throb, a menacing electrical buzzing sweeps from one side of the darkened venue to the other.

The sound must be playing from a DAT or a mini disc, because, in so far as I can make out, none of the musicians are holding instruments. Instead, they grip industrial torch-lights, the beams raking across the audience, making us blink, making us squint. It's a perverse and confrontational gesture, more rooted in the Theatre of Cruelty than in rock and roll. In the blackness, Colin begins to intone over the uneasy pulse. *"Faith never skirted sense, Man has a wooden master"*. The taut, arcing noise builds and builds. Colin's voice grows in volume and aggression, until he's barking out the words.

The song's climax is followed by a mass of applause. Unfortunately, it's also followed by a power cut. Every piece of equipment on stage is dead. The band and a couple of roadies attempt to rectify matters. This goes on for several minutes. After such a strong opening, the delay is especially cruel. I suspect both band and audience will struggle to refocus after such an awkward hiatus. Wrong.

As soon as power is restored, Colin chops out the barbed riff of 'Germ Ship'. The kick drum punches, the hi-hat hisses, the bass circles like a vulture. The volume is extreme. Bruce begins to drop in icy two note slivers of guitar noise. I'm standing fifteen feet from the front of the stage. The sound is so severe, so stormy, standing in its hail freezes me to the spot.

Tonight's set is made up of tracks from their two *Read & Burn* EPs and a few more new pieces forged from a similarly serrated metal. Once again, Wire have emerged with a clean slate, dealing exclusively in new work. Some reviews have been suggesting the current material's spiky style harks back to the band's debut *Pink Flag*. In reality, the songs that make up the show tonight are so abrasive and astringent they make the band's 1977 incarnation sound positively stately by comparison.

"It's excellent." Says Lance. "But what do men of their age have to be so angry about?" It's 2002. Take your pick.

* * * * *

Saturday 26th April 2003, age 39.

I've travelled up to the Barbican, London. For an event entitled *(flag:burning)*. In line with the current vogue for bands revisiting classic albums on stage, Wire have agreed to play the whole of their 1977 debut

Pink Flag. This is a very un-Wire like gesture. In fact, it's pretty much the last thing I expected them to do. To celebrate their past.

Of course, being Wire, this can't be just a straightforward retelling of the same story. They've collaborated with the contemporary fine artists Jake and Dinos Chapman, who will be providing an additional element to tonight's performance. But I have no idea what that element is going to be. As a serious Chapmans fan, I asked Colin a few weeks ago about their contribution. "Everything is under wraps." He said with a smile.

Now I'm sitting on my own, in the front row, right hand side of the stage. The lights go down. Wire step out to applause and cheers and go straight into *Pink Flag*'s opening number: 'Reuters'. As the music begins, the screen behind them is illuminated with video footage of four handsome, muscle-bound men and women involved in a step exercise class. They are smiling, performing for the camera. The costumes are in bright primary colours, the camera angles are slanted, the lighting brash. This is the Chapman Brothers' contribution. Any vestiges of reverence for *Pink Flag* are sent springing and bounding from the hall.

Every single track is accompanied by its own tightly choreographed video aerobic routine. For the first few songs I feel vaguely irritated. This is possibly the least appropriate visual accompaniment imaginable. The music is from 1977 – the images look like they've been plucked from 1987. The songs are monochromatic – the videos are tastelessly garish. The compositions display seemingly infinite variation – the step routines are numbingly repetitious. The band radiate seriousness – the dancers project superficiality and camp.

Eventually, the grinding absurdity of the situation wears me down. I find myself sniggering. Yet, despite the innate daftness of the videos, after the first ten minutes or so, I end up ignoring them. The music is more than enough on its own, Wire's performance, a perfect copy of the recorded versions. At the set's conclusion, they play the title track 'Pink Flag' for a second time. As if to bludgeon the idea home, the band is joined on stage by a real life exercise step class. As Wire power through the song's forceful mono-chording, the brightly clad, brightly smiling exercisers run through their aerobic sequence over and over. This is without doubt the most unlikely spectacle I've ever seen on a rock stage.

During the interval, I notice a number of audience members wandering around wide-eyed, as if they've just experienced something they can neither name nor quantify. The remarkable thing is, the second half is even weirder. On stage a row of four screens, each around ten feet square. Upon these are projections of read outs from cardiographs.

Lights come on, revealing boxes behind the screens. Each one contains a member of Wire with their instruments and amp, each figure isolated in a ten foot square cube, its walls, floor and ceilings covered in some kind of reflective foil. From inside their boxes, the band proceeds to present a short selection of songs from their recent album *Send*. A series of terse, caustic bulletins.

They play the simply titled '1ˢᵗ Fast' – which was presumably the first fast song they wrote when they started writing again. With its harsh guitar noises and near gabba drum pattern, it's as uncompromising a statement of intent as you could wish for. And it's over and done in a minute and a half. Its cessation is greeted with a deafening burst of applause, as if the audience is keen to match the volume and intensity of the music coming from the four boxes.

The meeting of rock and art can often be an awkward overblown affair. But this visual augmentation is perfectly in tune with a band whose musical aesthetic is frequently defined by reduction and subtraction. The different boxes light up in time with the songs' strict rhythms. And over each musician's box, there are projections of extreme close ups of Bruce's left eye, Colin's mouth, Robert's nose and Graham's right eye. As the band play, the image of Colin's mouth moves in time to the lyrics. Wire looks less like a band, more like a row of medical exhibits.

On reflection, *this* is without doubt the most unlikely spectacle I've ever seen on a rock stage.

* * * * *

Friday 16th September 2011, age 47.

Pete and I wander up the steps to Manchester's Academy 3. Before we came out tonight, we each took a dab of MDMA. It's a drug I've treated with a blend of disinterest and suspicion ever since my less than satisfactory experiences in the late 80s. But tonight, stepping out to see my favourite band, with my best friend, it felt like the right time for a modest dab.

We walk through the double doors, into the darkened, low ceilinged space, into a capacity crowd. MDMA always makes me very aware of other people's physicality, how they are connected to the ground, how their bodies move through space, how they are literally breathing the same air as me.

We thread our way through the thicket of people to somewhere just a few feet from the front of the stage. This will be the third time I've seen Wire play this year. Yet I'm keyed up. Even if I hadn't rubbed a small cluster of grey crystals on my gum, I'd still be keyed up. The prospect of hearing new songs, the prospect of sonic overload. These days, Wire's performances are executed at supremely high volume.

The band is currently in international touring mode. Tonight is the 67th date they've played so far this year. Tonight, there will be no performance art interventions, no stage sets, no films, no blinding torchlights, no on stage dancers, no on stage exercise teams. Tonight it's just the music.

Bruce left the band back in 2004. His desire to approach sound in more abstract terms, was a core element of the band's appeal. Much as I was glad Wire had elected to carry on without him, it seemed highly unlikely that once the band's chemistry was altered, they could continue to produce work which possessed anything like the same strength and individuality. Wrong. And then some.

Guitarist Matt Simms is a natural fit. I've seen him play with Wire on numerous occasions over recent years, and his style is sonically very rich. Besides which, he has enough effects pedals to suggest he himself is more than a little fond of abstraction. His approach is perfectly suited to Wire's mode of expression, yet he never imitates Gilbert's style.

From the first note the band play tonight, it is obvious Wire are extremely tightly drilled, yet somehow still able to create moments of unfettered noise and experimentation. They take in songs from their last two albums, plus a lot of new material destined for their next one. As always, it's the new stuff that intrigues and excites the most. I am vibrating with pleasure throughout.

Following Bruce's departure, Wire have shifted away from the monochrome dramatics of *Send*, in favour of a sound which retains elements of stark rock, but also reconnects with the band's deeper, subtler and distinctly modernist psychedelic tendencies. The band's earlier 21st century work had inhabited a compressed and claustrophobic world. But tonight, when they play 'Please Take' it has an open, spacious feel, a bass which grooves and a guitar which glides.

The chorus of *"Fuck off out of my face, you take up too much space"* always makes me smile. The lines would seem merely blunt and crude if they were shouted or growled or hissed. But Wire seldom opt for the obvious. Instead, Lewis delivers this most vicious of couplets in a smooth croon, his baritone lending the words a lyrical gravity.

Tonight Wire climax with 'Boiling Boy'. I thought this a very fine song when it was released in 1988. But unfortunately, like many tracks from that era, the studio interpretation kept things too smooth, too digital. However, over recent years, in its various live interpretations, 'Boiling Boy' has become the highlight of many Wire gigs.

Matt picks out a repeating arpeggio whilst Robert plays an unwavering motorik – just the beat of the bass drum, the skitter of the hi-hat. Colin sings the opening lines *"Gifts of the west winds, dark and deep, in secret sunset, spaces creep."* If the lyrics commence with an intimation of poetic romance, then the chorus of *"Lock up your hats"* has echoes of early Dada.

Robert's metronomic rhythms send a warm prickling sensation up my arms and the back of my neck. This feels so good. So right. I've been such a prude about MDMA. Honestly. I think of all the times I could have enjoyed this buzz at gigs.

Half way through the song, Robert's snapping snare joins the fray, and Lewis doubles the force of his delivery. My heart rate increases.

The dual guitar assault powers onward, Colin unspooling the riff, Matt overlaying layers of scree. The simple riff rolls on becoming increasingly jagged and distorted, a continuing accumulation of elevating energy. In structural terms, the song couldn't be much simpler. Yet here, as elsewhere, Wire turn repetition into a form of transcendence.

The stage is streaked with blue and yellow light. The chemicals ripple through my system, nerve endings firing to the music's inner motor. Eyes closed, I sway to the music, my face split with a wide smile. This may be chemically assisted happiness. But it is happiness nonetheless.

For the next three days I find myself wading through a thick residue of anxiety, self doubt and all purpose misery. Ah, of course. *This* is why I never take MDMA.

* * * * *

Saturday 23rd March 2013, age 49.

Jesus I'm nervous…

Wire are curating their own music festival called *Drill*. It's spread across three days and several different London venues. This is the first of what will become an on going series of international *Drill* festivals, attracting both new, cutting edge acts and big names such as Swans, Earth and St. Vincent.

Right now, I'm sitting in Cafe Oto, in Dalston. It's a live music venue with an eye on the more experimental end of the spectrum. As part of the *Drill* festival, Colin has asked me to do an on stage interview with Wire. For some reason, I've arrived at the venue over an hour early. Wire themselves won't be here until about ten minutes before the interview is due to start. Jesus I'm nervous!

Alone, at a tiny table in the corner, I've read my handwritten notes over and over until they now seem to have jettisoned all meaning. I glance out of the window to see fat heavy snowflakes are falling. And sticking. Snow is already building up on the street. I check the time. Still 50 minutes before the interview is scheduled to start. "Perhaps it'll be cancelled due to the weather" I think optimistically. But no. People are stamping the snow off their boots outside and stepping into the warmth. The venue is steadily filling up. Jesus I'm nervous!

I've done stand up gigs where I've had to walk out in front of over a thousand people. I've had tiny acting roles where I've had to display my puny skills next to big stars. I've given evidence in crown court. But I've never felt anything approaching the nervousness I feel at this moment. Which is frankly a ludicrous state of affairs. Because by now I know the whole band fairly well and Sarah and I regularly hook up with Colin and Malka socially. In fact, my ever-increasing attendance at the band's live shows, means there are members of my own family I see far less than I do the members of Wire. And yet, despite all this, Jesus I'm nervous! Because no matter what the context I encounter them in, there is always something inside me shouting "This is *fucking Wire!*"

The venue is almost full. I had no idea the event would draw such a crowd. I read through my notes again. By now they are just abstract black marks on a white background. Finally the band arrives. A voice inside me shouts "This is *fucking Wire!*" To be exact, Colin, Graham and Matt arrive. Robert has been delayed as he's currently snowed in at home. A young guy from the venue sets up some chairs and mics.

Should I ever end up on *Mastermind*, Wire would be my specialist subject. In fact, I feel fairly confident I could actually win the whole show. Just so long as the general knowledge round also contained mainly Wire related questions. And yet, I know I am not alone in my devotion. Wire is a band that engenders obsessive and completist attitudes amongst their fans, both old and new. I'm well aware there are many here in the audience at Cafe Oto, who will know far more than me. Jesus I'm nervous!

I stand on stage. I introduce the band. There's no point in me looking at my notes – they are like anti-notes now. I somehow manage to say a few words about who Wire are. I somehow manage to not forget their names. I somehow get my first question out. Thankfully, both Graham and Colin are exceptionally articulate and whilst Matt doesn't say a huge amount, his contributions are both smart and thoughtful. During the audience Q&A, a couple of guys ask questions which sure enough display Wire-knowledge verging on the absolute. Thankfully I'm not the one who has to answer them. As the event concludes, I feel my muscles, my brain and my soul all gently unclenching. I have no recollection of what I have said.

The following evening, I go with Malcolm and my friend Paul Putner to the Heaven nightclub. Wire are launching their new album *Change Becomes Us*, which is being released tomorrow. They play the whole album in sequence. Another perverse gesture, as the majority of the audience are essentially being presented with an evening of entirely new material. Indeed, some songs are played for the first and only time. The band is accompanied on keyboards by Tim Lewis (aka Thighpaulsandra of Coil and Spiritualized). It's a rare treat to hear Wire play live with this additional colouring and it helps give the performance a very different feel. But it's with tonight's encore the show really marks itself out. For a performance of the song 'Pink Flag', Wire have assembled a guitar orchestra.

Along with around 50 other men and women, I join the band on stage. It's a diverse assembly of friends and fellow musicians including Malka, Steve Chandra Savale of Asian Dub Foundation, Julie Campbell aka Lone Lady, Emma Anderson of Lush, Robin Rimbaud of Scanner, Margaret Fiedler of Laika, the aforementioned Thighpaulsandra and numerous other faces, some I recognise, most I don't. We are all milling about. Scores of guitar leads snake across the floor of the stage. It takes an age for everyone to find an amp. The sound of buzzing jack-plugs fills the sound system. I feel like an imposter. I can't play guitar. But I guess any noises I make will be subsumed by the others.

Suddenly, Colin shouts "One, two, three!" and the massed guitarists begin to play. The song only has one chord; 'E'. That is part of its strength. And to hear the chord being hit over and over on 50+ guitars is breathtaking. The noise fizzes in my head, the physical impact of the waves of electricity repeatedly hit me in the gut as they roll out from the stage. If this is what it sounds like up here, who knows what it must sound like out in the auditorium. This is the loudest thing I have ever heard. The loudest thing I have ever *felt*. The song powers on for over 8 minutes. The tinnitus lasts for over 48 hours.

* * * * *

Thursday 19th September 2013.

I'm working in Manchester, filming the second series of *Hebburn*. It's been a long day. Yesterday was also a long day. I forgot to measure the day before that, but that also felt quite long. I was up working until well after midnight last night doing rewrites, then I got up at 5:30 this morning and worked in the studio right through until 7pm. I am exhausted. And there's another similar day looming up tomorrow. What's required is a very early night.

It's now just before 8pm and I'm standing at the end of Oldham Street, waiting for Pete to pick me up, so we can drive over to Brudenell Social Club in Leeds.

This will be the fifth time I've seen Wire play this year. I know, I *know*. It's obsessive. And it could be seen as unhealthy. But it makes me so happy. After The Fall, Wire are the group I've seen play live the most times. And their strike rate for top quality gigs is the highest of any band I know. Tonight I want to surrender to sound in a way that's only possible at a great gig. Pete pulls up in his black Mazda RX8. I climb into the passenger seat. "A'right fella?" He smiles and we squeeze each other's hand and drive off.

It's just three short months since Dad died. Four weeks ago we buried his ashes. A big portion of my identity right now still seems to be 'bereaved person'. Not that I'm still sobbing all the time. It's just that he's on my mind so much. It feels like in repeatedly pondering on Dad's death what I'm actually doing is not grieving, but convincing myself to accept the reality of the situation.

Pete parks up and we walk into the venue. It's a warm night and the club is packed. We go to the bar. Pete orders a pint of lager but I just want a cranberry juice. It was only two nights ago that I went out on a bar crawl around Manchester with Jim Moir and Mark E. Smith. The shadow of a monumental hangover has only just lifted.

The journey turns out to have been more than worth it. It's the best show I've seen Wire play this year. The venue's acoustics are top notch, the audience is enthusiastic and energetic and the band play with concentrated power.

They launch into 'Adore Your Island'. It opens up like The Who's 'Baba O'Riley' in a parallel universe, with Colin delivering a series of compressed power chords. No song has entertained me more this year than 'Adore Your Island'. And yet there's a sadness to the song too. The lyric *"It holds a fragile head, in intensive care"* always summons up thoughts of the recent deaths of both my Dad and Sarah's Mum.

Suddenly, the group surge into a wall of thrashing guitar. It sounds artfully unhinged. And it proves yet again that for all their intellectual rigour, Wire are still more than capable of out-punking the competition. Then a sudden switchback to the tension of the power chords. *"First I say I love you. Then you're silent."* Again, this line always gives me chills. The fear of rejection, the fear of loss of love within us all.

The band surge back into the wall of thrashing guitar. After 4 bars of this cacophony, Graham, Colin and Robert thump to a halt, but Matt continues to batter his guitar. Not strumming or picking, but slapping and punching the strings. The noise he generates sounds like the metal panels of an automobile grating together as they are squeezed inside a compactor. This barrage only lasts maybe 10 seconds, but the impact is enormous. The instant Matt stops, the silence is deafening, the audience too taken aback to respond. "Get *him*." Jokes Colin. "Sparkle Simms!" Then the room bursts into raucous applause.

Tonight Wire also play 'Map Ref. 41°N 93°W'. One of the numerous diamonds in *154*'s coronet, it's a song in the British deviant psychedelic tradition, which takes in Kevin Ayers, Syd Barrett's vision of The Pink Floyd and Brian Eno's early song based albums. This is a psychedelia which lacks any Americanisms, or 60s retro touches. Harder and pacier than its recorded counterpart, tonight's version soars with a lysergic grace.

I nod contentedly to myself. Nothing is going to top that. But then they play 'Stealth of a Stork'. I've loved this song since first hearing it age 16, on the live album *Document And Eyewitness*. It's a fast and frenzied piece, kept in combustible motion by Robert's brutal yet precise drumming.

It opens with Colin chopping out a straightforward riff, but each time the group shift from the riff to a more atonal bass driven section, Colin calls out the word "Change!" And he shouts it again when the group shifts back to the riff. But this isn't a bandleader calling out instructions. After all, they have been playing this song live since 1980. Wire know exactly what they are doing. Rather, this is another example of the group's diagrammatic approach to songwriting. On one level, 'Stealth of a Stork' is a hard driving piece of unadorned rock – the template that was picked up by the likes of The Minutemen and Fugazi. Yet at the points where the song neatly switches modes of expression, instead of allowing the audience to appreciate how smoothly the group affect the transitions, Wire choose to point up the vicissitudes.

Most songs try to seduce us into believing the song itself is a discreet world, where poetry, melody and rhythm are inhabited by a performer who transfers these to the listener via a form of intimate and direct communication. But here, Wire appear able to stand outside this song, commenting on its arrangement, whilst simultaneously also serving up a piece of music of such impact it's impossible to remain still.

Tonight, 'Stealth of a Stork' sounds like one of the most exciting songs ever written. And I'm not alone in thinking this. As the crowd applaud, just a few feet away from Pete and I, a man in his 30s shouts out with a mixture of amazement and reverence "People!! We're watching *fucking Wire*!!"

* * * * *

Sunday 13th April 2014.

I woke up. I was old.

Today is my birthday. I have been alive for 50 years. And I have seen many things. I have seen clothing fashions change and change again. I've seen lapels go in and out and in and out. I've seen flares go in and out and in and out. I was there in 1974, when flares were in, flares were cool.

I was there in 1977, when flares, through no fault of their own, became uncool and went out. And I was there in 1987, when flares came back in and were cool again. Now of course, we live in an age where flares refuse to occupy a definitive point on the cool/uncool spectrum. Are flares cool? We *just don't know*. And I think we may never know again. I think that knowledge has been lost to us.

This morning, like every morning, my ears are ringing. Whenever I'm lying in bed, late at night or early morning, when there are fewer sounds to distract me, I become aware of the ringing in my ears, especially my right ear. A 'war wound' from that very first rock gig, still making its presence felt.

Last night, I topped up my tinnitus. Sarah and I went to see Chrysta Bell and her band perform at the Pavilion Theatre. I've been playing Bell's album *This Train* quite a lot over the last couple of years. Produced by David Lynch, who also co-wrote several of the songs, it has the kind of dreamy yet passionate gleam that I find irresistible. Live however, Bell's performance was mannered in the extreme. Her between song banter so breathy, calculated, insincere and corny it felt like a brand of show business being beamed in directly from the early 1950s.[3]

Tonight I'm going to top up my tinnitus even further. Because tonight, for my 50th birthday party, I've hired The Haunt, a venue in Brighton's Pool Valley, near the seafront. My good friends Barry Adamson and Louise Manzaroli are DJ-ing and Wire are playing a set. *Fucking Wire!*

Over a year earlier, I'd phoned Colin and first floated this idea. "What would you want us to do?" He asked, initially sounding slightly suspicious. "Well, y'know, play a set." There was a pause. I imagined him thinking about all the worst-case scenarios a fan could ask for. That they

---

3. Three years later, Chrysta Bell would appear in the re-launched *Twin Peaks*, playing FBI Agent Tammy Preston, acting alongside David Lynch himself, in his role as Gordon Cole. In a series encompassing a whole spectrum of strangeness, Bell managed to give perhaps the most mannered performance of the show's 21st century incarnation.

play only tracks from the 1970s? That they play a set of Pussycat Dolls covers? That they jump out of four individual giant cakes? "You mean like a... normal gig?" He asked. "Yes."

I want them to play as if it *isn't* my birthday. I want them to do just what Wire do. I'm excited. But I'm also quite nervous about the party. Outside of my work, I'm a fairly shy individual who doesn't require much attention. In fact I'm the kind of person who, if they ever wrote their autobiography would make it mainly about something else. Music perhaps.

In truth, I'd happily walk the streets in a cloak of invisibility. Except I think the temptation to shop lift would be too great. But tonight I've invited a few hundred friends and colleagues to celebrate my birthday. The feeling of responsibility is unlike anything I've ever felt. The only way I've been able to cope with this is by turning it into a project.

Since I first saw it, late one Sunday night, age 17, my most loved film has always been Lindsay Anderson's 1973 satire *O Lucky Man!*. Written by David Sherwin, it's a thee hour picaresque epic which sees Michael Travis (played by the youthful Malcolm McDowell) travelling the country, meeting pretty much every element of society and falling victim to corruption in each and every sector. And yet, in the final scene, a happy, smiling Travis attends a party. Here, in a large hall, all the characters he has encountered on his journey dance together in celebration, as on stage, Alan Price and his band perform the film's theme song. I want my 50th birthday party to be like that. Except without Alan Price. But with Wire. Also, I should clarify I'm not implying any of my friends are corrupt.

* * * * *

I awake the following morning. My ears are ringing *very loudly*. If last night doesn't turn out to be the best night of my life, then I'm at an absolute loss as to what might top it.

Mum, my sisters Carolyn, Gillian and Susan and my brother-in-law Simon were there. Sarah, looking stunning in a long yellow satin gown, Misha so tall and sharp with his partner the smart and sylphlike Amy. Malcolm and his wife Lucy. And of course my oldest friend Pete.

Naturally, I hardly got a chance to talk with anybody for more than a couple of minutes. Like a wedding reception, it was a continuous flow of smiling faces and shaking hands and hugging. So many men and women whom I am proud to be able to call my friends. There were people I see most weeks and there were people I hadn't seen for well over a decade. Hell, the one thing there wasn't was any Goths.

And the music! Louise delivered an eclectic set, including some of my most beloved tunes of the last 50 years. Barry played a set of dark funk and slick grooves and managed, as ever, to be the coolest man in the room.

And best of all Wire were Wire. They opened with 'Drill', a song formed from a tight, spinning rhythm with guitars sparking like Catherine wheels. They played 'Another The Letter', 'Stealth of a Stork' and 'Adore Your Island'. But best of all, they played several bold and bristling new songs. I welled up three times and laughed hysterically once. They finished with another so far unreleased song: 'Harpooned'. Eight minutes of slow-moving Sabbath-like riffage climaxing in a viscous tempest of distortion.

Pete and I stand next to each other, thirty-five years after we attended our first rock gig together. He rests his head on my shoulder and says "I love you brother".

For the encore, I join Wire on stage. Jesus I'm nervous! About a month ago, Colin suggested I sing '12XU' with them. I declined. The song is so fast I just knew I would get lost in it. Then he suggested I play guitar with them on a version of 'Boiling Boy'. I felt compelled to remind him that I can't play guitar. "It's all in 'E'." He said. "Just like 'Pink Flag'. You could play that okay." It's true. "But, when I, for want of a better word 'played' that, I was hidden amongst over 50 other guitarists, who knew what they were doing." Colin finally convinced me it was a good idea. Or rather he convinced me to ignore the fact that it was a bad idea. For all my devotion to music I have to say I am far from musical.

Nevertheless I practiced for weeks in my office in the loft. Playing a live recording of Wire playing 'Boiling Boy' through the speakers and strumming along in 'E' on a red acoustic guitar. After a while, I began to feel a tiny, tiny bit more confident.

But then I find myself standing on stage with Wire. Around my neck, Colin's white Ovation Breadwinner guitar. It's a weirdly shaped instrument, with the main body resembling an axe head. To many, it's a guitar that will always be associated with Ace Frehley of KISS. Although to someone like me, who believes KISS are for music fans who place actual music very low down on their list of priorities, the Breadwinner will be forever synonymous with 1970s Wire.

The group begins to play the song. I close my eyes and listen. It sounds magnificent. I'm just so happy to be here in amongst the music. After a couple of bars I open my eyes. Across the stage Matt nods, encouraging me to join in. My fingers stiff and tense I gather myself together. I play the chord.

It's the wrong chord. It's not E. I'm not sure if it's even one of the chords which has been assigned a letter yet. It clangs out, tuneless and dissonant. I have dented the magnificence. I burst out laughing. I should not be here. I struggle gamely to find the right chord, the sound of the group surging around me. By the time I eventually hit my stride, the song is over.

* * * * *

There are audio recordings of it. But I can't bring myself to listen to them. There are video recordings of it. But I can't bring myself to watch them. In reality, I would have been far happier standing in the audience, watching Wire play it on their own. They are *fucking Wire*. And I'm not. However, there are photographs of it. And I am more than happy to look at those. There's *me* playing guitar with *Wire*! And the sound I imagine in my head is far better than any I made on that stage.

Tonight, I'm heading out to yet another gig. I know, I *know*. My good friend Lee Oliver and I are going to see Jesca Hoop at the Komedia. I've been playing her albums since 2007's goose pimple inducing *Kismet*.

But this will be my first chance to see her play live. Apparently she's performing an acoustic set, so I'm thinking this shouldn't contribute too much to my tinnitus mountain.

I climb out of bed, get dressed and go down to the kitchen. Mum is staying with us and we make breakfast together. Aside from the ringing in my ears, I'm actually not feeling too fragile. I spent so much time talking last night I didn't have a chance to do a great deal of drinking.

We sit together and sip mint tea. I mention Wire. "I've never heard anything so loud." Says Mum. In my blind enthusiasm, it never occurred to me that before the end of their second song, she and my sisters would have been so overwhelmed by the volume they'd have snuck off to seek sanctuary in a nearby bar. "I could feel it, physically." She says, patting her chest. "I know." I nod keenly. "That's one of the things I've always loved about live music." She reminds me about my fainting after The Jam gig. I nod. "But of course my first live music experience was going to see Cliff with you and Gran and Carolyn." She shakes her head. "No. There was one before that." I'm amazed. "Really?"

"You'd have been four, so it must have been 1968. I took you to see a pantomime of 'Babes in the Wood', and they had Freddie and The Dreamers doing a few songs." Perhaps unsurprisingly, I have absolutely no recollection of this.

Freddie and The Dreamers were a pop beat group who, despite coming from Manchester, got lumped in with the Merseybeat sound. Although smartly dressed in suits and thin ties, they were a deeply unprepossessing quintet. Lead singer Freddie Garrity was skinny and bespectacled and his constantly smiling stage presence was the opposite of rock and roll cool. He would prance and skip about the stage waving his arms and legs in choreographed glee. Between 1963 and 1965 they scored three number threes and a number five. By 1968, they would have been on the slide. Hence the panto.

"You were very frightened." Says Mum. This seems unlikely. "Frightened? Of Freddie and The Dreamers?" She laughs and takes my hand. "Before that, I think I'd only ever taken you to the pictures. So you must have assumed what you were watching was a film. But then, during one of the songs, Freddie jumped off the stage and came dancing down the aisle towards us. Well, you just couldn't understand how a character from a film had suddenly come to life. So you hid under your seat. You cried and cried. You were too scared to come out."

So that's the truth of the matter. I had always believed that my first gig was about as uncool as you could get: Cliff Richard singing gospel songs. Turns out I was doubly wrong. That wasn't my first gig. And it wasn't as uncool as you could get. Hiding in fear from Freddie and The Dreamers is as uncool as you could get.

CODA

On 24th January 2018, exactly a week after I finish writing *Foreground Music*, I'm sitting working at my laptop when a message comes up on Facebook from Keiron Melling. A kind and straightforward man, Keiron has been drumming with The Fall for the last decade; "What's your number mate? Could do with speaking to you." I sit for a moment with my face in my hands. I know what this is going to be.

The last time I saw The Fall play was one year ago; Sunday 29th January 2017 at the Concorde 2 in Brighton. The rhythm section of Keiron and Dave Spurr was like an efficient war machine, Peter Greenway's guitar incisive and intractable, the sound further beefed up by an additional drummer. The group was bullet-proof. Over this, Mark sang, ranted and extemporised, stalking the stage, a charismatic and acute presence.

Afterwards, in the dressing room, although he looked washed out, Mark was still lively, mercilessly taking the piss out of the additional drummer who was, as Mark put it, "used to working with the fuckin' Australian Pink Floyd! So fuck knows what he makes of this set up!"

He said he'd recently been really sick with a chest infection, bed bound for nearly a month. But I could see then Mark was still very ill. When we spoke on the phone a few weeks later, he revealed he'd been diagnosed with cancer. Something he described with typical economy as "quite disappointing actually".

Although Mark's exact medical condition has never been officially announced, it's been widely reported in the music press that he's seriously ill. During the final Fall shows of last year Mark was singing from a wheelchair, his arm in a sling. Opinion on his decision to go ahead with these gigs has been divided. Some have labelled it a morbid freak show, whilst others – including many who've witnessed the gigs themselves – say the shows are a testament to Mark's force of will.

Years ago, the two of us were sitting drinking in the Space Bar in Manchester. I'd been saying how I couldn't imagine ever wanting to stop writing, how I didn't think I could retire. Mark shook his head. "Retire? No." He screwed up his face, talking in a sarcastic half growl. "I mean what do you wanna be, somebody who used to do something?"

Due to his declining health, the remaining scheduled live dates of 2017 were indefinitely postponed. The last time I saw Mark in person was on 12th November. I visited him at his girlfriend Pam's house in Prestwich, where he was recuperating after a course of chemo. He looked so small, skinny and careworn. Yet he was in remarkably good spirits. Although we talked a little about his illness, Mark was full of plans for the future. A week-long residency in Brooklyn, more recording and an idea for a documentary.

He'd been watching lots of DVDs and had recently enjoyed *The Greasy Strangler*, as well as revisiting Lindsay Anderson's wonderful *Britannia Hospital*. I gave him a copy of Philip K. Dick's post-apocalyptic sci-fi novel *Dr. Bloodmoney*, as I'd remembered him saying it was one of the very few of Dick's books he hadn't read. He remarked how disappointed he'd been with *Electric Dreams,* the recent TV series of adaptations of Dick's short stories, targeting the glossy title sequence in particular; "It's like they're trying to get you to join Nat West!"

But most of all, we laughed. Mark is one of the funniest men I've ever known. The fact that you never know where the humour is going to come from, or what the target might be makes his company all the more exhilarating. As I rode in the taxi on the way back to Manchester, my cheeks were aching from laughing. Yet I was also well aware that this would probably be the last time I'd ever see him.

I look at Keiron's Facebook message again. I send him my number. I know exactly what this is going to be. A few moments later my mobile rings.

AFTERWORD

The majority of the time, when we experience music, we are experiencing it as background. When we play music at home, we usually listen to it whilst engaged in some other activity – from doing the washing up to making love.

We hear music on the soundtracks of motion pictures, television programmes, computer games and commercials. We hear it on the radio whilst we work. We hear music in pubs and bars as we drink, in restaurants as we eat. We hear music whilst driving. We hear it through headphones whilst commuting on public transport, whilst going for a walk or a run, or whilst exercising in the gym.

Music soundtracks our experience of the world. Music is one of life's great enhancers. But music is seldom the main event. It is only really when we attend concerts and gigs, or go clubbing, that music becomes the main event. Only then do we experience foreground music.

Meanwhile, the majority of music writing tends to be focused on recorded works, classic albums, top 50 lists and so on. Writing about these might seem like a safer bet. After all, the recordings are all still there. Fixed. They can be examined and reexamined. Whereas a gig is an ephemeral event. A matter of minutes. A matter of opinion. But then isn't it all opinion anyway? As David Cronenberg said "All reality is virtual."

I've always had a sharp memory. Well, that is as long as it involves something that interests or excites me. Or irritates me. If it fulfils one of those criteria then it's lodged in my mind for good. If it doesn't interest, excite or irritate then it is hit and miss if I'll even recall it five minutes after it's occurred. Nevertheless, whilst writing this book, there were various resources I could call upon.

Up until my mid 20s, I was a devoted diarist and I've remained a keen note taker and list maker. All of the scripts, articles or essays I've written started out as a note or a list. For some of the earlier gigs, I could also refer to reviews I wrote for my abandoned fanzine. Further *aide-mémoires* included stolen set lists, bootleg recordings, the recollections of other audience members, or of the performing musicians themselves.

For a few of the shows covered, there was contemporaneous performance footage available from just a week or so before or after the gig in question. For four of the shows, there was YouTube audience footage from the actual gigs themselves. Although all of these were incomplete, and of course had questionable sound quality and had been shot from someone else's perspective.

Once I started writing I realised – my passion for music aside – this was also a book concerned with three other key subjects; friendship, love and mortality. Yet, somehow, each of these led me back to the music.

Firstly friendship. I have been blessed with good and loyal friends. Some friends feature prominently in these pages. Others have slipped between the wide gaps between gigs. Being deeply disinterested in sport, I've never had access to the topics of football or cricket as an aid to social interaction. Music however is another great 'connector'. Music can help forge human connections, seal friendships and bind us together.

It may seem a superficial form of assessment, but there are certain bands whom I must confess to using as barometers of other people's friendship potential: Wire, The Fall and Coil primarily. If they dig any of these bands, then I think there's an increased likelihood we might be able to connect. Then, if the conversation goes a little 'deeper', I may well bring up Ludus, The Passage, Marshall Jefferson, Cotton Mather or Black Dresses.

Secondly, love. As youngsters, when we become besotted with a song, or a style of music, many of us find ourselves involved in a dry run for the act of falling in love with another human. A song or album or band will seize our imaginations, trigger endorphins and dominate our thoughts. In much the same way a boy or girl does when we fall for them. And, when we *do* finally fall for another human, the music soundtracking those moments becomes a hugely potent element of our love stories, whether in private or in public, on the dance floor or in the bedroom.

Thirdly mortality. Our friends and family die. Our heroes die. We die. Yes, that's an obvious statement of fact. Yet, as a society, we often behave as if death is something that happens to some people some times. Rather than something that happens to everybody. Always.

The deaths of Ian Curtis, John Peel, Peter Christopherson and David Bowie all felt like personal losses. I say this not to imply there was some kind of special bond between these people and myself. Quite the opposite. It wasn't the personal individual stuff that mattered. Rather it was the stuff that was accessible to everyone. The music. With each death – even with Curtis who, when he took his own life aged 23, could not have guessed the increasingly high regard he and his work would be held in by future generations – what I experienced was not just the sadness of their passing, but a reminder of how their music, or in Peel's case, his curating of music, had helped shape both my life and my approach to life.

And with each of these deaths, I was aware that across the country, across the world, other people were feeling variations of these same emotions. In certain respects, the death of my own father felt more unreal, because of the very private nature of the loss. Mark E. Smith's death on the other hand was a triple whammy; death of a hero, death of a friend, death of an era.

There are of course any number of ways we can look back and plot our journey through time. For my Dad, it was always via the various cars he'd driven during different periods of his life. But for me, it's always been music. Swiftly followed by films, television, art and books.

All the gigs covered in this book affected me both physically and emotionally. A number of them occurred at points of personal transition or crisis. A few of them were the triggers for those transitions. Some of them were nights of true epiphany. A couple, were lessons in industrial strength disappointment.

There are plenty of other gigs that I considered writing about. An alternate timeline might follow up that Cliff Richard gospel concert with Siouxsie and the Banshees at King George's Hall, Blackburn in 1978, Magazine at the same venue in 1979, The Passage at Derby Hall, Bury in 1981, Ludus at the Green Room, Manchester in 1982, NON at The Zap, Brighton in 1985, Michael Nyman at Bloomsbury

Theatre, London in 1985, Sonic Youth at The Zap in 1986, Orbital at Glastonbury in 1995, Chicks on Speed at the Richmond, Brighton in 1999, Domestic4 at the Lift, Brighton in 2000, Gorillaz at the Opera House, Manchester in 2005, Robyn at the Concorde 2, Brighton in 2010, Mazzy Star at Shepherd's Bush Empire in 2012, and Laurie Anderson at the Dome, Brighton in 2015.

It won't surprise you to learn I still attend gigs. Although, not as many as I'd like. The thing about writing is it takes a lot of time. And then it takes lot of *extra* time on top of that. But there are certain bands, both new and old, who are pretty much guaranteed to get me to step away from the laptop and head into town. To stand in the crowd, big or small. To move to the rhythm, to feel the throb of the bass inside my frame. To bask in the haze of electrical noise.

A great gig elevates my spirit like nothing else. And, despite my steadily increasing tinnitus, I very seldom resort to wearing earplugs. As I say, people who like music are stupid.

RECOMMENDED LISTENING

For each entry, I've suggested a live album, as this is a book about gigs, followed by a studio album.

CLIFF RICHARD
Cliff (1959)

Cliff's self-titled debut was recorded live at EMI Recording Studios (later renamed Abbey Road) in front of an invited audience. Backed by The Drifters (later renamed The Shadows), he gives a committed performance of a selection of original US rock 'n' roll songs such as 'That'll Be The Day' and 'Baby I Don't Care'. The recording is a fascinating document of an era when British rock 'n' roll was still tightly constrained within the world of show business. However, the audience's response to Cliff's debut hit single 'Move It' provides a foretaste of the mania that would envelop The Beatles.

I'm Nearly Famous (1975)

Whilst there is arguably no such thing as an essential Cliff Richard album, this 1975 outing probably comes closest. Recorded after a slight dip in the singer's popularity, it sees him returning with a more AOR sound. The title track has a Stonesy strut, yet inevitably replaces Jagger's sneer with a cheeky grin. But it would be a flinty heart indeed that didn't warm upon hearing the upbeat 70s pop bounce of 'You've Got To Give Me All Your Lovin''. The standout is the tender ballad 'Miss You Nights' which wouldn't have sounded out of place on The Walker Brothers' *Lines*. Instead it ended up being covered by Westlife. Oh brutal fate.

THE JAM
Fire & Skill (2015)
This six album set covers the band's entire career. The third disc: *The Jam at Reading University in February 1979*, captures a show akin to the one described in Chapter Two. Eight months on, and the songs of *All Mod Cons* are firmly embedded in the set, with the band well able to generate the maximum tension and release from the material. There's also an undertone of repressed violence to some of the songs that adds a dangerous glint to the performance. Highlights include a pugnacious 'Billy Hunt' and a spikey version of 'Mr. Clean' in which Weller absolutely seethes with distaste.

All Mod Cons (1978)
When a set of songs Paul Weller had written for the band's third album were rejected by their producer, The Jam were forced to go back to the drawing board. The result is an album that has everything to prove and sets about proving it with verve and precision. The inclusion of the Kinks' 'David Watts' was an indication that Weller's own lyrics were becoming as much concerned with storytelling as with articulating his ideas and passions. If 'Down in the Tube Station at Midnight' was the clearest example of this, then 'Billy Hunt' and the wide eyed and wired 'To Be Someone' have their own tales to tell. These are also – lest we forget – songs written by a 19 year old lad, feeling his way into the adult world.

2-TONE
Dance Craze (1981)
Dance Craze serves as a reminder that 2-Tone was indeed an entire movement. The album captures all the key bands of the ska revival at peak performance. Aside from The Specials, Madness and The Selecter, there are also live workouts from The Beat, The Bodysnatchers and Bad Manners. Highlights include a crisp and forceful 'Ranking Full Stop' courtesy of The Beat, whilst The Selecter's performance of 'Too Much Pressure' is a sparking jolt of pure energy. Throughout we're reminded

of how much of an influence the spirit and attack of punk was on the 2-Tone sound – something the studio cuts sometimes underplay.

The Specials (1979)
Released the same day as Madness' debut album, *The Specials* creates a vision of urban lives and loves which weds social realism to celebratory rhythms. It's an impressive feat that an album containing so many cover versions has such a cohesive feel and identity. From here on, Jerry Dammers would become increasingly interested in expanding the band's sound palette and experimenting with different musical stylings. But *The Specials* represents the high watermark of the original 2-Tone sound – vital, bright and burning to communicate with its audience.

JOY DIVISION
Les Bain Douches (2001)
On stage Joy Division were always a far more aggressively defiant proposition than their studio incarnation. This album comprises nine songs from a December 1979 performance in Paris, and a further seven from January 1980 shows in Amsterdam and the Netherlands respectively. Bernard Sumner is on particularly fine form on the Paris recordings, his guitar work on 'Shadowplay' and '24 Hours' a perfect balance of volatility and control. Elsewhere, 'Autosuggestion' is rendered as a fluid stutter, suddenly accelerating into frenzy as Ian Curtis' anguished vocal grips on for dear life.

Unknown Pleasures (1979)
Just ten songs make up perhaps the most perfectly realised soundworld of the post-punk era, with Martin Hannett's production moving the music light years away from the sound of live performance. As Curtis' sensitized lyrics explore both exterior and interior space, the instrumentation is turned inside out. Bass lines become lead lines, guitars sound like synths, the echo is more important than the source. Despite the band's reputation as purveyors of sadness, that is only part of their story. Opening track

'Disorder' is the sound of a headlong surrender to fate, whereas 'Interzone' is a jittery rush of exhilaration in dark times.

PSYCHIC TV
Those Who Do Not (1984)
Psychic TV have released a vast number of their live shows as albums, although the quality is variable, in terms of both musical style and sonic fidelity. But here, with selections recorded in Reykjavik, they come over like a fractured British version of The Velvet Underground, powered by magickal process, ritualistic intention and unshakable self-belief. The instinctive playing, especially in the more improvisatory sections, is exceptional and, on pieces such as 'Those Who Do Knot' and 'What's A Place Like You…' they sound truly unique.

Dreams Less Sweet (1983)
Beauty and the grotesque walk hand in hand through a landscape that is as much indebted to the spirit of William Blake as it is to Industrial music. Musically we can hear Peter Christopherson developing a number of the ideas he would explore much further in Coil, whilst Genesis P. Orridge's lyrics have never been more finely wrought. The album is the work of many collaborators, but a good portion of the glory is clearly due to Andrew Poppy's gorgeous yet sparing orchestrations. A genuinely experimental collection, *Dreams Less Sweet* contains songs you can hum, as well as ones that will jangle your nerves. It's also an important work, in that it foregrounds a number of obsessions which would gradually permeate both the wider counter culture and the mainstream – from chaos magick to tattoos and piercings. You need to hear this at least once.

THE SHAMEN
Synergy Live Mix Live On KISS 100 FM / Live in Manchester (2016)
Recorded in 1992, but not released until 24 years later, this album offers up two contrasting sets. The first is a live mix of prerecorded tracks and samples for KISS with DJ Stika and the preternaturally perky Mr. C in

full effect. The second set features The Shamen riding their newfound tsunami of popularity, including the wave-your-hands-in-the-air splurge of 'Comin' on Strong' and the please-let-it-end-soon gurn-fest of 'Ebeneezer Goode'. Whilst this is an album only of genuine interest to fervid completists, it does provide a freeze frame of the moment when the mores of the acid and E-powered underground went fully overground.

In Gorbachev We Trust (1989)

The sound of a group caught between several worlds and making the most of all of them. At this stage in their development, The Shamen knew the dynamics of psychedelic rock inside out, as is on full display on the phasing glory of 'Adam Strange'. But their embrace of modernist production techniques and numerous strains of dance floor music meant that they had so many more weapons in their arsenal. It remains largely unheralded as a collection, possibly due to the band's hurried exit from hipsterdom. But *In Gorbachev We Trust* is a bold, ambitious and entirely successful bricolage of psychedelic pop, art rock, hip hop and acid house. As such it prefigures what Primal Scream would do with *Screamadelica* two years later.

PRIMAL SCREAM

Live in Japan (2003)

Recorded in Tokyo, with a set list that draws most heavily from the *XTRMNTR* and *Evil Heat* albums, this is Primal Scream very much in electro-rock mode. The sound is lean and edgy with an unstoppable momentum. From the second 'Accelerator' crashes into inflammable motion, Primal Scream never really let up. With 'Shoot Speed/Kill Light' they comprehensively improve on the studio version, whilst 'Swastika Eyes' is transformed into some kind of mutant psychedelic gabba excursion. No recording can truly capture the charge of a live gig. But this album comes as close as damn it.

Screamadelica (1991)

Like so many pivotal recordings – such as the debut albums by The Velvet Underground, Roxy Music or Massive Attack – *Screamadelica* offers up not so much a new style, as a unique mix of existing styles. A magpie's collection made up of soul, house, gospel and so on. What makes this an even bolder set is the inclusion of songs such as 'Damaged' and 'Inner Flight'. Most bands would have hesitated to interrupt the album's dance floor flow with down tempo country blues and chill-out room introspection. But in the end, *Screamadelica*'s success is the result of masterful cross genre songwriting and a wisely assembled host of collaborators.

THE VELVET UNDERGROUND

The Complete Matrix Tapes (2015)

The Velvets were a creatively restless live band, frequently overhauling their material from one night to the next, resulting in performances of songs which could differ wildly in length, tempo and tone. Therefore the band's live recordings are often things of unique beauty. Comprising four entire sets professionally recorded over two nights in San Francisco 1969, *The Complete Matrix Tapes* proves that The Velvets didn't lose their willingness to experiment when John Cale left the band. The 4:31 version of 'What Goes On' is superb. But when it comes to the 8:53 minute version, nothing else matters.

The Velvet Underground & Nico (1967)

One of the most important musical recordings of the 20th century. Period. The Velvets' debut album was a signpost planted in the late 1960s pointing to absolute elsewhere. Not many people followed it initially, but some of those who did, such as David Bowie, Brian Eno or Jonathan Richman, went on to plant signposts of their own. Contemporary rock music without the influence of The Velvet Underground is thankfully unimaginable. We would be living in a completely different world. And it would be crap.

SLEATER-KINNEY
Live in Paris (2017)

When Sleater-Kinney returned to the studio and stage following an eight-year hiatus, they did so as an acknowledged influence on a generation of bands. However, as this album recorded in March 2015 attests, they weren't primarily focused on re-treading their best-known 'hits'. A pin sharp performance sees the trio deliver a set largely made up of songs from their just released *No Cities To Love* and their pre-pause album *The Woods* (2005). The gesture squarely positions the band as a relevant on going concern and also allows them to explore the live possibilities of the newly recorded material. Highlights include the crooked fury of 'What's Mine is Yours' and a terse febrile take on 'Surface Envy'.

All Hands on the Bad One (2000)

Sleater-Kinney's fifth long player is possibly their strongest and certainly the most varied in tone. With lyrics that flit from the intensely personal to the overtly political, they deliver a set of songs such as 'You're No Rock 'n' Roll Fun' and 'Ballad of a Ladyman' which show a band operating entirely on their own terms. Meanwhile, 'The Professional' is their sparkling punk-pop moment. Yet it's all over in one minute twenty-eight seconds. All these and more show why, at this point in their career, Sleater-Kinney were the greatest rock 'n' roll band in the world.

THE STROKES
Live in Iceland (2002)

Recorded at the Broadway in Reykjavik, this is an extremely short and snappy split CD/DVD. With only six songs, it serves more as a live sampler than a full document of the band on stage. Nevertheless, it does offer up a snapshot of The Strokes three years into their career, brimming with confidence and couldn't care less charm. The full-tilt performance of 'Soma' is probably the standout, with the guitars of Nick Valensi and Albert Hammond Jr. constantly meshing and diverging. The closing 'Take It Or Leave It' is a master-class in musical urgency and brevity, leaving a very vocal audience ecstatic but hungry for more.

Is This It (2000)

It would be easy to describe this album as reinventing the wheel. And, whilst there may be little to truly surprise here, there is much to enjoy. Garage rock had been largely nudged to the sidelines during the 1990s, but The Strokes helped bring it out into the spotlight with what became the definitive turn of the century garage band album. Despite giving the impression of being rock rebels, The Strokes are clearly a very clever pop band in the tradition of The Kinks or Blondie. In fact, this is such a smart and poised collection you're left with the distinct impression pretty much every song on the album could have been released as a single.

THE FALL

Totale's Turns (1980)

There are as many live albums by The Fall as there are studio recordings. This early entry into their live discography is notable for its skeletal rockabilly sound and for the off kilter wit of Mark E. Smith's inter-song banter. Of the other live recordings from this era, the barbed majesty of *In A Hole* (1983) is well worth your attention, as it showcases the group at its most tense, mesmeric and Beefheartian. Late period picks would have to include the thrilling *Last Night at the Palais* (2009) and the delightfully titled *The Fall Group – Live Uurop VIII-XII Places In Sun & Winter, Son* (2014) both of which prove The Fall of the 21st century were still exploring areas other bands could scarcely dream of.

Live At The Witch Trials (1979)

With a band as long running and prolific as The Fall it's a tricky task to select just one studio album. But their debut still stands as a staggeringly individual statement of intent. The majority of the elements that would remain constant throughout The Fall's forty-one year lifespan are already in place and punching hard; taut garage band riffs, uncompromising arrangements, and lyrics that blend the magical and arcane with the earthy and the quotidian. And at the heart of it all is the sound of a man who declares in the album's title track "I still believe in the 'R'n'R dream, 'R'n'R' as primal scream". The first essential album in a lifetime of essential albums.

DAVID BOWIE
Welcome to the Blackout – Live London '78 (2018)

This set was recorded in 1978, from the same tour that spawned the earlier live album *Stage*. However, whereas that release cherry picked from several international tour dates, this one is a complete performance from London Earl's Court. And it's a pretty special show. 'Beauty And The Beast' is funkier than its studio counterpart, even as it seems to travel further away from conventional song form. 'Sound and Vision', which received its first ever live performance that night, has an uncharacteristically summery spring in its step, and the weird, clipped version of 'Jean Genie' is virtually unrecognisable.

Low (1977)

Despite the revolutionary stance of the punk movement, Bowie's *Low* was almost certainly the most musically radical 'rock' record released in 1977. By this point, he'd already adopted, adapted and discarded numerous musical styles. But *Low* feels like a completely clean slate. Side one features two instrumentals and five short songs with frequently atypical structures. The mood is introspective, the instrumentation lacking in adornment. Side two goes even further; four lengthy and largely instrumental works which owe little if anything to the world of rock 'n' roll but much to the serialist compositions of Steve Reich and of course the influence of Bowie collaborator Brian Eno's privileging of atmospheres and textures. The track 'Warszawa' takes its wordless vocal melody from the Polish song 'Helokanie' performed by folk choir Śląsk, a recording of which Bowie had bought whilst in Warsaw.

THROBBING GRISTLE

Thee Psychick Sacrifice (1979)

Recorded at the Adjanta Cinema in Derby in April 1979, *Thee Psychick Sacrifice* snares so much of what is great about live Throbbing Gristle. The performance opens with 'Weapons Training', which progresses from a straight recording of army weapons training into a darkly seductive electronic rhythm laced with slivers of sonic poison. The set closes with a blunt and frenetic take on 'Five Knuckle Shuffle'. And in between the group pushes their sound to the limits. It's a harsh and aggressive but nevertheless deeply nuanced hour of music that must surely have been exciting to witness.

Heathen Earth (1980)

This is an album poised somewhere between a live show and a studio recording. Performed in front of a small invited audience at their Industrial Studios, it sees Throbbing Gristle setting down a version of their then current live set without the sometimes uncontrollable aspects of various venues. Perhaps due to the audience of friends, the usual combative element of a live TG show is largely absent. Yet in its place we can hear a group of very intuitive non-musicians at their most rhythmic and playful. If you are new to TG this is a good place to start.

MASSIVE ATTACK

Live At the Albert Hall (1998)

A bootleg which has enjoyed surprisingly wide distribution, this is a superb performance by a group who, by this stage, had completely mastered the art of on-stage dynamics. Opening with a dubby and disorienting version of 'Rising Son', the show builds and builds. The set is composed primarily of selections from *Mezzanine*, including a stripped down interpretation of 'Man Next Door' with Horace Andy's vocals in top form. Andy also delivers another sweet soulful performance on 'Hymn of the Big Wheel'. A rare moment of bright eyed optimism in a night dominated by bass pressure.

Mezzanine (1998)

If the 1990s UK music scene had kicked off in a blaze of hedonism and bravado then it concluded in a far more fragmented mood. Dread, in both its musical and existential forms, had always played a major role in Massive Attack's soundscapes, and on *Mezzanine* it has achieved primacy. Paranoia and suspicion are everywhere on this album. And yet the pure, heartfelt vocals of Elizabeth Fraser help leaven this often claustrophobic collection. Like all of Massive Attack's albums, *Mezzanine* obviously has a well thought out arc, yet it also feels like a personalized mixtape.

WIRE

Document And Eyewitness (1981)

Following the release of *154*, Wire parted company with EMI. Nevertheless they were bursting with fresh and unconventional ideas and keen to show them to potential new labels. The resulting set of live recordings displays a band engaged in the development of material that stretches the rock form whilst simultaneously editing it down to its essence. The shows were undertaken with the assistance of dancers and performance artists and were as much Dada cabaret as rock gig. Something that only served to create hostility in certain portions of the audience. *Document And Eyewitness* remains raw, uncompromising and frequently very confrontational.

154 (1979)

From the art-pop of 'The 15th' to the dark tone poem of 'The Other Window' this is an album that knows no bounds. Recorded at a point when inter-band tensions were at an all time high, the result is an album that summons both immediacy and grandeur. One of the many impressive things about *154* – released in September 1979 – is not just how it so keenly anticipates the coming decade. Rather that it predicts so many different versions of the 1980s. From the icy synths of the Futurists, to the compressed thrash of the DC Hardcore scene, from the doomy landscapes of the emergent Goths, to the optimistic neo-psych of the incoming Liverpool bands. Here, Wire make all these leaps first, whilst applying their own very special treatments. Thirteen songs, forty-five minutes, not a wasted second.

THANKS & ACKNOWLEDGEMENTS

For additional recall on individual chapters, I am indebted to…

Christine Duff (*Cliff Richard*), Pete Cowie (*The Jam*), Pete Cowie, Bernard Hall-Falconer and Paul Putner (*2-Tone*), John Blackett, James Wilson Ogden and Mark Hoyle (*Joy Division*), Pete Cowie, Brian Nicholson and Paul Reeson (*Psychic TV*), Malcolm Boyle and Rebekah Kortokraks (*The Shamen*), Sarah Cheang (*David Bowie*), Chris Carter, Cosey Fanni Tutti and Claus Laufenburg (*Throbbing Gristle*), Christine Cort, Damon Reece and Euan Dickinson (*Massive Attack v. Adam Curtis*), Colin Newman (*Wire*). And thank you to Mark Refoy for your excellent guitar identification skills.

* * * * *

Without the following people, this book would never have been written. And I give my thanks to them from the depths of my heart.

Christine Duff – for introducing me to this world. For introducing me to the genius of Tony Hancock. For putting up with endless bursts of 'weird music' coming from my bedroom. For dealing with my grumpy teenage years with more grace than I deserved. For providing an entire lifetime of love and encouragement. And for protecting me from Freddie and the Dreamers.

Pete Cowie – for making me laugh so much and so hard for so long. For making me feel like my strangeness was only as strange as your strangeness. For winning those tickets to see The Jam. For helping bring Cartoon Head into the world. For a lifetime of friendship, support and silliness. For being the brother I always had.

Sarah Cheang – for your care, patience and love. For bringing our two amazing sons into this world. For putting up with 25 years of someone who places art before life. I would not be who I am now, doing what I'm doing, without your emotional, financial and organisational support and I am a far better man for having known you. Thank you.

Malcolm Boyle – for your wit and your positivity. For removing a few musical blinkers. For scores of mix-tapes, mix-CDs and recommendations. For your knowledge of musical theory. For aiding and abetting numerous excursions behind culture's enemy lines. And for recognising the rightful lineage of the Portuguese Anti-King.

Mike Bradshaw – for removing a few more musical blinkers, and broadening my horizons. For teaching me about music radio broadcasting. For making me laugh and making me think. For being half of Team Tentacles. For your far-reaching musical knowledge and impeccable taste. For your good company which I dearly miss.

Imogen Christie – for your enthusiasm and encouragement with the initial chapters and helping me believe I could write a book in the first place. For our meetings in cafés, our exchange of ideas, and for listening to 'Skyscraper' by Elephant with me. For times both thrilling and calming. Meet next life.

Henry Normal – for being my mentor. For your rare wisdom and very special nous. For making me laugh over and over. For being patient with my arrogance. For always surprising me. For teaching me so many things about writing, I shudder to think how I might have fared without you.

Very special thanks also go to…

Thanks & Acknowledgements

Barry Adamson – for the many hours of free counselling and deep wisdom, and for always being the coolest man in the room.

Bukie Aja Lloyd – for your calmness, your generosity and your intensity, and for reminding me of who I am. You are a star.

Sean Baldwin – for remaining unruffled, witty and dry in all circumstances and for years of Whofulness.

Misha Begley – for your years as a bean and your years as a man, for all that you've taught me. My pride is unconfined.

Vicki Bennett – for being a renaissance woman, a true friend and an inspiration.

John Blackett – for your insightful and sensitive mind, for our unbroken friendship and for always being able to pick up where we left off.

Lucy O'Brien – for your encouragement and wisdom.

Dave Bramwell – for level headed conversations on off kilter topics. For making the effort.

Leonor Cano – for believing I was worth your time, and for a friendship I value higher than you could ever imagine.

Chris Carter – for your part in the creation of one of the major achievements of the 20th century. And for being such a lovely man.

Billy Chainsaw – for your honesty, openness, your love, your art and your willingness to always embrace the future.

Lucian Cheang Duff – for lighting up my heart with your dancing, your empathy and your timing. And for being The Monsignor.

Marius Cheang Duff – for lighting up my heart with your insightful and inquisitive mind. And for being The Exquisite Gentleman

Steve Coogan – for taking a chance on my writing and for sticking with it. For your support and endless creativity.

Jessica Cooper – for your wit, patience and insight.

Steve Delaney – for your high creative standards and for making hard graft feel like pure fun.

Ted Dowd – for keeping a cool head and for being a joy to work with.

Cosey Fanni Tutti – for your constant inspiration, for fighting and winning so many battles so early on.

Alice Fox – for years of support and help, and being a most patient, attentive and caring doula.

Tanja Gangar – for your listening and your talking and your reading, and for sharing your strength.

Mark Gatiss – for your support, your wisdom, your friendship and your faith. And for setting an example of how to operate with class in a crass cultural landscape.

Tim Harrold – for building the Obelisk and sparking the purest inspiration and incentive to create.

Dave Haslam – for your encouragement and for services above and beyond.

Gill Isles – for the hours of endless fun. Thanks for making some of the best times even better.

Douglas Jones – for your wisdom, your images and your hospitality, for truly getting it from day one and for always making me laugh.

Miriam King – for your kindness, your positivity and your unwavering commitment to creativity.

Rebekah Kortokraks – for your inspiring musical brain. For your wisdom, your understanding and your compassion. For everything. Thank you.

Tim Leopard – for your humour, your inventiveness and for your lack of compromise.

Graham Lewis – for your lust for life and your experimentation. But most of all for your words.

Sean Longcroft – for your wit and your keen eye and for being the noblest Silurian of them all.

Jim Moir – for your help, your support and your very special brain

Anna Moulson – for your help and for putting on so many superb gigs.

Daniel Nathan – for your support and encouragement, for your passion for the medium of radio and for your friendship and your honesty.

Colin Newman – for your generosity, your inspiration and your friendship. For your drive and your openness and for proving it isn't always a bad thing to meet your heroes.

Brian Nicholson – for fanning the flames, for your dedication to quality work and for encouraging others to create it.

Jeff Noon – for your subtle mind and for our many hours of talking about the addiction of writing.

Lee Oliver – for your good taste, insightful mind and for being so generous with your scanning skills.

Mary Photiou Knight – for your friendship, your endless support and your Greek wisdom. For being Electra.

Mark Pilkington – for taking a chance on the book, and for your broad knowledge and continuing enthusiasm.

Greg Pope – for being a shining light and a true inspiration. Thanks for all the Memory Vicars.

Elena Poulou – for our phone calls, for always cheering me up and for always thinking of others.

James Poulter – for our hundreds of performances together, our hundreds of hours of conversation and for talking sense when I was at my lowest.

Paul Putner – for your removal work at a delicate time and your encyclopaedic knowledge of 2-Tone.

Tim Sagar – for your endless support and your innate dudeness.

Jack Sargeant – for sticking to your guns, for following your obsessions and for walking the walk.

Mark E. Smith – for decades of inspiration, for being a dream to collaborate with and a true friend. For giving the least amount of fuck possible. And for the three Rs.

Malka Spigel – for your kindness, your optimism and for elevating my life with both your music and your photography.

Chris Stagg – for hours of enthusing about Hancock. For our conversations and collaborations that sharpened my mind. For your friendship, insight and wit.

Stephen Thrower – for your encouragement, your expertise and for setting the bar so high with your writing.

Deborah Turnbull – for your insight, your honesty, your skill with language and the solid connection.

Johnny Vegas – for your enthusiasm, your devotion to your craft and for having time for everyone.

Natalia Whiteside – for your love and belief, and for turning me from an unsophisticated oik into a sophisticated oik.

Richard Witts – for your wide-angled cultural engagement and inspirational music.

* * * * *

Over the years, the following people have all enriched my life. Many by offering friendship and love and inspiration, many by collaborating creatively and elevating my work by sharing their considerable talents, many by offering advice, insight or guidance. Many by doing all of these things. So thank you…

Haruka Abe, Carl Abrahamsson, Adam Acidophilus, Liz Aggiss, Darius Akashic, Graham Alexander, Sarah Alexander, Kenton Allen, Toby Amies, Jeff Amos, Chris Anderson, Ronni Ancona, Adrian Annis, Curtis Appleby, Pank Armodee, Rick Antonsson, Alexander Armstrong, Claire Asbury, Stephen Ashworth, Rebecca Atkinson, Avy, Stephanie Bagshaw, Robert E. Baker, Yvonne Baker, Steve Barber, Andy Barski, Jane Bassett, Jenny Bassett, Dave Battersby, Roy Bayfield, Andy Baynton-Power, Katherine Beacon, Tim Beater, Helen Begley, Jenny Begley, Mike Begley, Tom Bell, Trudy Bellinger, Mark Bennett, Mark Benton, Naomi Bentley, Jane Bertoud, Claude Bessy, Leanne Best, Honor Blackman, Rachel Blackman, Tobi Blackman, Karl Blake, Nicky Bligh, Richard Boon, Chris Bohn, John Bolton, Cass Bonner, Josephine Bourne, Lawrence Bowen, Steve Bowman, Lorraine Bowen, Jackie Bowker, Joanna Boyce, David Bradley, Sue Bradley, Paul Brasch, Sally Bretton, Sue Bricknell, Lucy Broadbent, Philip Brodie, Nick Briggs, Owen Brindle, Heather Brown, Jim Brown, Ossian Brown, Tim Brown, Roger Browning, Kat Buckle, Adrian Bunting, Tony Burgess, Gavin Burrows, Andrew Bury, Neil Butler, Pat Butler, Nick Burbridge, Mark Bursa, David Butterworth, Patrick Cahill, Amy Carr, Karen Cass, Larry Cassidy, Vincent Cassidy, Rosie Cavaliero, Phil Chapman, Mary Cheang, Min Yin Cheang, Nick Cheang, Andy Cheng, Peter Chrisp, Robert Cohen, Anita Christy, Fabrizio Clemenza, Donna Close, Jackie Clune, Nathan Coles, Austin Collings, Sean Connell, Pat Conner, J.C. Connington, Angela Conway, Jason Cook, Tania Corbett, Cara Courage, Christine Cort, Billy Cowie, Ernest Cowgill, Eva Cowgill, Davy Craig, Elinor Crawley, Ben Crompton, Graham Crowden, Sarah Crowden, John Cunningham, Julia Dalkin, Dawn Dann, Lance Dann, Ralph D'arcy Higgins, Mark Davenport, Al Davies, Jess Davies, Melanie Davies, Miles Davies, Julia Davis, Warwick Davis, Peter Davison, Richard Daws, Julia Deakin, Anna Deamer, Grania Dean, Josh Dean, Sophia Deeprose, Francis De Groote, Dolorosa Del La Cruz, Gail Denham, Val Denham, Melita Dennett, Chris Devlin, Mark Devlin, Caroline Dewey, Dan Dewsnap, Dicky, Sophia Di Martino, Beverley Dixon, Leticia Dolera, Ben Donald, Willie Dowling, Eric

Drass, Stephen Drennan, Nick Driftwood, Drum, Greg Duffield, Pat
Dunn, Steve Dunn, Lorraine Dwight, Richard Dyball, Chloe Dymott,
Mark Dyvig, Rob Earl, Caitlin Easterby, George Egg, Janette Eddisford,
Idris Elba, Paul 'Josh' Elliot, Victoria Elliott, Josephine Enright, Rob
Entwistle, Alex Evans, Dan Evans, Elaine Evans, Lourdes Faberes,
Mercy Faith, Tim Fallows, Simon Fanshawe, Ginny Farman, Tim
Farman, Maggie Feeny, James Fennings, Phil Fennings, Colette
Ferguson, Murray Ferguson, Daniel Finlay, Adele Firth, Fist, Beth
Fitzgerald, Fran Flood, Frank Flood, Cylvie Flynn, Johnny Flynn,
Simon Flynn, Paul Forshaw, James Foster, Maria Fusco, Jane Fox,
Elizabeth Frazer, Mark Freeland, Petra Fried, Emma Fryer, Michael
Gale, Michael Gambon, Gina Gangar, Zoe Gardiner, Terry Garoghan,
Janeane Garofalo, Rhona Garvin, Ed Gaughan, Fraser Geesin,
Christine Gernon, Jonathan Gershfield, Neil Gibbons, Rob Gibbons,
Mel Giedroyc, Nick Gillespie, Bruce Gilbert, Tracey Gillham, Tim
Goffe, Kevin Goldsborough, Gary Goodman, Tom Goodman Hill,
Lorna Gordon, Martin Gordon, Ben Gosling Fuller, Mark Goucher,
Kevin Gough, Len Gowing, Neil Grainger, Craig Grannell, Stephan
Grant, Rupert Graves, Liliana Gozdecka-Daniel, Rachel Grant, Frank
Gray, Venus Green, Simon Greenall, Pauline Greenhalgh, Peter
Greenhalgh, Peter Greenway, Andy Greetham, Gonia Greetham, Ben
Gregor, Robert Grey, Roger Griffiths, Doreen Grimshaw, Steve Groves,
Mercedes Grower, Natalie Gumede, Ross Gurney-Randall, Tony Haase,
Toby Hadoke, Daisy Haggard, Ian Hallard, Chris Hallam, Bernard
Hall-Falconer, Sheila Hancock, Lee Hardman, Damian Harris, Mel
Harris, Richard Harris, Adele Hartley, Ian Hartley, Jonathan Hearsey,
Sophie Hebron, Celia Hemmings, Jeff Hemmings, Wayne Hemmings,
Hayley Henderson, Sarah Henderson, Verity-May Henry, Sam Hewitt,
James Hicks, Robin Hill, Paul Hodson, Robin Hodson, Elizabeth
Holden, Andy Hollingworth, John Holloway, Will Hollinshead, Jamie
Holman, Stewart Home, Peter Hook, Paul Hope, Leslie Hoyle, Mark
Hoyle, Roy Hudd, Nick Hudson, Dave Hughes, Kerrie Hughes,
Lindsay Hughes, Amy Hunt, Greg Hunt, Judith Hurley, Danny
Hussain, Roy Hutchins, Bob Isles, Lou Isles, Xavier Itter, Sarah Ivinson,

Tom Jackson, Curtis James, Simon James, Simon Jameson, Matt Jarvis, Steve Jeanes, Jimeion, Alfie Joey, David Johnson, Steve Johnson, Paul Jones, Freya Judd, Ronny Jhutti, Kaleigh Kahl, Andrew Kay, Katie Kearney, Sheila Keith, Paul Dean Kelly, Beatrice Kelley, Paul Kendall, Alistair Kerr, Jez Kerr, Jeremy Kidd, Niall Kidd, Paul T. Kirk, Terry Kilkelly, Emma Kilbey, Matt King, Jess Knappett, Phil Knight, Michael Kofi, Nick Kool, John Krausa, Haruka Kuroda, Andrew Lahman, Kit Lam, Dave Lamb, Dave Lambert, Claus Laufenburg, Jerry Laurence, David Lavender, Andrew Lawrence, Alf le Flohic, Stewart Lee, Andrew Lee Potts, Christy Lee Rogers, Charlie Leech, Julian Lees, John Leonard, Michelle Leung, Alan Levy, Gavin Lewis, Rachel Lewis, Donna Leyland, Mercy Liao, Dan Li, Donna Lin, Lesley Lin, Martin Lin, Matt Lipsey, Sean Lock, Stephen Loska, Tania Love, Ken Lowe, Lucy Lumsden-Cook, Gil Luz, Doug Lyon, Seymour Mace, Ali MacPhail, Octavia Mackenzie, Louise Mackintosh, Sue MacLaine, Torquil MacLeod, Paul Mahoney, Andrew Mailing, Stephen Mallinder, Jason Manford, Miriam Margolyes, Robin Manuell, Louise Manzaroli, Alan Marke, Jason Marshall, Samantha Marshall, Stuart Martin, Charlie Martineau, Suely Martinez, Roger Mason, Jonny Mattock, Sinead Matthews, Pete McCarthy, Jo McClellan, Marcus McConnell, Jacqueline McCord, Rose McDowall, Paul McGann, Penelope McGhie, David McGillivray, Tara McGinley, Lisa McGrillis, Ashley McGuire, Gina McKee, Iain McKee, Joe Mckechnie, Pad Mclean, Emily McPowell, Keiron Melling, Jonathan Merrell, Jason Merrells, Simon Merrells, Richard Metzger, Mick Middles, Debbie Midland, Vicky Middles, Nick Miles, Ben Miller, Mick Miller, Brian Mitchell, Tamsin Monaghan, Tony Monaghan, Felicity Montagu, Jon Montague, Simon Montgomery, Tony Morewood, Danny Morgan, Sarah Morgan, Seth Morgan, Joel Morris, Richard Morris, Dave Mounfield, Phil Mouldycliff, Peter Mullan, Joe Murray, Ben Myers, Joanna Neary, Phil Newton, Mimi Nicholson, Joseph Nixon, Kimberley Nixon, Steve North, Benn Northover, Gemma Nunn, Joseph Nunnery, Sally Ann Oakenfold, Patrick Oldacre, Kim Oliver, Des O'Malley, Simon Ounsworth, Ruben Pang, James Papademetrie,

Toby Park, Emma Parker, Shaun Parkes, Rich Parrish, Richard Partridge, Simon Pascoe, Marcus Patrick, Thomas Patterson, Tom Patterson, Carol Payne, James Payne, Caroline Peacock, Jeni Pearson, Steffen Peddie, Simon Pegg, Jessica Peh, Angela Pell, James Pennington, Roy Pennington, Eugene Perera, Carolina Perez Richard, Sue Perkins, Julian Phillips, Maurice Phillips, Tim Piggott-Smith, Al Pillay, Hon Ping Tang, Angela Pleasance, Ivan Pope, Ryan Pope, Lindsay Posner, Richard Povey, Dan Powell, Jude Pratt, Tim Presley, Sian Prime, Dorothy Prior, Helen Pyle, Michael Queen, Nicholas Quirke, Mark Radcliffe, Claire Raftery, Chris Ramsey, Stephen Randall, Louise Ratcliffe, Jan Ravens, Vicki Rawlinson, Andy Ray, Damon Reece, Paul Reeson, Christopher Reeves, Justine Reeves, Mark Refoy, Simon Reglar, Louise Rennison, Nicola Reynolds, Glen Richardson, Mick Riddle, Paul Riding, Robin Rimbaud, John Robb, Nia Roberts, Steve Roberts, Tim Roberts, Philip Robertson, Tim Robins, Leon Robinson, Mellany Robinson, Maya Rochol, David Roger, Sooxanne Rolfe, Gillian Rooke, Sandra Roost, Laurie Rose, Jenny Ross, Andy Rossiter, Gary Russell, Olly Sagar, Sharuna Sagar, David Sant, Yaya Somsri, Hiba Sarraf, Sunetra Sarker, Jon Savage, Alexei Sayle, Donald Scott, Tim Searle, Judith Sharp, Robert Shearman, Dan Shea, Ned Sherrin, Adrian Shergold, Paul Shorrock, Nick Simmonds, Matthew Simms, Robert Simpson, Vanessa Sinclair, Gail Sixsmith, Peter Slater, Daniel Sloss, Roy Smiles, Bill Smith, Erica Smith, Ian Smith, Mal Smith, Nick Smith, Sean Smith, John Sorapure, Dave Spurr, Hayley Jayne Standing, Marcia Stanton, Catherine Starling, Stella Starr, Hanne Steen, Teresa Stewart-Goodman, Katie Stiles, Simon Stopher, Alistair Strachen, Adele Stripe, Simon Strong, Dave Suit, Liz Sutherland, Jonathan Swain, Julian Tardo, Michelle Tatters, Noah Taylor, Peta Taylor, Teho Teardo, David Tennant, Thighpaulsandra, Aimee Thomas, Antonia Thomas, David Thomas, Hugh Thomas, Richard Thomas, Sian Thomas, Alex Thompson, John Thompson, John Thursfield, David Tibet, Matt Tiller, Damian Toal, Oliver Tobias, Mary Tobin, Gavin Toomey, Faiza Tovey, Ira Trattner, Luke Treadaway, Jack Trevillion, David Tribe, Nic Tribe, Mick Tunstall, Sharon Tuppeny, Paul Tuppeny, Edwin Underwood,

Helena Uren, Anna Valdez-Hanks, Clea Venables, Guy Venables, Kerry Waddell, Bruce Wang, John Warr, Nick Ware, David Warner, Julia Waugh, Mark Waugh, Julian Weaver, Nick J. Webb, Jane Webb, Russell Webb, Martyn Weedon, Paul Weller, Josephine Welcome, Tim Wellington, Steven Wells, Andrew Wheatley, Ben Wheatley, Dennis Wheatley, Trevor Wheelan, Phil Whelans, Andrew White, Greg White, Vanessa White, Francesca Whiteside, James Wilby, Stuart Wilding, Kate Williams, Lee Williams, Paul H. Williams, Anthony H. Wilson, James Wilson Ogden, Ray Winstone, Alan Wise, Simon Witts, Matthew Wolf, Lisa Wolfe, Benedict Wong, John Woodvine, Jon Wozencroft, Stewart Wright, Stephen Wrigley, Pol Wynberg, David Yates, Alan Yentob, Dan Zeff and Marlene Zwickler.

* * * * *

A special thank you to I-Hui Lin. For taking the time to get to know me. For your hospitality and your many kindnesses both large and small. For your trust, faith, tenderness and love. For lifting me out of the mire of misery and pointing me at the future. I am blessed to have met you.

* * * * *

A very special thank you to my sisters Carolyn Duff, Gillian Duff & Susan Stopher. From the heady days of Womblemania to the early decades of the 21st century, thank you for putting up with a brother who disappeared into his own world. For being kind, understanding, funny, cynical and caring. For being the kind of sisters who make me very proud.

* * * * *

And finally to my lovely Dad Derrick Duff. You lived the life you wanted to live and you were kind and generous along the way. You were the man you wanted to be and you let me be the man I wanted to be. May the mirrors never catch you.

ILLUSTRATIONS

Page 126
Glastonbury 1993 lanyard
G.D. – Photo by Sarah Cheang

Page 144
Mike Bradshaw – Photo by Ashley Bird
Sleater-Kinney gig poster courtesy of Anna Moulson of Melting Vinyl.

Page 162
G.D. – Photo by Andy Farrington.

Page 174
Mark E. Smith & G.D. – Photo by Samantha Marshall

Page 192
Sarah Cheang & G.D. – Photo by Misha Begley

Page 208
Chris Carter & G.D. – Photo by Malcolm Boyle
Cosey Fanni Tutti & G.D. – Photo by Malcolm Boyle

Page 232
Christine & Derrick Duff with G.D. in 1964 – Unknown photographer
Christine & Derrick Duff in 2012 – Photo by Susan Stopher

Page 264
G.D. – Photo by Xavier Itter

Page 298
Colin Newman & G.D. – Photo by Fabrizio Clemenza

Page 329
Theatre of the Bleeding Obelisk (Julian Phillips, Pol Wynberg, Peta Taylor, G.D. & Greg Pope) – Photo by Paula Cox

INDEX

STRANGE ATTRACTOR PRESS 2019